Mathematics 1

*Foundation Skills
for 11-14 year olds*

Michael Ashcroft BSc

Head of Mathematics,
Berry Hill High School,
Stoke-on-Trent

Charles Letts & Co Ltd
London, Edinburgh & New York

First published 1986
by Charles Letts & Co Ltd
Diary House, Borough Road, London SE1 1DW

Design: Ben Sands
Illustrations: Keith Howard, Brian Stimpson

ISBN 0 85097 655 3

Printed in Great Britain by
Charles Letts (Scotland) Ltd

Acknowledgements

The author and publishers are grateful to the
following organizations for permission to reproduce
photographs for which they hold the copyright:

Aerofilms Limited: p 106; All Action Photographic:
p 39; The Bridgeman Art Library and DACS: p 51;
British Railways Board: p 72; Camera Press: p 105;
Ford Motor Company Limited: p 16; Pam
Isherwood/Format: pp 13,35,61,96; Brenda
Prince/Format: pp 13,36,96,98; The Meat Promotion
Executive: p 22; The *Radio Times*: p 39; Paul Robinson
Studios: p 95; The Royal Mint: p 27;

Preface

Although many parents do not realize it, probably the most traumatic happenings in a child's school-career take place during the transition from Primary to Secondary school at the age of 11/12/13 (depending upon the organization of their Local Education Authority).

Whilst most children take the upheaval in their stride, inevitably some children experience a very difficult period of adjustment. Coming from the much smaller Primary schools into the far greater populated Secondary schools, is a daunting prospect in itself. The changeover from a general teaching system to a strange system involving many teachers handling their own specialist subjects, can also lead to confusion and have an unsettling effect on the child.

'Tell-tale' signs are often evident to parents – such as sleepless nights, slight character changes, mystery illness on a morning before school, and even truancy in extreme circumstances.

More often than not, the root cause of the problem may appear – on the surface – to be quite trivial when it is eventually unearthed and, frequently, the problem can easily and painlessly be dealt with at school. However, in order for this to be done, parents must feel free to contact the school and enlist pastoral help. Most schools are only too pleased to be of assistance regarding such problems and, as parents, it is our duty to help not only the child but also the school who are, after all, not always aware that there is a problem.

As parents, we should also be aware of a large problem faced by the teaching staff of the Secondary school. My own school, for instance, admits 'new-intake' 11-year-olds from as many as ten different 'feeder' Primary schools. Imagine the problem of the teacher of a 'new-intake' class of thirty pupils who may have arrived from any of the ten 'feeder' schools. Whilst not in any way wishing to be critical of some 'feeder' schools and their differing 'systems', we have the very difficult task of moulding the class into a single unit rather than the fragmented unit as presented to us. Children are used to different teaching styles, methods and even variations in subject matter covered in their Primary Education. Liaison between 'feeder' Primary schools and their Secondary schools is improving all the time, and some of the problems in this area are gradually being overcome.

Due to the continuous nature of a subject such as Mathematics (probably more so than in any other school subject) most Secondary schools adopt a levelling and consolidation period of teaching, whereby the children are taken over the 'common ground' arithmetical work, in order to ensure a reasonable consistency amongst the group. Having achieved this consistency level, on which the whole of Secondary Maths depends, we then proceed to introduce new work built upon the child's previous arithmetical knowledge.

It is easy to see that, without these basic arithmetical concepts and skills, the foundation for further development and future success in Mathematics would be missing and would lead to recurring problems in the learning processes forthwith.

In conclusion, whilst it is fair to say that some of the arithmetical work in Volume One is quite basic, it is of extreme importance as far as the rest of the course is concerned, and we must always be mindful that the best buildings are the ones laid on good solid foundations.

Mike Ashcroft 1986

I wish to thank the following people for their help in producing these books: my consultant, Ray Williams (second in Maths. Dept., Berry Hill High School) who has given tremendous assistance with the assignments and for his general help, advice, criticism and encouragement; my wife Norma for her marvellous support and the professionalism of her typing; and the staff of Charles Letts & Co. Ltd, for their excellent assistance.

4

Contents

Introduction

and guide to using the book

As already mentioned in the Preface, in order to achieve success in Mathematics it is very important to acquire basic concepts and skills. This first volume is designed to 'bridge the gap' between Primary and Secondary school Mathematics, whilst at the same time developing the subject matter to greater levels, thus providing the basis for the first-year Secondary Mathematics course.

Most teachers would accept that much assistance and practice at home can be invaluable in the acquisition of mathematical skills. However, the order in which subject matter is tackled is not necessarily as shown in this volume. Other Secondary schools may tackle the different skills and concepts in a slightly different order but hopefully, whatever the order, the subject matter will be found somewhere in the book.

Volume One is basically aimed at the 11-year-old child.

Volume Two is basically aimed at the 12-year-old child.

Volume Three is basically aimed at the 13-14-year-old child.

Again, it must be emphasized that, because of the follow-through nature of mathematical study, there will be slight variations from school to school.

Much research has been done in recent years into methods of learning and much discussion has been directed at deciding what should constitute a Mathematics course up to 16+ years of age. The Assessment of Performance Unit (APU) was set up in 1975 as a branch of the Department of Education and Science (DES). The Unit aims to provide information about the levels of performance that pupils achieve in different subjects and how their performance changes over the years.

The terms of reference of the APU are: 'To promote the development of methods of assessing and monitoring the achievement of children at school, and to seek to identify the incidence of under-achievement'.

To this end, the APU, based at Chelsea College, University of London, and at the University of Leeds, has carried out a large number of tests of pupils aged 11, 13 and 15 years. The analysis of the results of these tests has enabled the researchers to identify the levels of understanding which we can expect pupils to have at different ages. *Foundation Skills – Mathematics*, in its three volumes, has been compiled along the broad outlines laid down by APU, which categorizes mathematics into five specific areas – Number, Measure, Algebra, Geometry and Statistics. Hence, the three volumes are designed with a section devoted to each of the five specific areas.

In Mathematics, the APU has developed both written and practical modes of assessment. In its reports, entitled *Mathematical Development*, published by HMSO, some very interesting results have come to light concerning mathematical 'under-achievement' – a problem to which we, as teachers and parents, should pay great attention.

It is also interesting to note that, in November 1981, Dr W. H. Cockcroft and his research team submitted a report entitled *Mathematics Counts*, published by HMSO, dealing with an Inquiry into the teaching of Mathematics in Primary and Secondary schools in England and Wales. It is the most authoritative document concerning school Mathematics to be published for many years. Known to most as the *Cockcroft Report*, it puts forward recommendations which call for 'early' action by all involved in mathematical education.

At this time, many teachers of Mathematics are greatly aware of the Cockcroft findings and of our own shortcomings, and are attempting to implement as many of its recommendations as possible. These include such things as enthusiasm and enjoyment for the subject and its 'rub-off' effect, discussion between teacher and pupils, the introduction of activity/practical work, consolidating and practising of fundamental skills and routines, problem solving relating to everyday situations, and investigational work.

The report also makes reference to the role of parents in a child's mathematical development. It does this along the lines that parents can exercise, even if unknowingly, a considerable influence on the attitudes of their children to Mathematics. The encouragement to make use of aspects of Mathematics during normal family activities can assist with the development and understanding of the number concept. Sometimes a negative attitude, by parents in failing to understand the nature of the work which their child is doing, can result in the child adopting the same negative thoughts and hence developing poor attitudes in general towards Mathematics. It can also happen that parents can expect too little or too much of their children. Total backing and encouragement from parents is a vital ingredient in assisting the teaching of Mathematics.

Most schools would be only too delighted to enlist the help of parents, by explaining the approaches to Mathematics which they are using and the purpose of mathematical activities – which parents, themselves, may not have undertaken while at school.

With this particularly in mind, these volumes have been designed to carefully explain to interested parents the concepts and skills of the Mathematics taught to 11 to 13 year olds in our Secondary schools.

As a result, parents may then feel in such a position as to be able to offer their children positive help and advice with most problems which the school Mathematics curriculum may cause them.

It is important to view these volumes not as a school textbook, but more as a back-up source for schoolwork, which can be used by the family in the confines of its own home.

The book can be used as a whole course i.e. worked through from start to finish, or by selecting particular problem areas. By use of the Contents (at the front) any particular skill/concept can be easily located. The analysis table (at the front) can be particularly helpful when matching a particular topic to its constituent skills and concepts. Assignment activities follow on from units or sections of units. Answers to activities in some detail can be found at the end of each volume. There is also a list of some school textbooks which may be helpful in further follow-up work, particularly in the area of further activities/exercises.

Finally, having used Volume One to good effect, it would be most fitting to follow through the basic ideas extended in Volume Two and taken even further in Volume Three.

Remember, Mathematics, well taught and understood, can be one of the most enjoyable subjects of the Secondary school's curriculum. My hope is, that these volumes will enrich and enhance the users' mathematical prowess.

SKILLS

	Problem Solving	Use of Equipment	Scale Drawing	Sketching	Information Processing	Decision Making
Units 1–9 NUMBER	•				•	•
Units 10–16 MEASURE	•	•	•	•	•	•
Units 17–23 ALGEBRA	•					•
Units 24–28 GEOMETRY	•	•	•	•		
Units 29–35 STATISTICS	•	•	•	•	•	•

CONCEPTS

	Computation	Place Value	+ve/–ve Numbers	Operation Order	Fraction	Money	Time	Measurement	Graphical Representation	Spatial Concept	Statistical Ideas	Area	Capacity	Inverse
Units 1–9 NUMBER	•	•	•	•	•	•					•			•
Units 10–16 MEASURE	•	•			•	•	•	•		•	•	•	•	
Units 17–23 ALGEBRA	•		•	•	•				•					•
Units 24–28 GEOMETRY	•							•		•		•		
Units 29–35 STATISTICS	•			•	•	•	•	•	•	•	•			

NUMBER

Unit 1

Whole numbers

1.1 Useful sets of numbers

We will firstly look at some sets of numbers which we will continually use throughout the three volumes of the series.

The set of **whole numbers** (counting numbers or integers)

$$= \{0, 1, 2, 3, 4, \ldots\ldots\}$$

Another useful set of numbers is the set of **natural numbers**

$$= \{1, 2, 3, 4, \ldots\ldots\}$$

Notice that the only difference between the above two sets is the 0 (zero).

We are also very familiar with the following sets.

The set of **even numbers** = $\{2, 4, 6, \ldots\ldots\}$
The set of **odd numbers** = $\{1, 3, 5, 7, \ldots\ldots\}$

A prime number is a whole number which can only be divided by itself and 1. 0 and 1 are not considered to be prime numbers.

Hence, the set of **prime numbers** = $\{2, 3, 5, 7, 11, \ldots\}$

A square number is formed by multiplying a whole number by itself. For example, $5 \times 5 = 25$, so 25 is a square number.

We often write 5×5 as 5^2 ('Five squared').

The set of **squares of whole numbers**

$$= \{1^2, 2^2, 3^2, \ldots\ldots\}$$
$$= \{1, 4, 9, \ldots\ldots\}$$

In diagram form, square numbers can be represented by dots in the form of a square, as in Fig. 1.1.

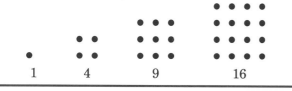

Fig. 1.1

Likewise, the set of **cubic numbers**
$$= \{1^3, 2^3, 3^3, 4^3, \ldots\}$$
$$= \{1, 8, 27, 64, \ldots\}$$

These numbers can be represented by cubes, as in Fig. 1.2.

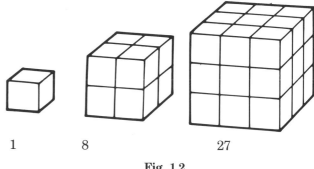

Fig. 1.2

The set of **triangular numbers** = $\{1, 3, 6, 10, \ldots\ldots\}$

As we did with square numbers, we can arrange triangular numbers in dot form to show how the equilateral triangles are formed (see Fig. 1.3).

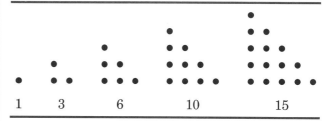

Fig. 1.3

Activities

1 List these sets of numbers:
(a) the integers less than 10
(b) the odd numbers less than 12
(c) the even numbers less than 11
(d) the prime numbers less than 15
(e) the square numbers less than 50
(f) the integers which are greater than 20 but less than 25
(g) the odd numbers between 30 and 40
(h) the even numbers between 40 and 50
(i) the square numbers between 80 and 150
(j) the prime numbers between 20 and 40
(k) the multiples of 8 less than 50
(l) the even multiples of 3 between 10 and 40.

2 The answer you get when you multiply two even numbers together is always .....

3 The answer you get when you multiply two odd numbers together is always .....

4 When you multiply an odd number by an even number, the answer is always .....

5 Examine this set of numbers,
$\{3, 8, 9, 15, 31, 39, 49\}$, and from this set
(a) list the prime numbers

(b) list the square numbers

(c) list the multiples of 3

(d) list the numbers that are a factor of 60

(e) what is the sum of the square numbers?

(f) what is the product of the prime numbers?

1.2 Sequences or series

When we arrange numbers in order according to some rule, the numbers form a sequence or series.

Each number is called a term of the sequence.

Example 1   3, 7, 11, 15, ...

We see that each term, after the first, can be formed by the rule 'add 4'. The next two terms will then be 19 and 23.

Example 2   27, 22, 17, 12, ...

The next two terms can be found using the rule 'subtract 5'. The next two terms will be 7 and 2.

Example 3   9, 16, 25, 36, ...

Since this sequence is a series of square numbers, i.e. $3^2, 4^2, 5^2, 6^2$, then the next two terms will be 7^2 and 8^2, that is, 49 and 64.

Activities

Consider the set of numbers 2, 4, 6, 8, ... (as in Fig. 1.4).

The numbers are in a definite order and there is a rule for obtaining the next number in the set. You need to try to find that rule.

1 Find the next two numbers in each of the following sequences:

(a) 1, 3, 5, 7, ...　　(g) 2, 4, 8, 16, ...

(b) 2, 4, 6, 8, ...　　(h) 160, 80, 40, 20, ...

(c) 5, 8, 11, 14, ...　　(i) 3, 9, 27, 81, ...

(d) 4, 11, 18, 25 ....　　(j) 5, 10, 20, 40, ...

(e) 29, 24, 19, 14, ...　　(k) 6, 60, 600, 6000, ...

(f) 99, 88, 77, 66, ...　　(l) 625, 125, 25, ...

Sometimes the rule is not so easy to find. It may even be a combination of two rules.

For example, in the set of numbers 2, 5, 11, 23, 47, the number is doubled and then 1 is added to the answer.

2 Try finding the next 2 in these:

(a) 1, 4, 9, 16, 25, ...　　(g) 5, 9, 15, 23, 33, ...

(b) 3, 5, 9, 17, ...　　(h) 99, 88, 79, 72, ...

(c) 1, 2, 5, 14, ...　　(i) 5, 10, 20, 35, 55, ...

(d) 3, 4, 6, 10, ...　　(j) 2, 3, 5, 8, 13, 21, ...

(e) 3, 5, 8, 12, 17, ...　　(k) 3, 7, 15, 31, 63, ...

(f) 39, 32, 26, 21 ....　　(l) 1, 2, 6, 22, ...

Houses in a street

Fig. 1.4

Unit 2

Factors and multiples

2.1 Factors

36 can be divided exactly by 2. The number 2 is called a factor of 36.

36 can also be divided exactly by 9. The number 9 is also a factor of 36.

In fact, the set of factors of 36 is

$$\{1, 2, 3, 4, 6, 9, 12, 18, 36\}$$

(**N.B.** 1 is a factor of every number.)

Dot patterns may be helpful in finding the factors of a number. For example, we can use them to find the factors of 12, as in Fig. 2.1.

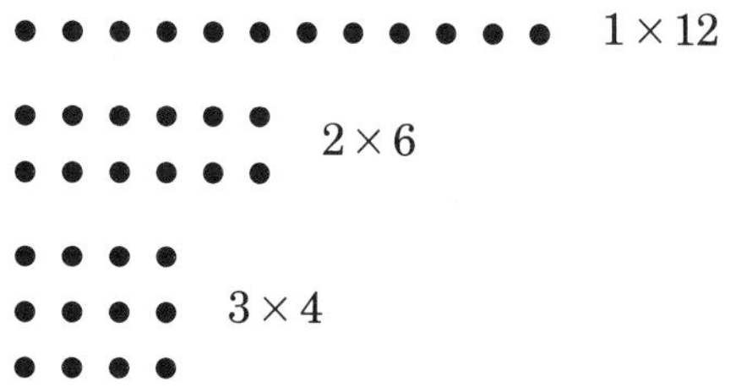

● ● ● ● ● ● ● ● ● ● ● ● 1×12

● ● ● ● ● ●
● ● ● ● ● ● 2×6

● ● ● ●
● ● ● ● 3×4
● ● ● ●

Fig. 2.1

So the set of factors is $\{1, 2, 3, 4, 6, 12,\}$

The **prime factors** of 12 will be the factors which are prime numbers, i.e. 2 and 3.

Example Find the set of prime factors of 84.

$$84 = 12 \times 7$$
$$= 4 \times 3 \times 7$$
$$= 2 \times 2 \times 3 \times 7$$

∴ the prime factors of $84 = \{2, 3, 7\}$

Activities

5 is a **factor** of 20 because 5 will divide into 20 exactly.

For the same reason we can say:

5 is a factor of 15   3 is a factor of 12

6 is a factor of 18   10 is a factor of 50

Also we can say that $\{1, 2, 3, 5, 6, 10, 15, 30\}$ are all factors of 30 because they will all divide into 30 without leaving a remainder.

1 Complete these sets of factors:

(a) $\{1, \_, \_, \_, \_, 12\}$ are all factors of 12

(b) $\{1, \_, \_, \_, \_, 20\}$ are all factors of 20

(c) $\{\_, \_, \_\}$ are all factors of 25

(d) $\{\_, \_, \_, \_, \_, \_, \_, \_\}$ are all factors of 40

2 Write down all the factors of 60 (there are 12 in all).

2.2 Highest Common Factor

The factors of 24 are $\{1, 2, 3, 4, \mathbf{6}, 8, 12, 24\}$

The factors of 30 are $\{1, 2, 3, 5, \mathbf{6}, 10, 15, 30\}$

Those factors common to both are $\{1, 2, 3, 6\}$ and **6** is called the **Highest Common Factor** of 24 and 30.

Activities

Find the Highest Common Factor of:

1	12, 16	**6**	35, 42
2	18, 24	**7**	6, 12, 42
3	15, 20	**8**	10, 20, 25
4	24, 60	**9**	18, 27, 81
5	32, 48	**10**	42, 56, 84

2.3 Multiples

We have already seen that multiples of 2 are given the special name of even numbers, i.e. $\{0, 2, 4, 6, ...\}$.

In a similar way $\{0, 5, 10, 15, ...\}$ are known as multiples of 5 and likewise $\{0, 9, 18, 27 ......\}$ are the multiples of 9.

Example List the set of multiples of 3 between 20 and 40.

This is $\{21, 24, 27, 30, 33, 36, 39\}$

2.4 Lowest Common Multiple

The multiples of 5 are

$$\{5, 10, 15, 20, 25, 30, 35, \mathbf{40}, 45\}$$

The multiples of 8 are

$$\{8, 16, 24, 32, \mathbf{40}, 48, 56, ...\}$$

40 is the **Lowest Common Multiple** of 5 and 8.

Activities

Multiples and Factors

$\{5, 10, 15, 20, 25, 30, ...\}$ are all multiples of 5 because they represent the number 5 multiplied by another number.

1 Now write down these sets of multiples:

(a) the first 4 multiples of 10

(b) the first 3 multiples of 8

(c) the first 5 multiples of 6

(d) any 3 multiples of 12 less than 50

(e) any 5 multiples of 4 less than 25

(f) the set of multiples of 5 less than 24

(g) the set of multiples of 3 that lie between 20 and 40

(h) the set of multiples of 8 less than 90

(i) which numbers between 1 and 101 are multiples of 25

(j) which numbers less than 50 are multiples of 7

2 Find the Lowest Common Multiple of these:

(a)	4, 5	(f)	3, 4, 5
(b)	8, 12	(g)	2, 3, 4
(c)	10, 25	(h)	2, 5, 8
(d)	3, 8	(i)	3, 5, 15
(e)	5, 15	(j)	4, 6, 9

3 Complete the mappings in Fig. 2.2:

(a)

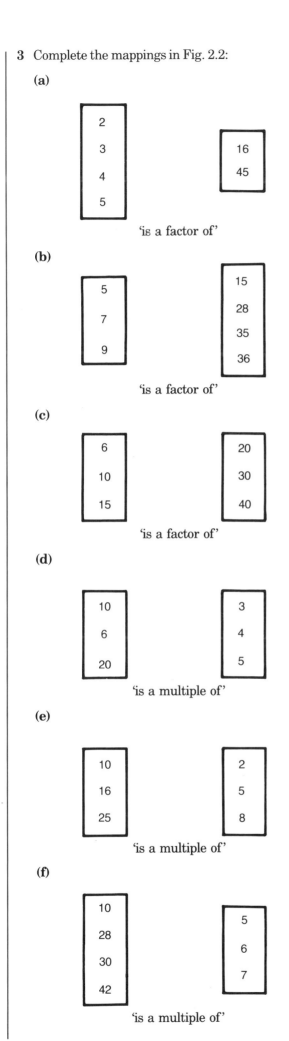

'is a factor of'

(b)

'is a factor of'

(c)

'is a factor of'

(d)

'is a multiple of'

(e)

'is a multiple of'

(f)

'is a multiple of'

Fig. 2.2

Unit 3

The four rules for whole numbers

3.1 Signs

+ Addition or Plus
− Subtraction or Minus
× Multiplication or Times
÷ Division or Share

3.2 Addition

This is concerned with putting things together.

For example, putting blocks together (as in Fig. 3.1),

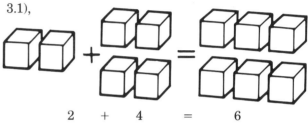

$$2 \quad + \quad 4 \quad = \quad 6$$

Fig. 3.1

or putting distances together on a map.

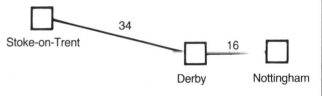

Fig. 3.2

In Fig. 3.2 it is $34 + 16 = 50$ miles from Stoke to Nottingham via Derby.

When we add numbers together it is important that units, tens, hundreds, thousands etc, are underneath one another.

Example Add $875 + 34 + 2779$

We must firstly re-write the numbers in column form with figures 5, 4 and 9 lined underneath one another.

```
   875      Start adding the units column either
    34      upwards or downwards (5 and 4 is 9,
  2779+     9 and 9 is 18 which is 1 ten and 8
  3688      units).
   111
```

Hence 8 is put in the units column, the 1 is carried over to the tens column and the process repeated for the tens column.

The answer, 3688, is called the **sum** of 875, 34 and 2779.

3.3 Subtraction

This means taking away.

For example, using blocks again, if we take 2 blocks away from 5 blocks we are left with 3 blocks (as in Fig. 3.3).

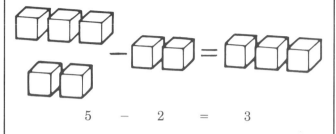

$$5 \quad - \quad 2 \quad = \quad 3$$

Fig. 3.3

As we did in addition, we must make certain that units, tens, hundreds etc, are underneath one another in columns before starting.

Example 1 Take 42 away from 156 or 156 − 42

```
156      Starting with units column, simply
 42 −    take the bottom line number away
114      from the top line number,
              i.e. 6 − 2 = 4
```

Then the tens column   5 − 4 = 1 etc

The answer, 114, is known as the **difference** between 156 and 42.

Unfortunately, we sometimes have a problem to deal with, as in the following case.

Example 2 186 − 47

In column form   1⁷8¹6
```
         4 7 −
         1 3 9
```

We cannot subtract 7 from 6 and, in order to overcome the problem, we reduce the 8 tens (on the top line), to 7 tens and use the spare ten to make 16 in the units column. Hence, we can then take 7 away from 16 to give us 9.

We then proceed as before, i.e.

    7 − 4 = 3 (tens column)

and   1 − 0 = 1 (hundreds column)

Example 3 567 − 398

In column form   ⁴5¹⁵6¹7
```
       3 9 8 −
       1 6 9
```

The problem here is that both the tens and units column have larger numbers on the bottom line. The method of solving is the same as in Example 2, i.e. reduce 6 tens on top line to 5 tens and hence take 8 from 17, this gives an answer of 9.

Then reduce 5 hundreds on top line to 4 hundreds and take 9 from 15 giving an answer of 6 (this is really taking 90 away from 150 to leave 60).

Finally, in the hundreds column, perform 4 − 3 = 1.

The difference between 567 and 398 is 169.

Example 4 We may come across some difficulty when there are noughts on the top line, e.g. 2000 − 162.

In column form   ¹2⁹0 ⁹0 ¹0
```
           1 6 2 −
         1 8 3 8
```

In this case, taking the units column first, we reduce the 10 tens by 1 ten to 9 tens, which in turn reduces the hundreds by 1 hundred to 9 hundreds, which again in turn reduces the thousands column to 1 thousand.

In effect, what we have done is to reduce 200 to 199 with a 1 by the 0 in the units column.

The subtraction then commences.

    10 − 2 = 8 (units column)
    9 − 6 = 3 (tens column)
    9 − 1 = 8 (hundreds column)
    1 − 0 = 1 (thousands column)

3.4 Checking your answers

It is always a good idea to check your answer by adding your answer to the second row. If you are correct, then your answer will be the same as the top line.

Remember Example 1,   156 − 42
```
         1 5 6
          4 2 −
         1 1 4
```

If this is correct then, if we add 114 and 42, we should arrive at 156 as the answer, if our subtraction was correct.

```
         1 1 4
          4 2 +
         1 5 6
```

Hence subtraction correct.

We could even use this as another way of subtracting. We could express 156 − 42 as:

What number, when added to 42, will give us an answer of 156? i.e., 42 + ? = 156.

```
Solve by saying      4 2 to 5 0   =      8
                and  5 0 to 1 5 6 = 1 0 6 +
                                     1 1 4    is the
                                              difference

        or even      4 2 to 1 0 0 =     5 8
                and  1 0 0 to 1 5 6 =   5 6 +
                                      1 1 4
```

Activities

Adding and subtracting

1 (a) $162 + 416$ (b) $278 + 87$

   (c) Find the sum of 386 and 746

   (d) $604 - 285$ (e) $132 - 96$

   (f) Find the difference between 125 and 98.

2 There are 5485 spectators at a football match. Of these 3750 are adults.

   (a) How many are children?

   635 of the children are girls.

   (b) How many are boys?

3 There are spaces for 250 cars on a car park. If there are 79 empty spaces one day, how many cars are parked?

Fig. 3.4

4 The number of litres of petrol stored in a garage's tank is recorded each day at the close of business (see Table 3.1).

At the start of business on Monday morning the tank held 42 500 litres.

Day	Litres left
Mon	35 000
Tues	29 365
Wed	24 524
Thurs	17 967
Fri	12 250
Sat	4880

Table 3.1

Work out how many were sold each day.

Then work out how many litres were sold for the six days that the garage was open.

3.5 Multiplication

This is a quick way of adding equal numbers.

```
  5
  5      3 × 5 = 15
  5 +    (three times 5 equals 15)
 ———
 15
 ———
```

15 is called the **product** of 5 and 3.

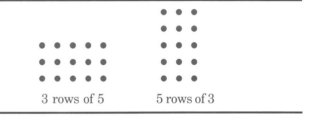

3 rows of 5   5 rows of 3

Fig. 3.5

We do not need to count the dots, in Fig. 3.5, since 3 rows of 5 dots or 5 rows of 3 dots gives us a total of 3×5 or 5×3, which are both 15.

The order in which the factors are written down does not matter, for instance:

$$24 = 2 \times 3 \times 4$$
$$\text{or } 4 \times 3 \times 2$$
$$\text{or } 3 \times 4 \times 2$$

This is known as the **commutative property** of the process of multiplication.

Addition also has this property since the order of an addition is unimportant.

We must always remember, however, that subtraction and division are not commutative (or non-commutative) since the order of the numbers is very important in both cases, i.e.

$$8 - 6 \neq 6 - 8$$
and $8 \div 4 \neq 4 \div 8$

It is very helpful if we know the multiplication tables up to 12×12, as shown in Table 3.2.

1	2	3	4	5	6	7	8	9	10	11	12
2	4	6	8	10	12	14	16	18	20	22	24
3	6	9	12	15	18	21	24	27	30	33	36
4	8	12	16	20	24	28	32	36	40	44	48
5	10	15	20	25	30	35	40	45	50	55	60
6	12	18	24	30	36	42	48	54	60	66	72
7	14	21	28	35	42	49	56	63	70	77	84
8	16	24	32	40	48	56	64	72	80	88	96
9	18	27	36	45	54	63	72	81	90	99	108
10	20	30	40	50	60	70	80	90	100	110	120
11	22	33	44	55	66	77	88	99	110	121	132
12	24	36	48	60	72	84	96	108	120	132	144

Table 3.2

Activities

Number pictures

Useful words to remember should include:

> **Product** – the answer you get when you multiply; e.g. the product of 7 and $11 = 7 \times 11 = 77$

> **Sum** – the answer you get when you add; e.g. the sum of 7 and $11 = 7 + 11 = 18$

Let us, in Fig. 3.6, build up a picture of the number 36, using all the words we have learned.

Now, in Fig. 3.7, build up pictures to describe the numbers 16 and 100.

3.6 Short multiplication

Example Multiply 47 by 4. (This means 'how many is 4 lots of 47?')

Once again we set the problem up in column form as shown.

$$\begin{array}{r} 4\,7 \\ \underline{4 \times} \\ 1\,8\,8 \\ \scriptstyle 2 \end{array}$$

Firstly multiply 7 in the units column by 4.
The answer is 28 of which the eight are units and the 2 are tens.
Then the 4 in the tens column is multiplied by 4.
The answer is 16 to which is added the 2 tens from the units column giving a total of 18, which actually represents 180.

The product of 47 and 4 is 188.

However, we must always look for short methods. For example, to multiply by ten simply add a nought to a number. Also to multiply by a hundred add two noughts to the number.

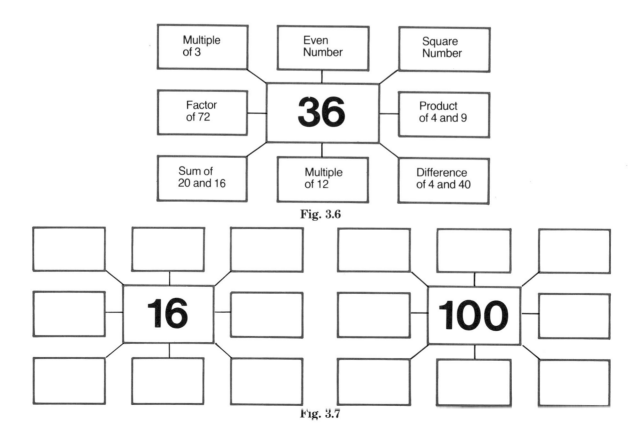

Fig. 3.6

Fig. 3.7

Example 1

H. T. U.   H. T. U.

$$4\ 3 \times 10 = \quad 4\ 3\ 0$$

Example 2

Th. H. T. U.   Th. H. T. U.

$$5\ 9 \times 100 = 5\ 9\ 0\ 0$$

Obviously, since $2\ 0 = 2 \times 10$

$3\ 0 = 3 \times 10$ etc.

so $2\ 8 \times 20$ will be

$2\ 8 \times 2 \times 10$

which is $56 \times 10 = 560$

3.7 Long multiplication

Example Multiply 184 by 37.

$$\begin{array}{r} 1\ 8\ 4 \\ 3\ 7 \times \\ \hline 1\ 2\ 8\ 8 \\ 5\ 5\ 2\ 0 \\ \hline 6\ 8\ 0\ 8 \\ \hline \end{array}$$

We solve this problem by doing 184×7 (as for short multiplication and get 1288). Then we multiply by 30 by putting a nought in the units column and multiplying by 3 (3 times 184 gives 552). Hence the second row is 5520. The two rows are then added together to give the product of 184 and 37 as 6808.

3.8 Division

Division is sharing into equal parts.

Example Divide 12 sweets equally amongst 3 people.

$12 \div 3 = 4$ or

Twelve divided by three equals 4. Each person will have 4 sweets.

Notice that there are many ways of writing division.

12 divided by 3 can be written, for example, as

$$12 \div 3 \quad \text{or} \quad 3\overline{)12} \quad \text{or} \quad \frac{12}{3}$$

3.9 Short division

Example 1 Divide 434 by 7. This means 'how many 7s are in 434?'

$$\begin{array}{r} 0\ 6\ 2 \\ 7\overline{)4\ 3\ ^1 4} \end{array}$$

Each of these numbers has a special name.

434 is known as the **dividend**

7 is known as the **divisor**

62 is known as the **quotient** (answer)

The method of performing the above division is as follows:

$$\begin{array}{r} 0\ 6\ 2 \\ 7\overline{)4\ 3\ ^1 4} \end{array}$$ $4 \div 7 = 0$ (above the 4)

$43 \div 7 = 6$ (above the 3)

remainder 1

The remainder 1 is then added as 10 to the unit 4, to make a total of 14,

then, $14 \div 7 = 2$ (above the 4)

hence, $434 \div 7 = 62$

Example 2 $1234 \div 9$ (an example with a remainder)

$$\begin{array}{r} 0\ 1\ 3\ 7 \quad \text{rem 1} \\ 9\overline{)1\ 2\ ^3 3\ ^6 4} \end{array}$$

When 9 is divided into 1234 there will be a remainder of 1.

3.10 Long division

Any divisor greater than 12 will create a long division.

The method is very similar to short division except that we write the problem out more fully.

Example 1 $2408 \div 14$

$$\begin{array}{r} 0\ 1\ 7\ 2 \\ 14\ \overline{)2\ 4\ 0\ 8} \end{array}$$

$1 \times 14 =$ $\dfrac{1\ 4\downarrow}{14\ \overline{)\ 1\ 0\ 0}}$

$7 \times 14 =$ $\dfrac{9\ 8\downarrow}{14\ \overline{)\quad 2\ 8}}$

$2 \times 14 =$ $\dfrac{2\ 8}{0\ 0}$

Method

$2 \div 14 = 0$

$24 \div 14 = 1$ rem 10

$100 \div 14 = 7$ rem 2

$28 \div 14 = 2$

$\therefore \ 2408 \div 14 = 172$

Example 2 $54\ 322 \div 24$ (remainder example)

$$\begin{array}{r} 0\ 2\ 2\ 6\ 3 \\ 24\overline{)5\ 4\ 3\ 2\ 2} \end{array}$$

$2 \times 24 =$ $\dfrac{4\ 8\downarrow}{24\ \overline{)\ 6\ 3}}$

$2 \times 24 =$ $\dfrac{4\ 8\downarrow}{24\ \overline{)1\ 5\ 2}}$

$6 \times 24 =$ $\dfrac{1\ 4\ 4\downarrow}{24\ \overline{)\quad 8\ 2}}$

$3 \times 24 =$ $\dfrac{7\ 2}{1\ 0}$

$\therefore 54\ 322 \div 24 = 2263$ rem 10

3.11 Checking your answers

Once again, as we did with subtraction, it is a good idea to check your answer.

We can do this by reversing the operation and performing a multiplication.

In Example 2, long division,

$54\ 322 \div 24 = 2263$ rem 10.

If this is correct, then 2263×24 with 10 added should give us 54 322.

$$\begin{array}{r} 2\ 2\ 6\ 3 \\ 2\ 4 \times \\ \hline 9\ 0\ 5\ 2 \\ 4\ 5\ 2\ 6\ 0 \\ \hline 5\ 4\ 3\ 1\ 2 \quad + 1\ 0 = 54\ 322 \\ \hline \end{array}$$

$\therefore$ Result was correct.

Activities

Multiplication and division

1 (a) 256×5 (b) 45×12
  (c) What is the product of 21 and 18?
  (d) $\begin{array}{r} 35 \\ \times 4 \end{array}$ (e) $\begin{array}{r} 254 \\ \times 8 \end{array}$ (f) $\begin{array}{r} 275 \\ \times 10 \end{array}$ (g) $\begin{array}{r} 2246 \\ \times 11 \end{array}$

2 (a) $\begin{array}{r} 23 \\ \times 14 \end{array}$ (b) $\begin{array}{r} 123 \\ \times 22 \end{array}$ (c) $\begin{array}{r} 245 \\ \times 51 \end{array}$ (d) $\begin{array}{r} 322 \\ \times 85 \end{array}$

3 (a) $75 \div 5$ (b) $92 \div 4$ (c) $756 \div 7$ (d) $852 \div 6$
  (e) $25\overline{)875}$ (f) $13\overline{)182}$ (g) $15\overline{)735}$ (h) $33\overline{)7755}$

4 A newsagent sells 48 copies of the *Sun*, 55 copies of the *Mirror* and 72 copies of the *Express* every day.

(a) How many copies of the 3 newspapers altogether does he sell daily?

(b) How many copies of the *Sun* does he sell in a 25 weekday period?

(c) How many copies of the *Mirror* does he sell in a 50 weekday period?

(d) How many copies of all 3 together, does he sell in an 80 weekday period?

5 A car travels 448 kilometres on 32 litres of petrol.

(a) How many kilometres will the car travel on 1 litre?

(b) How far will the car travel on 25 litres of petrol?

Unit 4

Order of performing operations

If we look at the following problems, it is obvious that we can achieve different answers by performing the operations in a different order.

(a) $5 + 12 \div 4 =$

(b) $4 \times 9 + 3 =$

(c) $19 - (7 - 3) =$

(d) $(6 + 8) \div 2 =$

We must always observe a particular sequence when we are faced with a jumble of operations.

The order is as follows:

  (i) Brackets
  (ii) Multiplication/Division
  (iii) Addition/Subtraction

For instance

(a) $5 + 12 \div 4 = 5 + 3 = 8$

(b) $4 \times 9 + 3 = 36 + 3 = 39$

(c) $19 - (7 - 3) = 19 - 4 = 15$

(d) $(6 + 8) \div 2 = 14 \div 2 = 7$

Unit 5

Fractional numbers

5.1 Definition

When one number divides another we have a fraction, for example,

$$3 \div 4 = \frac{3}{4}, \text{ i.e. three quarters}$$

$$5 \div 9 = \frac{5}{9}, \text{ i.e. five-ninths}$$

They are also represented by parts of a unit circle. The shaded part of the circle in Fig. 5.1 represents 3 parts of the total 8 parts.

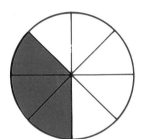

Fig. 5.1

The fraction it represents is $\frac{3}{8}$, i.e. three-eighths.

5.2 Numerator and denominator

In a fraction, the top line number is called the **numerator**. The bottom line number is called the **denominator**.

5.3 Equivalent fractions

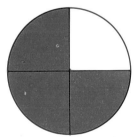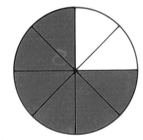

Fig. 5.2

We can see in Fig. 5.2 that $\frac{3}{4} = \frac{6}{8}$ and these are known as equivalent fractions.

If we divide $\frac{6}{8}$, both numerator and denominator, by 2 we finish with $\frac{3}{4}$. Another fraction equivalent to $\frac{3}{4}$ would be $\frac{12}{16}$

Activities

1 In Fig. 5.3 shade $\frac{1}{2}$

How many **quarters** have been shaded?

We can say $\frac{1}{2} = \frac{2}{4}$

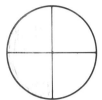

Fig. 5.3

2 In Fig. 5.4 shade $\frac{1}{2}$

How many **eighths** have been shaded?

We can say $\frac{1}{2} = \frac{4}{8}$

Fig. 5.4

3 In Fig. 5.5, shade $\frac{1}{3}$

How many **sixths** have been shaded?

We can say $\frac{1}{3} = \frac{2}{6}$

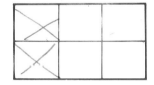

Fig. 5.5

4 In Fig. 5.6 shade $\frac{2}{3}$

How many **sixths** have been shaded?

We can say $\frac{2}{3} = \frac{4}{6}$

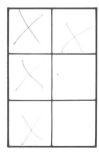

Fig. 5.6   Fig. 5.7

5 In Fig. 5.7, shade $\frac{3}{4}$

How many **eighths** have been shaded?

We can say $\frac{3}{4} = \frac{6}{8}$

6 In Fig. 5.8 shade $\frac{3}{4}$

How many **twelfths** have been shaded?

We can say $\frac{3}{4} = \frac{?}{12}$

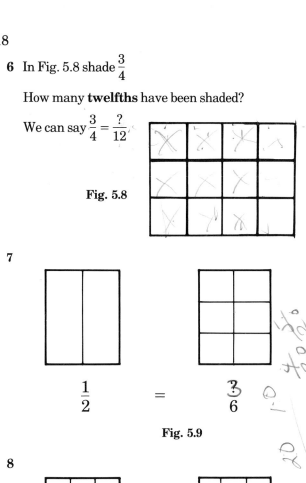

Fig. 5.8

7

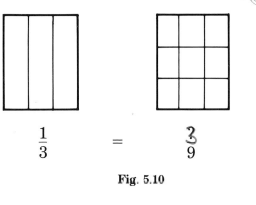

$$\frac{1}{2} = \frac{3}{6}$$

Fig. 5.9

8

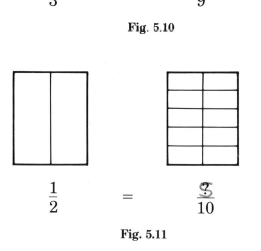

$$\frac{1}{3} = \frac{3}{9}$$

Fig. 5.10

9

$$\frac{1}{2} = \frac{5}{10}$$

Fig. 5.11

10

$$\frac{2}{5} = \frac{4}{10}$$

Fig. 5.12

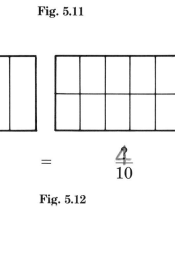

11

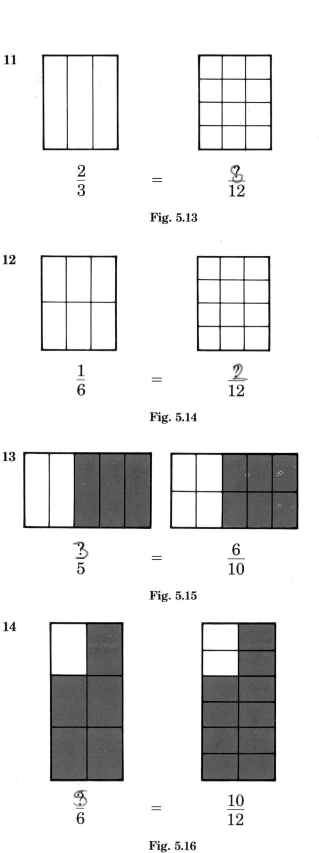

$$\frac{2}{3} = \frac{8}{12}$$

Fig. 5.13

12

$$\frac{1}{6} = \frac{2}{12}$$

Fig. 5.14

13

$$\frac{3}{5} = \frac{6}{10}$$

Fig. 5.15

14

$$\frac{5}{6} = \frac{10}{12}$$

Fig. 5.16

15 (a) $\frac{1}{2} = \frac{4}{8}$ **(b)** $\frac{1}{4} = \frac{2}{8}$ **(c)** $\frac{1}{5} = \frac{2}{10}$ **(d)** $\frac{1}{6} = \frac{2}{12}$

(e) $\frac{2}{5} = \frac{8}{20}$ **(f)** $\frac{3}{4} = \frac{15}{20}$ **(g)** $\frac{2}{3} = \frac{8}{12}$ **(h)** $\frac{2}{3} = \frac{6}{9}$

Instead of multiplying the **denominator** and the **numerator** by the same number, we can sometimes **divide** the **denominator** and **numerator** by the same number. This reduces the fraction to its lowest terms, e.g. $\frac{12}{18} = \frac{2}{3}$

16 Try these:

(a) $\frac{6}{15}$ (b) $\frac{5}{25}$ (c) $\frac{9}{27}$ (d) $\frac{9}{15}$ (e) $\frac{40}{60}$

(f) $\frac{25}{100}$ (g) $\frac{20}{48}$ (h) $\frac{15}{65}$ (i) $\frac{32}{48}$ (j) $\frac{75}{125}$

17 Copy and complete these to make sets of **equivalent fractions**

(a) $\frac{1}{2} = \frac{?}{4} = \frac{?}{6} = \frac{4}{8} = \frac{5}{12} = \frac{6}{12} = \frac{?}{20}$

(b) $\frac{1}{3} = \frac{2}{6} = \frac{?}{9} = \frac{4}{12} = \frac{?}{15} = \frac{6}{18} = \frac{?}{30}$

(c) $\frac{1}{4} = \frac{2}{8} = \frac{4}{16} = \frac{5}{20} = \frac{6}{24} = \frac{8}{32} = \frac{10}{40}$

(d) $\frac{3}{4} = \frac{6}{8} = \frac{9}{12} = \frac{12}{16} = \frac{15}{20} = \frac{24}{32} = \frac{30}{40}$

(e) $\frac{2}{3} = \frac{4}{6} = \frac{6}{9} = \frac{8}{12} = \frac{10}{?} = \frac{16}{?} = \frac{20}{30}$

(f) $\frac{3}{5} = \frac{6}{10} = \frac{9}{15} = \frac{12}{20} = \frac{15}{25} = \frac{24}{40} = \frac{30}{50}$

5.4 Lowest terms

When the numerator and denominator of a fraction have no common factor, the fraction is then in its **lowest terms**, i.e.

$\frac{3}{15}$ (common factor of 3) $= \frac{1}{5}$ in lowest terms

$\frac{7}{19}$ (no common factor) $= \frac{7}{19}$ in lowest terms

So the value of a fraction remains unchanged, if the numerator and denominator are both divided by the same number.

5.5 Proper fractions

If the numerator of a fraction is smaller than the denominator, the fraction is called **proper**.

Example $\frac{2}{3}$ is a proper fraction.

5.6 Improper fractions

If the numerator of a fraction is larger than the denominator the fraction is called **improper**.

Example $\frac{8}{5}$ is an improper fraction.

5.7 Mixed number

If a number consists partly of an integer and partly of a fraction, it is called a **mixed number**.

Example $2\frac{4}{5} = 2 + \frac{4}{5}$ i.e. a mixed number.

Example 1 Rewrite the improper fraction $\frac{19}{8}$ as a mixed number.

$$19 \div 8 = 2 \text{ rem } 3$$

This represents 2 whole numbers, and the remainder 3 will be $\frac{3}{8}$

Hence the mixed number is $2\frac{3}{8}$.

Example 2 Rewrite the mixed number $3\frac{2}{7}$ as an improper fraction.

$$3\frac{2}{7} = 3 \text{ whole numbers} + \frac{2}{7}$$

$$= 3 \times 7 \text{ sevenths} + \frac{2}{7}$$

$$= \frac{21}{7} + \frac{2}{7} = \frac{23}{7}$$

Activities

Improper fractions and mixed numbers

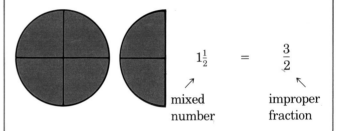

$$1\frac{1}{2} \quad = \quad \frac{3}{2}$$

mixed number = improper fraction

Fig. 5.17

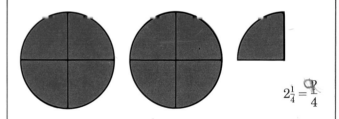

$$2\frac{1}{4} = \frac{?}{4}$$

Fig. 5.18

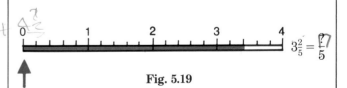

$$3\frac{2}{5} = \frac{?}{5}$$

Fig. 5.19

Now write these **mixed numbers** as **improper fractions**.

1 $1\frac{3}{4} = \frac{?}{4}$ **2** $2\frac{1}{5} = \frac{?}{5}$ **3** $3\frac{2}{3} = \frac{?}{3}$ **4** $1\frac{4}{5} = \frac{?}{5}$

5 $2\frac{3}{8} = \frac{?}{8}$ **6** $5\frac{1}{3} = \frac{?}{3}$ **7** $1\frac{7}{10} = \frac{?}{10}$ **8** $4\frac{1}{5} = \frac{?}{5}$

9 $2\frac{1}{6} = \frac{?}{6}$ **10** $10\frac{1}{3} = \frac{?}{3}$ **11** $5\frac{1}{2} = \frac{?}{2}$ **12** $1\frac{5}{6} = \frac{?}{6}$

Now write these **improper fractions** as **mixed numbers**.

13 $\frac{5}{4}$　　14 $\frac{7}{3}$　　15 $\frac{15}{2}$　　16 $\frac{23}{6}$

17 $\frac{30}{7}$　　18 $\frac{23}{5}$　　19 $\frac{53}{10}$　　20 $\frac{17}{8}$

21 $\frac{21}{2}$　　22 $\frac{19}{3}$　　23 $\frac{25}{12}$　　24 $\frac{20}{9}$

5.8 L.C.M. (Least Common Multiple)

If we consider the following fractions

$$\frac{2}{3}, \frac{7}{12}, \frac{3}{4}, \frac{5}{8} \text{ and } \frac{5}{6}$$

it is worthwhile attempting to find the largest of these fractions down to the smallest.

In order to do this, we must find a common denominator which is suitable for all the denominators, i.e. 3, 12, 4, 8 and 6.

In other words, what is the smallest number that all the above numbers will divide into?

The answer is of course 24, and so 24 is known as the **least common multiple** or least common denominator of 3, 12, 4, 8 and 6.

We then convert all the fractions into twenty-fourths.

$$\frac{2}{3} = \frac{2 \times 8}{3 \times 8} = \frac{16}{24}, \qquad \frac{7}{12} = \frac{7 \times 2}{12 \times 2} = \frac{14}{24},$$

$$\frac{3}{4} = \frac{3 \times 6}{4 \times 6} = \frac{18}{24}, \qquad \frac{5}{8} = \frac{5 \times 3}{8 \times 3} = \frac{15}{24},$$

$$\frac{5}{6} = \frac{5 \times 4}{6 \times 4} = \frac{20}{24}.$$

In order then, $\frac{20}{24}, \frac{18}{24}, \frac{16}{24}, \frac{15}{24}, \frac{14}{24}$, shows that $\frac{5}{6}$ is the largest and $\frac{7}{12}$ the smallest of the fractions.

Activities

Comparing fractions

Insert the correct sign using >, < or =, in place of each box.

1 $\frac{3}{5} \,\boxed{?}\, \frac{10}{15}$　　2 $\frac{3}{5} \,\boxed{?}\, \frac{6}{10}$　　3 $\frac{2}{5} \,\boxed{?}\, \frac{1}{4}$

4 $\frac{2}{3} \,\boxed{?}\, \frac{6}{9}$　　5 $\frac{4}{5} \,\boxed{?}\, \frac{3}{4}$　　6 $\frac{5}{6} \,\boxed{?}\, \frac{2}{3}$

7 $\frac{2}{5} \,\boxed{?}\, \frac{3}{7}$　　8 $\frac{5}{8} \,\boxed{?}\, \frac{3}{5}$　　9 $\frac{4}{7} \,\boxed{?}\, \frac{7}{14}$

10 $\frac{3}{4} \,\boxed{?}\, \frac{9}{12}$　　11 $\frac{7}{10} \,\boxed{?}\, \frac{3}{4}$　　12 $\frac{3}{4} \,\boxed{?}\, \frac{5}{6}$

Write in order of size, smallest first:

13 $\frac{1}{3}, \frac{1}{4}, \frac{1}{2}$

14 $\frac{3}{8}, \frac{1}{2}, \frac{1}{3}, \frac{1}{6}$

15 $\frac{3}{5}, \frac{3}{4}, \frac{2}{3}, \frac{7}{12}$

16 $\frac{1}{2}, \frac{3}{4}, \frac{7}{12}, \frac{4}{6}$

17 $\frac{2}{5}, \frac{3}{8}, \frac{1}{4}, \frac{3}{10}$

Unit 6

Operations on fractions

6.1 Adding fractions

When fractions with the same denominator are added or subtracted, the result is a fraction with the same denominator.

Example 1

$$\frac{2}{9} + \frac{5}{9} = \frac{2+5}{9} = \frac{7}{9}$$

Example 2

$$\frac{4}{9} + \frac{8}{9} = \frac{4+8}{9} = \frac{12}{9} = \frac{4}{3} \text{ (improper)}$$

$$= 1\frac{1}{3} \text{ (mixed number)}$$

When the denominators are different, the fractions must first be expressed with the same denominator.

Example 3

$$\frac{5}{6} + \frac{3}{8} = \frac{20}{24} + \frac{9}{24} = \frac{20+9}{24} = \frac{29}{24} = 1\frac{5}{24}$$

When mixed numbers are involved, we must add the whole numbers separately from the fractional parts.

Example 4

$$1\frac{1}{2} + 2\frac{1}{3} = 3 + \frac{3}{6} + \frac{2}{6}$$

$$= 3 + \frac{3+2}{6} = 3\frac{5}{6}$$

Example 5

$$2\frac{3}{4} + 4\frac{7}{12} = 6 + \frac{9}{12} + \frac{7}{12}$$

$$= 6\frac{16}{12} = 7\frac{4}{12} = 7\frac{1}{3} \text{ (in lowest terms)}$$

Obviously more than two numbers can be added.

Example 6

$$1\frac{5}{8} + 5\frac{11}{12} + 3\frac{5}{6} + 4\frac{3}{4} = 13\frac{15+22+20+18}{24}$$

$$= 13\frac{75}{24}$$

but, $\frac{75}{24} = 3\frac{3}{24} = 3\frac{1}{8}$

hence, $13\frac{75}{24} = 13 + 3\frac{1}{8} = 16\frac{1}{8}$

6.2 Subtracting fractions

We use exactly the same method as we used, above, for addition.

Example 1 $\quad \frac{8}{9} - \frac{5}{9} = \frac{3}{9} = \frac{1}{3}$

Example 2 $\quad \frac{3}{4} - \frac{2}{5} = \frac{15}{20} - \frac{8}{20} = \frac{7}{20}$

As before, when whole numbers are involved, they must be dealt with separately.

Example 3 $\quad 4\frac{7}{8} - 2\frac{5}{6} = 2 + \frac{21}{24} - \frac{20}{24}$

$$= 2\frac{1}{24}$$

The biggest problem we are likely to come across is with the type of example which follows.

Example 4 $\quad 3\frac{2}{5} - 1\frac{3}{4} = 2 + \frac{8}{20} - \frac{15}{20}$

$$= 2\frac{8-15}{20}$$

Obviously, $8 - 15$ is a problem. In order to overcome the problem, we must use one of the 2 whole numbers and convert it into $\frac{20}{20}$ which is then added to the $\frac{8}{20}$ to give $\frac{28}{20}$.

The problem can then be re-written as $1\frac{28-15}{20}$, which we can then finish to give $1\frac{13}{20}$.

6.3 Multiplying fractions

To multiply a fraction by a fraction, we must multiply the numerators together to give the numerator of the answer and then multiply the denominators together to give the denominator of the answer.

Example 1 $\quad \frac{2}{3} \times \frac{4}{5} = \frac{2 \times 4}{3 \times 5} = \frac{8}{15}$

If the numerator and denominator have common factors, it is best to divide them both by these factors before doing the multiplications.

Example 2 $\quad \frac{7^1}{8_2} \times \frac{20^5}{21_3} = \frac{5}{6}$

7 and 21 are both divided by 7
8 and 20 are both divided by 4

If we have mixed numbers to be multiplied, then they must be converted to improper fractions before the multiplications are done.

Example 3 $\quad 5\frac{1}{3} \times 2\frac{1}{4} = \frac{16}{3} \times \frac{9}{4}$

$$= \frac{16^4 \times 9^3}{3_1 \times 4_1} = \frac{12}{1} = 12$$

Once again, it is possible to multiply more than two numbers together.

Example 4 $2\frac{1}{3} \times 4\frac{1}{2} \times \frac{1}{14}$

$$= \frac{7}{3} \times \frac{9}{2} \times \frac{1}{14} = \frac{7^1 \times 9^3 \times 1}{3_1 \times 2 \times 14_2} = \frac{3}{4}$$

6.4 Dividing fractions

To understand this process, we must realize that dividing by 2 is the same as multiplying by $\frac{1}{2}$.

Likewise, dividing by $\frac{2}{3}$ is the same as multiplying by $\frac{3}{2}$.

Using this idea, we can change any division problem into a multiplication problem and then proceed as for any multiplication problem as shown above.

Again, before starting, any mixed numbers must be converted into improper fractions.

Example 1 $6\frac{3}{7} \div 5$

$$= \frac{45}{7} \div \frac{5}{1} = \frac{45^9}{7} \times \frac{1}{5_1} = \frac{9}{7} = 1\frac{2}{7}$$

Example 2 $2\frac{5}{8} \div 8\frac{1}{6}$

$$= \frac{21}{8} \div \frac{49}{6} = \frac{21^3}{8_4} \times \frac{6^3}{49_7} = \frac{9}{28}$$

N.B. We can see that the techniques for addition and subtraction are basically the same as are the techniques for multiplication and division.

But, we must be very careful never to confuse the two basic techniques.

Addition and subtraction

1 (a) $\frac{1}{10} + \frac{7}{10}$ (b) $\frac{1}{2} + \frac{1}{4}$ (c) $\frac{1}{4} + \frac{7}{8}$ (d) $\frac{2}{5} + \frac{7}{10}$

(e) $\frac{2}{3} + \frac{3}{4}$ (f) $1\frac{1}{5} + 2\frac{1}{2}$ (g) $2\frac{1}{2} + 3\frac{2}{3}$ (h) $2\frac{1}{3} + 3\frac{1}{5}$

2 (a) $\frac{7}{8} - \frac{3}{8}$ (b) $\frac{2}{3} - \frac{1}{6}$ (c) $\frac{5}{12} - \frac{1}{6}$ (d) $\frac{2}{3} - \frac{2}{5}$

(e) $1\frac{1}{6} - \frac{1}{2}$ (f) $2\frac{7}{10} - 1\frac{3}{4}$ (g) $3\frac{2}{5} - 1\frac{1}{2}$ (h) $4\frac{1}{4} - 2\frac{2}{3}$

3 A boy spends $\frac{1}{4}$ of his pocket money on sweets, $\frac{1}{3}$ on entertainment and saves the rest. What fraction of his pocket money does he save?

Multiplication and division

1 (a) $\frac{3}{8} \times 5$ (b) $\frac{4}{5} \times 3$ (c) $2\frac{1}{4} \times 7$ (d) $\frac{2}{5} \times \frac{5}{8}$

(e) $\frac{4}{9} \times \frac{3}{10}$ (f) $4\frac{1}{4} \times 2\frac{2}{3}$ (g) $3\frac{2}{3} \times 1\frac{1}{11}$ (h) $7\frac{1}{2} \times 3\frac{3}{5}$

2 (a) $\frac{3}{4} \div 3$ (b) $2\frac{1}{2} \div 5$ (c) $3\frac{1}{3} \div 1\frac{1}{2}$ (d) $2\frac{1}{4} \div 2\frac{2}{3}$

(e) $1\frac{1}{5} \div 2\frac{1}{10}$ (f) $3\frac{3}{8} \div \frac{3}{5}$ (g) $10 \div 2\frac{1}{2}$ (h) $5\frac{2}{5} \div 1\frac{1}{8}$

3 If it takes a cooker $1\frac{1}{2}$ hours to cook 1 kg of meat, how long will it take to cook a piece of meat weighing $2\frac{1}{4}$ kg?

Unit 7

Decimal numbers;

operations on these

7.1 Addition

This is very similar to what we found when adding ordinary numbers (Addition, Unit 3.2), the main difference being the use of decimal points.

The purpose of the decimal point is to separate the whole numbers from the fractional parts, i.e. 14.7 represents 14 whole ones and 7 tenths and 3.25 represents 3 whole ones and 25 hundredths etc.

In order to overcome the problem, we must work in columns and the decimal points must be underneath one another.

Example $0.328 + 7.63 + 19.4$

```
   0.328        Noughts can easily be added
   7.630        without changing the problem.
  19.400+
  27.358        We shall be linking this work very
                closely with Unit 10−16 (Measure).
```

7.2 Subtraction

Once again this is similar to subtraction of ordinary numbers. Again we must work in columns and line-up the decimal points, as in addition.

Example $17.42 - 6.635$

```
  17.420        A nought is added to the top
   6.635−       line.
  10.785
```

Check
```
  10.785
   6.635+
  17.420        ∴ Correct answer.
```

7.3 Multiplication

To perform this operation we ignore the decimal points and multiply as before, placing the decimal point in its correct position afterwards.

Example 14.7×0.59

```
    147         (This is 10 times too big)
     59×        (This is 100 times too big)
   1323
   7350
   8673         (This is 10 × 100 times too big
                 = 1000 times too big)
```

Hence, $14.7 \times 0.59 = 8.673$

We can say that the answer will have as many decimal places (numbers after the decimal point) as the number of decimal places in the two numbers we are multiplying, added together.

In the above case, $1 + 2 = 3$ decimal places.

7.4 Division

In order to do this operation, we must always have the divisor as a whole number.

Example $130.76 \div 2.8$

In this case we need the divizor as 28, not 2.8. To do this we multiply 2.8 by 10, but also we have to multiply 130.76 by 10 giving 1307.6.

The problem now reads, $1307.6 \div 28$, which can now be dealt with in long division manner, leaving the decimal point in the dividend.

```
                0046.7
           28)1307.6
   4 × 28 = 112
           28)  187
   6 × 28 =    168
           28)   196
   7 × 28 =     196
                000
```

Hence, $130.76 \div 2.8 = 46.7$

Activities

Addition and subtraction

1 (a) $3.6 + 9.7$ (b) $5.7 + 3.67$ (c) $0.97 + 4.6 + 6$
   (d) $3.375 + 15.25 + 9.18$ (e) $16 + 0.05 + 3.2$

2 (a) $6.8 - 4.3$ (b) $2.3 - 0.7$
(c) $4.5 - 2.95$ (d) $11 - 7.5$
(e) What change from £10 will I get if I spend £7.95?

3 In the Olympic Games 100 metres sprint, the Gold Medal Winners have been:

       1976 H. CRAWFORD   10.06 seconds
       1980 A. WELLS   10.25 seconds
       1984 C. LEWIS   9.99 seconds

(a) How much faster was LEWIS than WELLS?
(b) How much faster was LEWIS than CRAWFORD?

Multiplication and division

1 (a) 2.55×4 (i) 1.375×100
   (b) 3.25×1.2 (j) $66.7 \div 10$
   (c) 9.7×2.5 (k) $255.5 \div 100$
   (d) $12.8 \div 4$ (l) $55.5 \div 50$
   (e) $3.95 \div 5$ (m) $2.4 \div 0.5$
   (f) $91.6 \div 8$ (n) $3.0 \div 0.4$
   (g) 34.68×10 (o) $10.5 \div 1.5$
   (h) 2.35×20

2 Velvet material costs £5.94 per metre.
   Cotton material costs £3.48 per metre.
(a) What would 2.5 m of velvet cost?
(b) What would 1.25 m of cotton cost?

Unit 8

Percentages

Percentage means 'part of a hundred'.

We usually use percentages when we talk about examination marks at school, or about money involving discounts, profits etc.

We use the symbol % to mean 'percent'. If you look carefully, % is the same as 100 re-arranged.

For instance, 50% means 50 parts of a hundred parts, which can be written as a fraction

$$\frac{50}{100} \text{ or } \frac{1}{2} \text{ (in its lowest terms).}$$

30% means 30 parts of a hundred parts, which can be written as a fraction

$$\frac{30}{100} \text{ or } \frac{3}{10} \text{ (in its lowest terms).}$$

If 15% of a village population are teenagers, it means that 15 out of every 100 people are teenagers.

If there are 1800 people in the village then there are 18 lots of 15 teenagers, i.e. 270 teenagers.

It follows that 15% can be written as $\frac{15}{100}$ or $\frac{3}{20}$

Percentages are simply fractions with a denominator of 100,

$$\text{e.g. } 20\% = \frac{20}{100} = \frac{1}{5} = 0.2$$

Activities

1 Complete Table 8.1

$10\% = \frac{10}{100} = \frac{1}{10} = 0.10$	$15\% = \frac{15}{100} = \frac{3}{20} = 0.15$
$30\% = \quad = \quad =$	$25\% = \quad = \quad =$
$40\% = \quad = \quad =$	$75\% = \quad = \quad =$
$50\% = \quad = \quad =$	$5\% = \quad = \quad =$
$60\% = \quad = \quad =$	$2\frac{1}{2}\% = \quad = \quad =$
$70\% = \quad = \quad =$	$7\frac{1}{2}\% = \quad = \quad =$
$80\% = \quad = \quad =$	$12\frac{1}{2}\% = \quad = \quad =$
$90\% = \quad = \quad =$	$150\% = \quad = \quad =$

Table 8.1

Unit 9

Linking fractions, decimals and percentages

9.1 Changing fractions to decimals

To change a fraction into a decimal, we divide the numerator by the denominator.

Example 1 $\dfrac{3}{4} = 4\overline{)3.000}$ giving 0.75

Example 2 $\dfrac{5}{6} = 6\overline{)5.0000}$ giving $0.8333 = 0.8\dot{3}$

A dot over the 3 means that the 3 is recurring, and this is the accepted shorthand way of writing such decimals.

9.2 Changing decimals to fractions

To change a decimal into a fraction, we must see how many decimal places are involved and act accordingly.

Example 1 0.5 (one decimal place)
Denominator will be 10.

Then $0.5 = \dfrac{5}{10} = \dfrac{1}{2}$ (in lowest terms)

Example 2 0.65 (2 decimal places)
Denominator will be 100.

Then $0.65 = \dfrac{65}{100} = \dfrac{13}{20}$ (in lowest terms)

Example 3 0.375 (3 decimal places)
Denominator will be 1000.

Then $0.375 = \dfrac{375}{1000} = \dfrac{3}{8}$ (in lowest terms)

9.3 Changing fractions/decimals to a percentage

To do this, we must multiply the fraction or decimal by 100, and work out the result.

Example 1 $\dfrac{1}{4}$ is equivalent to $\dfrac{1}{4} \times 100\% = 25\%$.

Example 2 0.85 is equivalent to $0.85 \times 100\% = 85\%$.

9.4 Changing percentages to fractions/decimals

To do this we must write the percentage as a fraction with denominator 100, and find the result by division.

Example 1

45% is equivalent to $\dfrac{45}{100} = \dfrac{9}{20}$ (in lowest terms)

or $\dfrac{45}{100} = 0.45$ (decimal form)

Example 2

$37\frac{1}{2}\%$ is equivalent to $\dfrac{37\frac{1}{2}}{100} = \dfrac{75}{200} = \dfrac{3}{8}$ (in lowest terms)

or $\dfrac{37.5}{100} = 0.375$ (decimal form)

Activities

To find a percentage of something

For example,

$$10\% \text{ of } £80 = \dfrac{10}{100} \times £80 = \dfrac{800}{100} = £8.00$$

$$5\% \text{ of } £60 = \dfrac{5}{100} \times £60 = \dfrac{300}{100} = £3.00$$

Now, find the values of:

1 10% of £120	**2** 10% of £30
3 5% of £250	**4** 5% of £12
5 20% of £40	**6** 30% of £15
7 25% of £30	**8** 75% of £8
9 $12\frac{1}{2}\%$ of £80	**10** 15% of £20
11 10% of 1500	**12** $2\frac{1}{2}\%$ of 400

To express a fraction as a percentage

$$\overset{\times 20}{\dfrac{4}{5}} = \dfrac{80}{100} = 80\% \text{ or } \dfrac{4}{5} \times 100 = \dfrac{400}{5} = 80\%$$

To change a fraction to a percentage, multiply it by 100.

1 Express these fractions as percentages:

(a) $\dfrac{1}{2}$ (b) $\dfrac{1}{4}$ (c) $\dfrac{2}{5}$ (d) $\dfrac{3}{4}$

(e) $\dfrac{3}{20}$ (f) $\dfrac{21}{25}$ (g) $\dfrac{9}{10}$ (h) $\dfrac{17}{20}$

2 A boy scores $\dfrac{7}{10}$ in a Maths test. What is his percentage mark?

3 A girl scores $\dfrac{15}{25}$ in an English test. What percentage mark is this?

4 In a school of 600 there were 90 pupils absent.

(a) What percentage were absent?

(b) What percentage were present?

MEASURE

Unit 10

Money

10.1 Introduction

The 'cost' of buying something is very important to us because we must know whether or not we can afford to buy the item/s required with the money we have. We will, therefore, start this unit by doing some simple operations on sums of money. One very obvious thing to remember is that since we use metric units for all our measure these days, our calculations depend very much on a good knowledge of decimal operations (previously discussed in Unit 7).

There are 100 pence in one pound; 100p = £1.

£3.75 is read as, 'three pounds, seventy-five pence'.

£4.03 is read as, 'four pounds and three pence'.

10.2 Adding and subtracting money

Example 1 Add £5.98 + £10.87 + £4.66

```
  £   p
  5 . 98
 10 . 87
  4 . 66 +
 ─────────
£21 . 51
```

Example 2 From £13.43 take £6.78

```
  £   p
 13 . 43
  6 . 78 −
 ─────────
 £6 . 65
```

10.3 Multiplying money

Example Multiply £23.49 by 8

We work on the problem with £23.49 converted to 2349p.

Then,
```
    2 3 4 9
        8 ×
  ───────────
  1 8 7 9 2 pence
```

This, we then convert back to pounds and pence by dividing the result by 100 (or moving the decimal point two places to the left) since 100 pence = £1.

In this example, the answer will be £187.92.

In the case of long multiplication, we simply follow the rules as in Unit 3.7, working once again in pence, and afterwards converting this to pounds and pence.

10.4 Division

Example Divide £28.44 by 6

```
    £   p
    4 . 74
  ──────────
6)28 . 44
```

In the case of long division, the method is exactly the same as in Unit 3.10.

10.5 Finding the cost of one item

Example Suppose 12 books cost £2.88, what will be the cost of one book?

We divide £2.88 by 12 to find the cost of one book, i.e.

```
      0 . 24
   ──────────
12)2 . 88
```
Each book costs 24p.

10.6 Finding the cost of several items

Example Suppose 15 pens cost £4.65, how much will 23 pens cost?

Step 1 We divide £4.65 by 15 to find the cost of one pen.

Step 2 We multiply the cost of one pen by 23 to find the cost of 23 pens.

i.e.
```
        0 . 3 1
      ───────────
   15)4 . 6 5
        4 . 5↓ −
   15)    1 5
          1 5 −
          ───
            0
```
Cost of one pen = 31p

Therefore, the cost of 23 pens is
```
    3 1
    2 3 ×
  ────────
    9 3
  6 2 0
  ────────
  7 1 3 p
```
= £7.13

10.7 Shopping bills

Although most shops and supermarkets these days have tills which print-out your total bill and even the change to be given by the cashier, it is still important for us to know how to keep a check on what we are spending.

For example, we can work out the following grocery bill.

1 Packet of Cornflakes	@	67p	0.67
2 Tins of Salmon	@	88p	1.76
3 Tins of Baked Beans	@	22p	0.66
1 Jar of Coffee	@ £1	18p	1.18
5 Packets of Crisps	@	12p	0.60
2 Packets of Biscuits	@	19p	0.38
4 Tins of Peas	@	17p	0.68
	Total	=	£5.93

Activities

Money operations

1 Which single coin is worth:

(a) 1 five pence, 2 two pence and 1 one pence? 10p

(b) 1 ten pence and 2 five pence? 20p

(c) 1 fifty pence and 2 twenty pence and 1 ten pence? 1·00

(d) 3 ten pence, 7 two pence and 6 one pence? 50p

(e) 5 two pence, 1 five pence and 5 one pence? 20p

2 How many 5 pence coins are worth 50p? 10R

3 How many 2 pence coins are worth 20p? 10R

4 How many 20 pence coins are worth £1? 5

5 How many 10p coins are there in a bag with £8.60 in 10p pieces? 86

6 Which three coins have a total of 20p? 10p 5, 5

7 Which three coins have a total of 50p? 20p 20p 10p

8 Which four coins have a total of 10p? 5, 2, 2, 1

9 Which five coins have a total of £3.70? 1, 1, 50 20

10 Which four coins have a total of £1.72? 100, 50p, 20, 2p

11 Find the cost of 3 bars of chocolate at 65p each. 1 95

12 If I buy 3 items costing £2.99, £1.25 and £6.15, what is the total cost of the 3 items? 10·39

13 If the adult fare on a train journey is £5.20 and children can travel at half price, what is the total cost for 2 adults and their 3 children to make the journey? 18·20

14 What change from £5 would you get if your bill came to £3.72? 1:28

15 I gave a shopkeeper £8 and he asked me for another 15p to save his change. He then gave me a 50p piece. How much did my goods cost? 7:80

16 If Pete saves £1.40 per week for 15 weeks and his brother Jim saves £4.50 per month for 4 months, who saves most and by how much?

17 (a) Add £6.95, £2.24 and £11

(b) £24.99 + £5.45 + £1.95

(c) 65p + £1.80 + £2.10

(d) Find the sum of 95p, 28p and 18p

18 (a) £15.50 − £8.75

(b) £50 − £38.82

(c) Take £11.89 from £25

(d) What change do I get from £5 if I spend £2.67?

19 (a) £35.45 × 8

(b) £3.85 × 12

(c) Double £99.50

(d) What is the total cost of 5 books at £2.95 each?

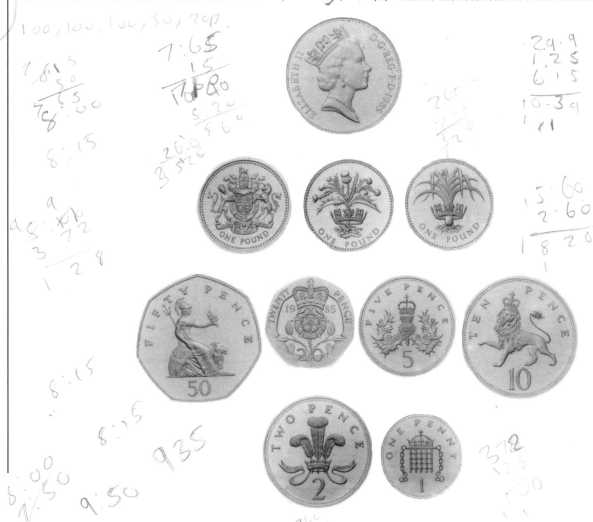

this week's specials

TIN BEANS 18p   JAR COFFEE £1·90   1kg BACON £2·40

" SOUP 16p   " JAM 41p   2 KITCHEN ROLLS 48p

" PEAS 21p   " MARMALADE 43p   250g BUTTER 42p

" PEACHES 44p   250g TEA 60p   GIANT SOAP-

      TEA BAGS 65p   POWDER 74p

Fig. 10.1

20 (a) £155.75 ÷ 5   (b) £708 ÷ 12

(c) Share a pools win of £7800 equally amongst 8 winners.

21 My weekly paper bill is £1.68 but I pay every 5 weeks. How much do I pay?

22 I buy a colour T.V. costing £375 on H.P. and have to pay the cost price in 12 equal instalments. How much is an instalment?

23 A T.V. is rented at £9.65 per month. How much rental is paid in 2 years?

24 Find the cost of one article in each of the following:
(a) 20 articles costing £11.60 altogether
(b) 100 articles costing £385
(c) 24 articles costing £27.60
(d) 1 dozen articles costing £5.40

25 (a) Make out a bill for the following:
3 loaves at 32p each
6 eggs at 8p each
4 packets of biscuits at 18p each
2 bottles of milk at 28p each

(b) What change will you get from £3?

(c) What is the smallest number of coins that you could be given for change?

26 A school orders 300 books at 22p each and 200 at 40p each. Find the total cost.

Shopping bills

1 Find the cost of these items from this week's 'Special Offers' in Fig. 10.1 and work out the cost of each list below.

(a)
1 tin of beans
1 jar of coffee
2 tins of soup
    Total

(b)
1 jar of jam
2 tins of peas
500 g of butter
    Total

(c)
1 kg of bacon
500 g of tea
4 kitchen rolls
3 tins of peaches
    Total

(d)
1 jar of marmalade
1 box tea bags
giant soap powder
4 tins of beans
    Total

2 From the list in Fig. 10.2:
(a) How much are apples per pound?
(b) How much are pears per pound?
(c) How much does 1 orange cost?
(d) How much are potatoes per pound?
(e) Find the cost of these items, and the total on this list:

15 lb of potatoes
4 lb of apples
6 lb of pears
10 oranges
    Total

FRUIT & VEG

5 lb of POTATOES 55p

2 lb of APPLES   48p

2 lb of PEARS   64p

BAG of 5 ORANGES 35p

PEACHES 5 for   40p

Fig. 10.2

10.8 Fractions of money

Another common problem we have to face is that of the type in the following example.

Example If 1 costs £22.40, how much will $\frac{1}{4}$ cost and also how much will $\frac{3}{4}$ cost?

Remember that $1 = \frac{4}{4}$, therefore if $\frac{4}{4}$ costs £22.40,

$\frac{1}{4}$ will cost $\dfrac{£22.40}{4} = £5.60$

Then, since $\frac{3}{4} = 3 \times \frac{1}{4}$, then $\frac{3}{4}$ will cost

$3 \times £5.60 = £16.80$

A similar problem to this might be:

Example If $\frac{3}{5}$ cost £3.69, what will 1 cost. (Remember again that $1 = \frac{5}{5}$.)

Hence, since $\frac{3}{5}$ costs £3.69

then $\frac{1}{5}$ costs $\dfrac{£3.69}{3} = £1.23$

So, $1 = \frac{5}{5}$ costs £1.23 $\times 5 = £6.15$

Activities

More money operations

1 **(a)** If 10 pens cost £1.60, find the cost of
    (i) 1 pen   **(ii)** 6 pens

  (b) If 4 books cost £3.20, find the cost of
    (i) 1 book   **(ii)** 5 books

  (c) If 3 LPs cost £11.85, find the cost of
    (i) 1 LP   **(ii)** 5 LPs

  (d) If 8 stamps cost £1.28, find the cost of
    (i) 1 stamp   **(ii)** 12 stamps

  (e) If 4 choc ices cost 64p, find the cost of
    (i) 1 choc ice   **(ii)** 7 choc ices

2 **(a)** Find $\frac{1}{2}$ of £8.20   **(b)** Find $\frac{1}{3}$ of £15
  (c) Find $\frac{1}{4}$ of £0.96   **(d)** Find $\frac{1}{8}$ of £120
  (e) Find $\frac{2}{3}$ of £12.60   **(f)** Find $\frac{5}{8}$ of £44
  (g) Find $\frac{3}{5}$ of £275   **(h)** Find $\frac{7}{10}$ of £1.60
  (i) Find $\frac{3}{4}$ of £56   **(j)** Find $\frac{7}{8}$ of £40

3 Find the cost of one article if:
  (a) $\frac{1}{4}$ cost £2.50   **(b)** $\frac{1}{3}$ cost £0.75
  (c) $\frac{1}{8}$ cost £1.10   **(d)** $\frac{2}{3}$ cost 72p
  (e) $\frac{3}{4}$ cost 60p

4 A father changes £5 and gives each of his 3 sons £1.40 pocket money. How much change does he have left over?

5 Tyres cost £19.50 each. **(a)** How much would it cost to buy a set of four new tyres? **(b)** What will be left out of £100?

6 **(a)** How many 15p Christmas cards can I buy for £5? **(b)** What money will be left over?

7 A money box contains twelve 20p coins, fifteen 10p coins, eight 5p coins and three 50p coins. How much is there in total?

8 The total numbers of tickets sold at the cinema one evening were 125 at £2.50, 86 at £1.80 and 145 at £1.20. What were the total takings?

Unit 11

Length

11.1 Introduction

Most countries of the world now use a metric system of measuring for length, based on the following units.

Using the abbreviations mm for millimetre, cm for centimetre, m for metre and km for kilometre, we have:

10 mm = 1 cm
100 cm = 1 m   also 1000 mm = 1 m
1000 m = 1 km

Table 11.1

In this country we do still use Imperial units which are non-metric, but apart from a brief mention of these, we shall not use them for problem purposes.

12 inches = 1 foot	
3 feet = 1 yard	220 yards = 1 furlong (used in horse racing)
	8 furlongs = 1 mile
and 1760 yards = 1 mile	

Table 11.2

11.2 Metric equivalents

1 inch is approximately 2.54 cm
1 yard is approximately 91.5 cm
1 mile is approximately 0.63 km

Table 11.3

The 'length' of a line gives us a measure of how far the line stretches from one end to the other, and we can use the instruments pictured in Fig. 11.1 to measure these distances.

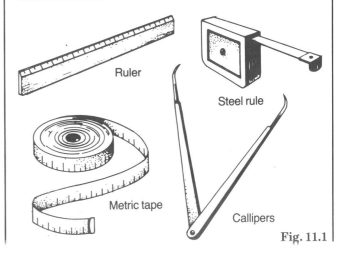

Fig. 11.1

30

The length of the line in Fig. 11.2 is 8 cm or 80 mm.

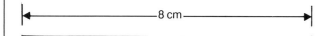

|← —————— 8 cm —————— →|

Fig. 11.2

We can measure short distances in mm (millimetres) and cm (centimetres) and longer distances in m (metres) and km (kilometres).

Pieces of wood may be measured in cm or mm. Curtain or clothes' material is sold by the m. Distances between two towns are measured in km.

It is very important that we can convert one set of units into another.

Example 1 How many mm are there in
      (a) 5 cm **(b)** 3.5 cm **(c)** 115 cm?

1 cm = 10 mm

So, to change cm to mm, we multiply by 10.

(a)   5 cm = 5 × 10 mm   = 50 mm
(b) 3.5 cm = 3.5 × 10 mm = 35 mm
(c) 115 cm = 115 × 10 mm = 1150 mm

Example 2 How many cm are there in
      (a) 7 m **(b)** 0.7 m **(c)** 35 m?

1 m = 100 cm

So, to change m to cm, we multiply by 100.

(a)   7 m =   7 × 100 cm =   700 cm
(b) 0.7 m = 0.7 × 100 cm =   70 cm
(c) 35 m = 35 × 100 cm = 3500 cm

Example 3 How many km are there in
      (a) 6000 m **(b)** 3500 m **(c)** 700 m?

1000 m = 1 km

So, to change m to km we divide by 1000.

(a) 6000 m = 6000 ÷ 1000 km = 6 km
(b) 3500 m = 3500 ÷ 1000 km = 3.5 km
(c)   700 m =   700 ÷ 1000 km = 0.7 km

N.B. To divide by 1000, move the decimal point three places to the left.

11.3 Adding, subtracting, multiplying and dividing units of length

Once again, we know more than enough from Unit 3 to be able to handle this type of problem.

We must, however, ensure that the units are the same before starting the operation.

Example 1   Add 6.5 cm + 32 mm

   Either   6.5 cm   or 65 mm
           3.2 cm +   32 mm +
           9.7 cm   97 mm

Example 2   Take 17 mm from 4.8 cm

   Either   48 mm   or 4.8 cm
           17 mm −   1.7 cm −
           31 mm   3.1 cm

Example 3   Multiply 9.7 mm by 8

     97
      8 ×
   77.6 mm   or   7.76 cm

Example 4   Divide 332 mm by 4

      83
  4)332   = 83 mm or 8.3 cm

Activities

Metric length

1 Measure the lines in Fig. 11.3 in
    (i) centimetres (cm)
    (ii) millimetres (mm)

(a)

(b)

(c)

(d)

(e)

(f)

Fig. 11.3

(g)

2 Convert these to millimetres (mm)

   (a) 2 cm   **(b)** 6 cm   **(c)** 4.5 cm   **(d)** 11 cm
   (e) 1.7 cm **(f)** 7.2 cm **(g)** 0.8 cm **(h)** 23.1 cm
   (i) 6.4 cm **(j)** 0.1 cm

3 Convert these to centimetres (cm)

   (a) 50 mm **(b)** 90 mm **(c)** 75 mm **(d)** 240 mm
   (e) 26 mm **(f)** 21 mm **(g)** 5 mm **(h)** 192 mm
   (i) 88 mm **(j)** 4 mm

4 Convert these to metres (m)

   (a) 200 cm **(b)** 900 cm **(c)** 450 cm **(d)** 780 cm
   (e) 145 cm **(f)** 50 cm **(g)** 5 cm **(h)** 309 cm

5 Convert these to centimetres (cm)

   (a) 5 m   **(b)** 11 m   **(c)** 5.5 m   **(d)** 2.85 m
   (e) 0.7 m **(f)** 0.25 m **(g)** 0.03 m **(h)** 5.1 m

6 Convert these to kilometres (km)

   (a) 5000 m **(b)** 3500 m **(c)** 1355 m **(d)** 750 m
   (e) 1950 m **(f)** 300 m **(g)** 30 m **(h)** 3 m

7 Convert these to metres (m)

   (a) 7 km   **(b)** 2.6 km
   (c) 1.250 km   **(d)** 0.485 km
   (e) 3.080 km   **(f)** 0.070 km
   (g) 0.7 km   **(h)** 0.009 km

8 Add these, giving your answers in the units specified.

(a) 3 m + 2.5 m + 165 cm + 1 m 63 cm (metres)

(b) 1.45 m + 78 cm + 1 m 43 cm (centimetres)

(c) 13 mm + 1.6 cm + 2 cm 6 mm + 4 cm (centimetres)

(d) 2.1 cm + 12 mm + 2 cm 6 mm (millimetres)

(e) 3 km + 2.566 km + 855 m + 2100 m (kilometres)

(f) 1.6 km + 335 m + 1 km 50 m + 2.450 km (metres)

9 Work out these, in the specified units:

  (a) 5 cm − 1.6 cm (cm)   **(f)** 3.6 m − 135 cm (m)
  (b) 7 cm − 23 mm (cm)   **(g)** 2.7 km − 950 m (m)
  (c) 2.6 cm − 11 mm (mm) **(h)** 6.850 km − 3995 m
  (d) 4.6 m − 245 cm (cm)   (km)
  (e) 1.75 m − 92 cm (cm)   **(i)** 10 km − 650 m (km)
                                     (j) 15 m − 2 m 75 cm (m)

10 How many wooden blocks, each 25 cm high, will stack to a height of 4.5 m?

11 If you saw a 4 m plank into ten equal pieces, how long will each piece measure in centimetres?

12 A 10p piece has a diameter of 2.8 cm. If five 10p pieces are placed in a line, how far will the line reach **(a)** in cm **(b)** in mm?

13 If you travel the same journey of 1.3 km to school each day, how far do you travel in 1 week?

Unit 12

Mass

12.1 Introduction

The metric system of mass used in most countries is as shown in Table 12.1, with abbreviations mg for milligrams, grams are shortened to g and kilograms to kg. We have

$$
\begin{aligned}
1000 \text{ mg} &= 1 \text{ g} \\
1000 \text{ g} &= 1 \text{ kg} \\
1000 \text{ kg} &= 1 \text{ tonne (metric)} \\
&= 1 \text{ t}
\end{aligned}
$$

Table 12.1

Scales

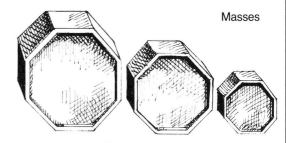

Masses

Fig. 12.1

Again, since we are using some Imperial measurements in this country, we shall just mention these (see Table 12.2):

16 ounces	= 1 pound
14 pounds	= 1 stone
112 pounds	= 1 hundredweight
20 hundredweights	= 1 ton

Table 12.2

12.2 Metric equivalents

4 ounces is slightly more than 100 g
2 pounds is slightly less than 1 kg

Table 12.3

We weigh light objects in mg or g (i.e. medicines, sweets etc).

Heavier objects are weighed in kg or tonnes (i.e. vegetables, coal, vehicles etc).

Once again, it is very important that we can change one set of units into another, as we did for length.

Example 1   Change 7000 g to kg

$$1000 \text{ g} = 1 \text{ kg}$$

so, $7000 \text{ g} = \dfrac{7000}{1000} = 7 \text{ kg}$

Example 2   Change 6275 g to kg

$$1000 \text{ g} = 1 \text{ kg}$$

so, $6275 \text{ g} = \dfrac{6275}{1000} = 6.275 \text{ kg}$

Example 3   Change 400 g to kg

$$1000 \text{ g} = 1 \text{ kg}$$

so, $400 \text{ g} = \dfrac{400}{1000} = 0.4 \text{ kg}$

Example 4   Change 3.64 kg to g

$$1 \text{ kg} = 1000 \text{ g}$$

so, $3.64 \text{ kg} = 3.64 \times 1000 \text{ g} = 3640 \text{ g}$

(A reminder, once again, that to divide by 1000, move the decimal point three places to the left; also, to multiply by 1000, move the decimal point three places to the right.)

12.3 Operations involving units of mass

Since we can now handle all decimal operations, we will not repeat the operations again for mass.

However, it is of course very important to be sure that the units in which we are working, are the same.

If not, then they must be converted before the problem is attempted.

*Remember, **'kilo'** means 1000

1 **kilogram** = 1000 grams
1 kg = 1000 g

Also,   1 gram = 1000 milligrams
and   1 tonne = 1000 kilograms

1   Choose a suitable unit to measure the mass of the following: (possible units are mg, g, kg, t,)

(a) a loaded lorry

(b) a small bar of chocolate

(c) a sack of potatoes

(d) a postage stamp

(e) a pencil

(f) a person

2   Express each quantity in terms of the unit given after it, in brackets.

(a) 5 t	(kg)		**(f)** 0.8 g	(mg)
(b) 9 kg	(g)		**(g)** 3420 kg	(t)
(c) 4 g	(mg)		**(h)** 475 mg	(g)
(d) 3.5 kg	(g)		**(i)** 2625 g	(kg)
(e) 2.3 t	(kg)		**(j)** 5 kg 340 g	(g)

3   A tin of beans has a mass of 250 g. What is the mass, in kilograms of 48 such tins?

4   A box of mass 450 g contains 20 boxes of soap powder, each of mass 900 g. What is the total mass of the box and powder?

5   10 identical parcels have a mass of 5.5 kg. What is the mass of an individual parcel in **(a)** kg **(b)** g?

6   Into an empty carton of mass 225 g, are placed a dozen eggs each of mass 220 g. What is the mass of the carton when full?

7   A box of 200 tins of fruit weighs 180 kg. The empty box weighs 25 kg. Find the mass of each tin, in grams.

Unit 13

Capacity

13.1 Introduction

Capacity is a measure of the amount of space that a liquid or other fluid takes up within the container in which it is held.

The metric units commonly used are the millilitre (ml), centilitre (cl) and litre (l); we have:

10 ml	= 1 cl
100 cl	= 1 litre (l)
1000 ml	= 1 litre (l)

Table 13.1

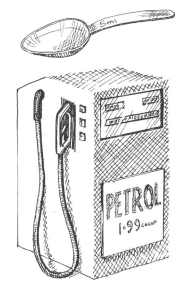

Fig. 13.1

We, in this country, are still using some of the Imperial units as follows: fluid ounces (fl oz), the pint (pt), the quart (qt) and the gallon (gall) and we shall mention these:

20 fl oz	= 1 pt
2 pts	= 1 qt
4 qts	= 1 gall
or 8 pts	= 1 gall

Table 13.2

Fluid ounces are used in baking (small quantities). Pints are used for measuring milk and beer, and gallons are used particularly in the sale of petrol.

13.2 Metric equivalents

1 litre is approximately $1\frac{3}{4}$ pints
30 ml is approximately 1 fl oz
1 gallon is approximately $4\frac{1}{2}$ litres

Table 13.3

As we did for length and mass, it is important to be able to convert one set of units into another.

Example 1   Change 4365 ml into litres

1000 ml = 1 litre

so, $4365 \text{ ml} = \frac{4365}{1000} \text{ litres} = 4.365 \text{ litres}$

or 4 litres 365 ml

Example 2   Change 75 cl into litres

100 cl = 1 litre

so, $75 \text{ cl} = \frac{75}{100} = 0.75 \text{ litres}$

Also, 0.75 litres = 750 ml

Example 3   Change 550 ml into cl

10 ml = 1 cl

so, $550 \text{ ml} = \frac{550}{10} = 55 \text{ cl}$

13.3 Operations involving capacity

As we did for length and mass, the operations are very simple, providing we start with all units of the same type.

Activities

*Remember, the unit is the **litre** (l)
= 1000 millilitres (ml)

1 Convert each quantity to the unit given after it, in brackets.

(a) 3 l	(ml)	**(f)** 7000 ml	(l)
(b) 2.4 l	(ml)	**(g)** 700 ml	(l)
(c) 1.265 l	(ml)	**(h)** 70 ml	(l)
(d) 0.8 l	(ml)	**(i)** 7 ml	(l)
(e) 1.050 l	(ml)	**(j)** 2555 ml	(l)

2 Each spoonful of medicine holds 5 ml. How many such doses can be served from a 1 litre bottle?

3 A glass of lemonade holds 600 ml. How many glasses can be filled from a 3 litre container?

4 150 milk bottles of 750 ml capacity are emptied into a container in order to fill it. What is its capacity in litres?

5 **(a)** How many 350 ml glasses can I fill completely from a 5 litres barrel? **(b)** How many ml will be left at the bottom of the barrel?

6 If I pour 3 litres of orange juice into six 300 ml glasses and the rest into 200 ml glasses, how many of the smaller glasses do I fill?

7 12 litres of water are poured into 16 identical containers. How many millilitres will each container hold?

8 A patient takes 10 ml of medicine 4 times per day. How long will a litre bottle of medicine last?

9 How many bottles of liquid of capacity 1.25 litres can be filled from a container of 50 litres?

10 1 litre of petrol lasts 15 kilometres. How far will 200 ml last?

Using metric units generally

kilometre (km)	centimetre (cm)	kilogram (kg)
metre (m)	litre (l)	gram (g)
millimetre (mm)	millilitre (ml)	milligram (mg)

1 Select from the metric units above, the unit you would choose to measure these:

(a) the mass of a packet of crisps

(b) the length of a fishing rod

(c) the height of a house

(d) the thickness of a pane of glass

(e) the capacity of a petrol tank

(f) how heavy your holiday luggage might be

(g) the distance from London to Manchester

(h) the mass of a page in this book

(i) the contents of small can of 'Coke'

(j) the length of a football pitch

(k) how heavy a small lock of your hair might be

(l) how heavy your television might be

2 If you drink 800 ml of milk per day, how many litres would you drink in a 30 day month?

3 How many 150 mm lengths of wood can cut from a 3 m length?

4 A wheel has a circumference of 60 cm. How far will it travel in metres, if it goes round 20 times?

5 A tin of fruit weighs 315 g. Find the weight in kg of 50 tins.

6 The distance around a running track is 400 m. How many laps must I run in an 8 km race?

7 A £5 bag of 10p coins weighs 1 kg. What is the mass of a single coin, in grams?

8 A fence post is 175 cm long. What length of wood, in metres, is needed to make 8 such posts?

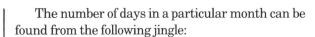

Unit 14

Time

14.1 Units of time

Time in this country in winter is measured using Greenwich Mean Time (GMT). In summer the clocks are put forward one hour and this is known as British Summer Time (BST).

Time is measured in non-metric units as shown in Table 14.1.

60 seconds (s) = 1 minute (m)
60 minutes = 1 hour (h)
24 hours = 1 day
7 days = 1 week
28/30/31 days = 1 month
365 days = 1 year
366 days = 1 leap year
13 weeks = 1 quarter
52 weeks = 1 year
12 months = 1 year

Table 14.1

The number of days in a particular month can be found from the following jingle:

●●

'Thirty days hath September,
April, June and November.
All the rest have thirty-one
Except February alone,
Which has twenty-eight days clear
and twenty-nine in each leap year.'

●●

The time of day can be expressed, either using the 12-hour clock, or the 24-hour clock. Our normal clocks and watches use the 12-hour clock and we tell morning from afternoon by using a.m. and p.m.

a.m. = ante meridiem (before midday) = morning
p.m. = post meridiem (after midday) = afternoon

Digital watches and clocks have, these days, enabled us to use the 24-hour clock system and most travel timetables are now written using the 24-hour clock running from 0000 hours (midnight) through to 2400 hours (midnight again). 7 a.m. (i.e. 7 o'clock in the morning) is written as 0700 ('seven hundred hours'). Midday would be 1200 hours and 4.30 p.m. would be 1630 hours ('sixteen thirty hours').

14.2 Operations involving units of time

Table 14.2 gives an extract from a Railway Timetable.

Crewe	Alsager	Kidsgrove	Longport	Etruria	Stoke
0600	0609	0615	0621	0625	0629
0720	0729	0735	0741	0745	0749
0810	0819	0825	0831	0835	0839
0920	0929	0935	0941	0945	0949
1020	1029	1035	1041	1045	1049
1120	1129	1135	1141	1145	1149
1220	1229	1235	1241	1245	1249
1320	1329	1335	1341	1345	1349
1420	1429	1435	1441	1445	1449
1530	1539	1545	1551	1555	1559

Table 14.2

Crewe

Kidsgrove

Stoke-on-Trent

Example 1 How long do the following journeys take?

(a) Crewe to Stoke (b) Alsager to Etruria
(c) Kidsgrove to Stoke

(a) Crewe to Stoke takes 29 minutes
(b) Alsager to Etruria takes 16 minutes
(c) Kidsgrove to Stoke takes 14 minutes

Example 2 Which train must I catch from Crewe in order to arrive at Stoke after 1.30 p.m.?

1.30 p.m. = 1330 hours. Next arrival at Stoke from Crewe due at 1349 hours.

So, I need to catch the 1320 hours train from Crewe.

Example 3 I arrive at Kidsgrove at 3.30 p.m. to catch the next train to Stoke. How long do I have to wait for the next train?

3.30 p.m. = 1530 hours. Next train to Stoke leaves at 1545 hours.

So, I have to wait 15 minutes or $\frac{1}{4}$ of an hour.

Other types of questions we may have to deal with, concerning **time**, are:

Example 4 How many minutes in $2\frac{1}{4}$ hours?

$$1 \text{ hour} = 60 \text{ minutes}$$
$$\text{so, } 2\tfrac{1}{4} \text{ hours} = 2\tfrac{1}{4} \times 60 \text{ minutes}$$
$$= 135 \text{ minutes}$$
$$\text{or } 2\tfrac{1}{4} \text{ hours} = 2 \text{ hours } 15 \text{ minutes}$$
$$\text{but, } 2 \text{ hours} = 120 \text{ minutes}$$
$$\text{and so, } 2\tfrac{1}{4} \text{ hours} = 120 + 15 = 135 \text{ minutes}$$

Example 5 Change 210 seconds into minutes.

$$60 \text{ seconds} = 1 \text{ minute}$$
$$\text{so, } 210 \text{ seconds} = \frac{210}{60} \text{ minutes} = \frac{7}{2} \text{ minutes}$$
$$= 3\tfrac{1}{2} \text{ minutes}$$
$$\text{(in mixed number form)}$$

Example 6 A man earns £6000 p.a. (p.a. means per annum or per year). How much is this per month?

$$12 \text{ months} = 1 \text{ year}$$

£6000 earned in 1 year is the same as

$$\frac{6000}{12} \text{ earned in 1 month}$$
$$= £500 \text{ per month}$$

Example 7 How many weeks are there from Wednesday 6 February to Wednesday 22 May? (See Fig. 14.1.)

Simply count down the Wednesday columns throughout February, March, April and May (to the 22nd).

February 6 – 13, 13 – 20, 20 – 27, 27 – March 6,
  Weeks   1,   2,   3,   4,

6 – 13, 13 – 20, 20 – 27, 27 – April 3, 3 – 10,
  5,   6,   7,   8,   9,

10 – 17, 17 – 24, 24 – May 1, 1 – 8, 8 – 15, 15 – 22
  10,   11,   12,   13,   14,   15.

Total is 15 weeks.

Calendar 1985

January		February		March	
S M T W T F S		S M T W T F S		S M T W T F S	
1 2 3 4 5		1 2		1 2	
6 7 8 9 10 11 12		3 4 5 6 7 8 9		3 4 5 6 7 8 9	
13 14 15 16 17 18 19		10 11 12 13 14 15 16		10 11 12 13 14 15 16	
20 21 22 23 24 25 26		17 18 19 20 21 22 23		17 18 19 20 21 22 23	
27 28 29 30 31		24 25 26 27 28		24 25 26 27 28 29 30	
				31	

April		May		June	
S M T W T F S		S M T W T F S		S M T W T F S	
1 2 3 4 5 6		1 2 3 4		1	
7 8 9 10 11 12 13		5 6 7 8 9 10 11		2 3 4 5 6 7 8	
14 15 16 17 18 19 20		12 13 14 15 16 17 18		9 10 11 12 13 14 15	
21 22 23 24 25 26 27		19 20 21 22 23 24 25		16 17 18 19 20 21 22	
28 29 30		26 27 28 29 30 31		23 24 25 26 27 28 29	
				30	

July		August		September	
S M T W T F S		S M T W T F S		S M T W T F S	
1 2 3 4 5 6		1 2 3		1 2 3 4 5 6 7	
7 8 9 10 11 12 13		4 5 6 7 8 9 10		8 9 10 11 12 13 14	
14 15 16 17 18 19 20		11 12 13 14 15 16 17		15 16 17 18 19 20 21	
21 22 23 24 25 26 27		18 19 20 21 22 23 24		22 23 24 25 26 27 28	
28 29 30 31		25 26 27 28 29 30 31		29 30	

October		November		December	
S M T W T F S		S M T W T F S		S M T W T F S	
1 2 3 4 5		1 2		1 2 3 4 5 6 7	
6 7 8 9 10 11 12		3 4 5 6 7 8 9		8 9 10 11 12 13 14	
13 14 15 16 17 18 19		10 11 12 13 14 15 16		15 16 17 18 19 20 21	
20 21 22 23 24 25 26		17 18 19 20 21 22 23		22 23 24 25 26 27 28	
27 28 29 30 31		24 25 26 27 28 29 30		29 30 31	

Fig. 14.1

Activities

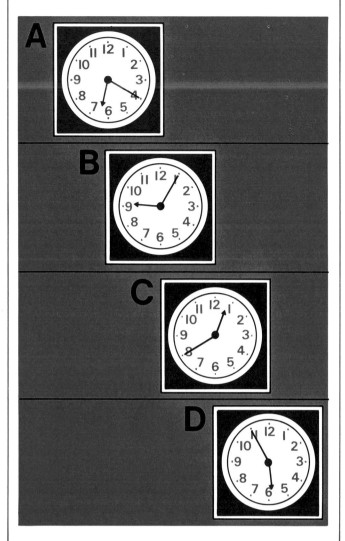

Fig. 14.2

1 In Fig. 14.2 the time shown on Clock A can be written:

Clock A = 6.20 = twenty minutes past six

Write the times shown on

Clock B =   =

Clock C =   =

Clock D =   =

2 How many seconds are there in the following?

  (**a**) 2 minutes   (**e**) $10\frac{1}{3}$ minutes

  (**b**) 5 minutes   (**f**) 1 hour

  (**c**) 20 minutes   (**g**) $6\frac{1}{4}$ minutes

  (**d**) $3\frac{1}{2}$ minutes   (**h**) $1\frac{3}{4}$ minutes

3 How many minutes are there in the following?

  (**a**) 2 h   (**b**) 3 h   (**c**) 5 h 30 m   (**d**) $3\frac{1}{4}$ h

  (**e**) $2\frac{1}{3}$ h   (**f**) $4\frac{3}{4}$ h   (**g**) 24 h   (**h**) 1 h 35 m

4 How many minutes are there between the following times?

  (**a**) 7.00 a.m. and 7.40 a.m.

  (**b**) 12.00 noon and 12.55 p.m.

  (**c**) 10.15 a.m. and 10.35 a.m.

  (**d**) 8.30 p.m. and 9.15 p.m.

  (**e**) 2.10 p.m. and 3.05 p.m.

  (**f**) midnight and 01.10 a.m.

  (**g**) 4.25 a.m. and 5.05 a.m.

  (**h**) 11.45 a.m. and 12.55 p.m.

  (**i**) 6.25 a.m. and 8.10 a.m.

  (**j**) 11.55 a.m. and 2.15 p.m.

5 How many hours and minutes between these times?

  (**a**) 8.15 a.m. and 9.30 a.m.

  (**b**) 6.45 p.m. and 9.15 p.m.

  (**c**) 10.45 p.m. and 02.55 a.m.

  (**d**) 10.34 a.m. and 12.52 p.m.

  (**e**) 6.05 a.m. and 8.55 a.m.

  (**f**) 7.55 a.m. and 12.00 noon

  (**g**) 11.54 a.m. and 2.18 p.m.

  (**h**) midnight and 02.30 p.m.

January							February							March						
M	T	W	T	F	S	S	M	T	W	T	F	S	S	M	T	W	T	F	S	S
						1			1	2	3	4	5				1	2	3	4
2	3	4	5	6	7	8	6	7	8	9	10	11	12	5	6	7	8	9	10	11
9	10	11	12	13	14	15	13	14	15	16	17	18	19	12	13	14	15	16	17	18
16	17	18	19	20	21	22	20	21	22	23	24	25	26	19	20	21	22	23	24	25
23	24	25	26	27	28	29	27	28	29					26	27	28	29	30	31	
30	31																			

April							May							June						
M	T	W	T	F	S	S	M	T	W	T	F	S	S	M	T	W	T	F	S	S
						1	1	2	3	4	5	6					1	2	3
2	3	4	5	6	7	8	7	8	9	10	11	12	13	4	5	6	7	8	9	10
9	10	11	12	13	14	15	14	15	16	17	18	19	20	11	12	13	14	15	16	17
16	17	18	19	20	21	22	21	22	23	24	25	26	27	18	19	20	21	22	23	24
23	24	25	26	27	28	29	28	29	30	31				25	26	27	28	29	30	
30																				

July							August							September						
M	T	W	T	F	S	S	M	T	W	T	F	S	S	M	T	W	T	F	S	S
						1		1	2	3	4	5							1	2
2	3	4	5	6	7	8	6	7	8	9	10	11	12	3	4	5	6	7	8	9
9	10	11	12	13	14	15	13	14	15	16	17	18	19	10	11	12	13	14	15	16
16	17	18	19	20	21	22	20	21	22	23	24	25	26	17	18	19	20	21	22	23
23	24	25	26	27	28	29	27	28	29	30	31			24	25	26	27	28	29	30
30	31																			

October							November							December						
M	T	W	T	F	S	S	M	T	W	T	F	S	S	M	T	W	T	F	S	S
1	2	3	4	5	6	7			1	2	3	4						1	2	
8	9	10	11	12	13	14	5	6	7	8	9	10	11	3	4	5	6	7	8	9
15	16	17	18	19	20	21	12	13	14	15	16	17	18	10	11	12	13	14	15	16
22	23	24	25	26	27	28	19	20	21	22	23	24	25	17	18	19	20	21	22	23
29	30	31					26	27	28	29	30			24	25	26	27	28	29	30
														31						

Fig. 14.3

6 From Fig. 14.3, how many days are there in the following periods?

  (**a**) 1st Jan. to 13th Feb.

  (**b**) 14th June to 3rd Aug.

  (**c**) 15th Aug. to 12th Oct.

  (**d**) 20th April to 25th May

  (**e**) 12th April to 19th June

  (**f**) 28th Oct. to 11th Dec.

  (**g**) 20th Feb. to 4th Mar.

  (**h**) Was this particular year a leap year?

7 Copy and complete this daily diary

	12-hour clock	24-hour clock
(a) Wake up		
(b) Arrive at school		
(c) Lunch begins		
(d) End of school		
(e) Eat tea		
(f) Come in from play		
(g) Go to bed		

Table 14.3

8 Re-write these using the 24-hour clock:

(a) 1.15 a.m. **(e)** noon **(i)** 6.30 p.m.
(b) 5.45 a.m. **(f)** 12.35 p.m. **(j)** 10.25 p.m.
(c) 8.37 a.m. **(g)** 1.05 p.m. **(k)** 11.55 p.m.
(d) 11.50 a.m. **(h)** 2.45 p.m. **(l)** 12.30 a.m.

9 Re-write these using the 12-hour clock. (Put in a.m. or p.m.)

(a) 0045 **(e)** 1210 **(i)** 1910
(b) 0320 **(f)** 1330 **(j)** 2140
(c) 0750 **(g)** 1400 **(k)** 2217
(d) 1015 **(h)** 1505 **(l)** 2349

10 Complete Table 14.4 of journey times (*see overleaf*):

11 Jim arrived at work at 7.50 a.m. and left at 5.15 p.m. For how long was he at work?

12 A coach left London at 1345 and arrived in Birmingham $2\frac{3}{4}$ hours later. What time did the coach reach Birmingham?

13 A milkman took 5 hours 50 minutes to complete his round. If he finished at 11.20 a.m., what time did he start his round?

14 A cinema show starts at 7.35 p.m. and lasts for 2 hours 40 minutes. At what time will the show finish?

15 In a marathon race, the winners time was 2 hours 13 minutes. If he crossed the finishing line at 12.03 p.m., at what time of day did the race start?

16 A video film lasts for 3 hours 17 minutes. What time will it end if the film starts at 8.45 p.m.?

17 A Cross-Channel ferry took 5 hours 38 minutes to make the trip. If it arrived at its destination at 1334, when did it start the journey?

18 Examine Table 14.5, an extract from a Local Bus Timetable:

	Bus A		Bus B		Bus C
Longton	0900	...	1100	...	1330
King St.	0907	...	1106	...	1337
Fenton	0912	...	1110	...	1342
Stoke	0918	...	1115	...	1348
Shelton	0925	...	1120	...	1354
Hanley	0940	...	1130	...	1410

Table 14.5

	Train Departs	Train Arrives	Time of Journey
(a)	10.30 a.m.	12.15 p.m.	1·45
(b)	11.30 a.m.	2.02 p.m.	2·32
(c)	0735	0905	1·30
(d)	1345	1623	2·38
(e)	0710	9.45	2 h 35 m
(f)	1505		1 h 55 m
(g)		1020	3 h 15 m
(h)		2240	2 h 25 m
(i)	0025		4 h 45 m
(j)	2312	0150	

Table 14.4

(a) How long does it take each of the buses to travel from Longton to Hanley?

(b) Which bus is quickest, and by how many minutes?

(c) If a woman gets on Bus A and gets off at Fenton to do some shopping, how long has she before she gets on Bus B to continue on to Hanley?

(d) If I have an appointment in Hanley at 2.00 p.m., will I be late if I catch Bus C from Longton?

(e) If so, by how many minutes will I be late?

(f) How many minutes between Bus A and Bus B at King St?

19 Examine the extract from a T.V. schedule in Table 14.6.

(a) How long does 'Breakfast Time' last?

(b) What fraction of an hour does 'The Flumps' last?

(c) How long between the end of 'Jackanory' and the start of 'News After Noon'?

(d) How long does the afternoon film last?

(e) How long is given over to News, both regional and national?

(f) If one page of 'Ceefax' is on the screen for 1 minute, how many pages can be shown during the early morning session of 'Ceefax'?

B.B.C.1

6.0 Ceefax AM.
6.30 Breakfast Time introduced by Selina Scott and Mike Smith.
9.0 Tarzan, Lord of the Jungle: Tarzan and the White Elephant.
9.25 Look Back With Noakes.
9.55 Jackanory with David Yip.
10.10 Take Hart with Tony Hart and Morph.
10.30 Play School.
10.55 Pages from Ceefax.
1.0 News After Noon.
1.25 Weather.
1.27 Regional News.
1.30 The Flumps.
1.45 The Life of a Lake: Windermere in Spring. A look at England's largest lake in the months before the crowds arrive.
2.35 Film: The French Line. Last of three films starring Jane Russell, also starring Gilbert Roland, Arthur Hunnicutt.
4.18 Regional News.
4.20 Play School: It's Friday.
4.40 Heathcliffe.
4.45 Jigsaw.

Table 14.6

Unit 15

Perimeter

Note In this section, diagrams are not always shown drawn to true size or to scale.

15.1 Definition

The perimeter is the distance all around the edge of a shape.

15.2 Perimeters of different shapes

Example 1

The distance around the square shape in Fig. 15.1 is

$$3 \text{ cm} + 3 \text{ cm} + 3 \text{ cm} + 3 \text{ cm} = 12 \text{ cm}$$
$$\text{Perimeter of this square} = 12 \text{ cm}$$

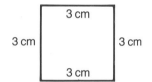

Fig. 15.1

Example 2

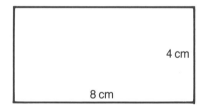

Fig. 15.2

The distance around the oblong (rectangular) shape in Fig. 15.2, is

$$8 \text{ cm} + 4 \text{ cm} + 8 \text{ cm} + 4 \text{ cm} = 24 \text{ cm}$$
$$\text{Perimeter of this rectangle} = 24 \text{ cm}$$

Example 3

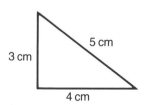

Fig. 15.3

The distance around the triangular shape in Fig. 15.3 is

$$3 \text{ cm} + 4 \text{ cm} + 5 \text{ cm} = 12 \text{ cm}$$
$$\text{Perimeter of this triangle} = 12 \text{ cm}$$

Example 4

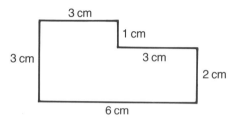

Fig. 15.4

The distance around the shape in Fig. 15.4 is

$$6 \text{ cm} + 3 \text{ cm} + 3 \text{ cm} + 1 \text{ cm} + 3 \text{ cm} + 2 \text{ cm} = 18 \text{ cm}$$
$$\text{Perimeter of shape} = 18 \text{ cm}$$

Example 5

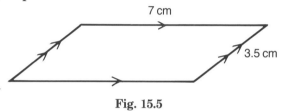

Fig. 15.5

The distance around the parallelogram shape in Fig. 15.5 is

$$7 \text{ cm} + 3.5 \text{ cm} + 7 \text{ cm} + 3.5 \text{ cm} = 21 \text{ cm}$$
$$\text{Perimeter of shape} = 21 \text{ cm}$$

Example 6

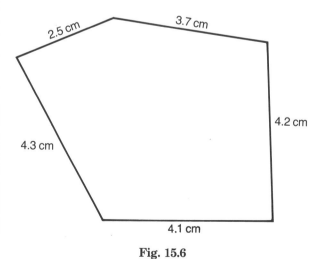

Fig. 15.6

Perimeter of the shape in Fig. 15.6
$$= 2.5 \text{ cm} + 3.7 \text{ cm} + 4.2 \text{ cm} + 4.1 \text{ cm} + 4.3 \text{ cm}$$
$$= 18.8 \text{ cm}$$

Activities

1 Find the perimeters of the shapes in Fig. 15.7
(remember, not always drawn to true size), giving
your answers in cm.

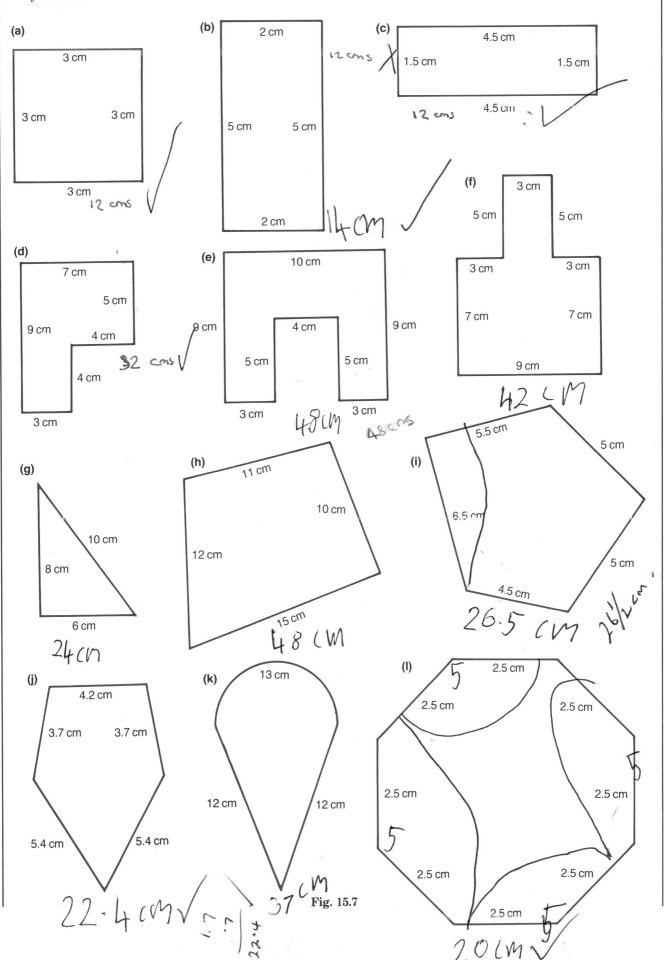

(a)

3 cm
3 cm 3 cm
3 cm
12 cms ✓

(b)

2 cm
5 cm 5 cm
2 cm
12 cms ✗ 14 CM ✓

(c)

4.5 cm
1.5 cm 1.5 cm
12 cms 4.5 cm

(d)

7 cm
5 cm
9 cm 4 cm
4 cm
3 cm
32 cms ✓

(e)

10 cm
9 cm 4 cm 9 cm
5 cm 5 cm
3 cm 3 cm
48 CM 48 cms

(f)

3 cm
5 cm 5 cm
3 cm 3 cm
7 cm 7 cm
9 cm
42 CM

(g)

10 cm
8 cm
6 cm
24 cm

(h)

11 cm
10 cm
12 cm
15 cm
48 CM

(i)

5.5 cm
5 cm
6.5 cm
4.5 cm 5 cm
26.5 CM 26½cm

(j)

4.2 cm
3.7 cm 3.7 cm
5.4 cm 5.4 cm
22.4 CM ✓ 22.4

(k)

13 cm
12 cm 12 cm
37 CM

Fig. 15.7

(l)

2.5 cm
2.5 cm 2.5 cm
2.5 cm 2.5 cm
2.5 cm 2.5 cm
2.5 cm
5
20 CM ✓

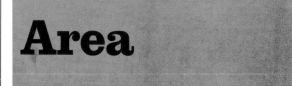

Unit 16

Area

Note In this section, diagrams are not always shown drawn to true size or to scale.

16.1 Squares and rectangles

Fig. 16.1

The small square in Fig. 16.1 measures 1 cm by 1 cm.

The amount of paper which it encloses is known as its **area** and this 1 cm square has an area of one square centimetre (written as 1 cm^2).

Suppose we have a square measuring 3 cm by 3 cm. This square is made up of nine 1 cm squares, as shown in Fig. 16.2 and so its area is nine square centimetres or 9 cm^2.

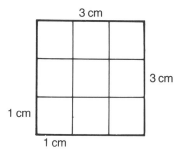

Fig. 16.2

In the case of a rectangle, such as the one shown in Fig. 16.3 (*see below*), it is made up of twenty cm squares and so its area is 20 square cm (20 cm^2).

We can see now that, rather than splitting the shape into 1 cm squares and then counting the number of squares to find the area, it is much easier to just multiply the length of the shape by its breadth (or width).

Hence, the area of the **square**, in Fig. 16.2 would be

$$3 \text{ cm} \times 3 \text{ cm} = 9 \text{ cm}^2$$

and the area of the **rectangle**, in Fig. 16.3, would be

$$10 \text{ cm} \times 2 \text{ cm} = 20 \text{ cm}^2$$

Length 10 cm

breadth (or width) 2 cm

Fig. 16.3

Example 1 Find the area of the rectangle in Fig. 16.4.

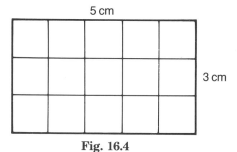

Fig. 16.4

There are fifteen 1 cm squares, so the area = 15 cm^2.

Or, area = length $\times$ breadth

$$= 5 \times 3 = 15 \text{ cm}^2$$

Example 2 Find the area of a rectangle measuring 8 cm in length and 4 cm in width.

We must always draw a diagram of the situation, so see Fig. 16.5.

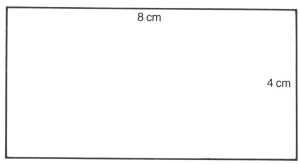

Fig. 16.5

area = length $\times$ breadth = 8 $\times$ 4 = 32 cm^2

Example 3 What is the area of a square of side length 3.5 cm?

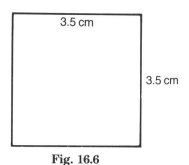

Fig. 16.6

Fig. 16.6 shows the square.

area = length $\times$ breadth = 3.5 $\times$ 3.5 = 12.25 cm^2

So far we have dealt with problems involving cm^2. Obviously there are other units for area, such as mm^2, m^2 and km^2.

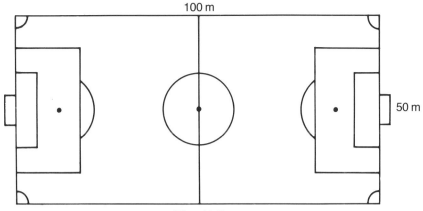

Fig. 16.7

The square millimetre (mm^2) is a very small unit of area measuring 1 mm by 1 mm.

The square metre (m^2) is a square of side length 1 m used for measuring areas of plots of land. For instance, a football pitch of length 100 m and width 50 m, as in Fig. 16.7.

This has an area of $100 \times 50 = 5000$ m^2.

The square kilometre is a square of side 1 km. It is used for measuring the areas of much larger plots of land, such as cities, counties or even countries.

It is very important that we can change easily from one set of square units to another.

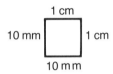

Fig. 16.8

For instance, a square measuring 1 cm by 1 cm, as shown in Fig. 16.8, also measures 10 mm by 10 mm.

Its area could be 10 mm $\times$ 10 mm = 100 mm^2

as well as 1 cm $\times$ 1 cm = 1 cm^2

Hence, 1 cm^2 = 100 mm^2.

Likewise, a square measuring 1 m by 1 m also measures 100 cm by 100 cm.

Its area could be 100 cm $\times$ 100 cm = 10 000 cm^2

as well as 1 m $\times$ 1 m = 1 m^2

Hence, 1 m^2 = 10 000 cm^2.

Similarly, a square measuring 1 km by 1 km also measures 1000 m by 1000 m.

Its area could be 1000 m $\times$ 1000 m = 1 000 000 m^2

as well as 1 km $\times$ 1 km = 1 km^2

Hence, 1 km^2 = 1 000 000 m^2

Below, is a table of areas

1 cm^2	= 100 mm^2
1 m^2	= 10 000 cm^2
1 km^2	= 1 000 000 m^2

Table 16.1

N.B. One very important thing we must remember is, that when we find the area of any shape, the units must always be of the same type.

Example 4 Find the area of a rectangle, 2 m 75 cm long and 40 cm wide.

Here we have a mixture of units and so we must start by either changing 2 m 75 cm into cm, i.e. 275 cm, or by changing 2 m 75 cm and 40 cm to m, i.e. 2.75 m and 0.4 m (see Fig. 16.9).

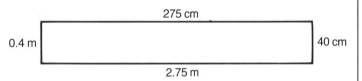

Fig. 16.9

area = length $\times$ breadth

     = 275 $\times$ 40 (in cm)

     = 11 000 cm^2 (in cm^2)

or,   area = length $\times$ breadth

     = 2.75 $\times$ 0.4 (in m)

     = 1.1 m^2 (in m^2)

Both answers are identical, since we have just discovered that 1 m^2 = 10 000 cm^2
and so 11 000 cm^2 = 1.1 m^2

44

Activities

1 Find the area of the squares in Figs. 16.10, 16.11 and 16.12, clearly stating the correct units.

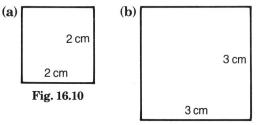

(a)
2 cm
2 cm
Fig. 16.10

(b)
3 cm
3 cm
Fig. 16.11

(c)
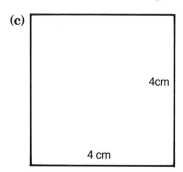
4cm
4 cm
Fig. 16.12

2 And these:

(a) A square of side 7 cm

(b) A square of side 10 cm

(c) A square of side 12 cm

(d) A square of side 1.1 m

(e) A square of side 20 mm

(f) A square of side $\frac{1}{3}$ km

(g) A square of side 0.5 m

(h) A square of side $\frac{1}{4}$ cm

3 Find the area of the rectangles in Figs. 16.13, 16.14 and 16.15, clearly stating the correct units.

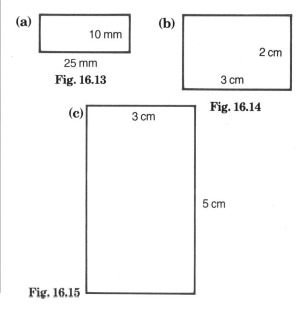

(a)
10 mm
25 mm
Fig. 16.13

(b)
2 cm
3 cm
Fig. 16.14

(c)
3 cm
5 cm
Fig. 16.15

4 And these:

(a) A rectangle measuring 5 cm by 8 cm

(b) A rectangle measuring 4 m by 11 m

(c) A rectangle measuring 9 cm by 30 cm

(d) A rectangle measuring 1.5 m by 6 m

(e) A rectangle measuring 0.75 km by 4 km

(f) A rectangle measuring 15 mm by 12 mm

(g) A rectangle measuring 25 mm by 5 mm

(h) A rectangle measuring $\frac{5}{8}$ m by 4 m

5 Find the area of a square of side length 9 cm.

6 Find the area of a rectangle measuring 7 mm by 11 mm.

7 What is the side length of a square whose area is 4 m^2?

8 What is the side length of a square whose area is 121 cm^2?

9 A rectangle has an area of 45 cm^2 and a length of 5 cm. What is the width of the rectangle?

10 A rectangular piece of card of area 48 cm^2 has a width of 6 cm. What is the length of the card?

11 What is the area of a tennis-court measuring 25 m by 12 m?

12 The area of my table is 6 m^2. If the width is 1.5 m, what is its length?

13 How many square pieces of card of side length 10 cm can I cut from a rectangular piece measuring 40 cm by 50 cm?

14 How many carpet tiles measuring $\frac{1}{2}$ m by $\frac{1}{2}$ m will be needed to cover a floor that measures 6 m by 5 m?

15 My patio floor measures 9 m by 6 m. How many concrete slabs of side length 1 m by $\frac{1}{2}$ m will I need to cover the floor?

With the following, you will need to change some of the units.

16 A photograph measures 10 cm long and 85 mm wide. What is the area of the photograph in (a) cm^2? (b) mm^2?

17 Square carpet tiles of length 50 cm are used to cover a floor of a room measuring 10 m by 12 m. How many tiles are needed?

18 How many square concrete paving slabs, each of side 75 cm, are required to pave a patio floor measuring 12 m by 15 m?

19 A postage stamp is 20 mm long by 15 mm wide. A sheet of 100 stamps has ten rows of ten stamps. (a) What is the length of the sheet? (b) What is the area of the sheet?

16.2 Area by addition

Look at the letter 'E' shape in Fig. 16.16.

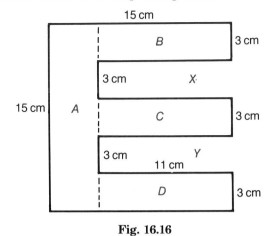

Fig. 16.16

If we wished to find the area of the shape, we would have to split up the shape into 4 rectangles and find the area of each, adding them together to give the total area.

i.e. area **A** + area **B** + area **C** + area **D**

16.3 Area by subtraction

A far easier way of tackling the problem would be to find the area of the outline shape and take from it the areas of the rectangles **X** and **Y**.

Area of total outline = length × breadth

$$= 15 \times 15 = 225 \text{ cm}^2$$

Area of **X** = length × breadth

$$= 11 \times 3 = 33 \text{ cm}^2$$

Area of **Y** $= 33 \text{ cm}^2$

Area of 'E' shape $= 225 - 66 = 159 \text{ cm}^2$

Activities

Areas of rectangular shapes

1 Find the areas of the shapes **(a)** to **(l)**, in Fig. 16.17 by splitting them into rectangles and then adding their areas, or by the subtraction method.

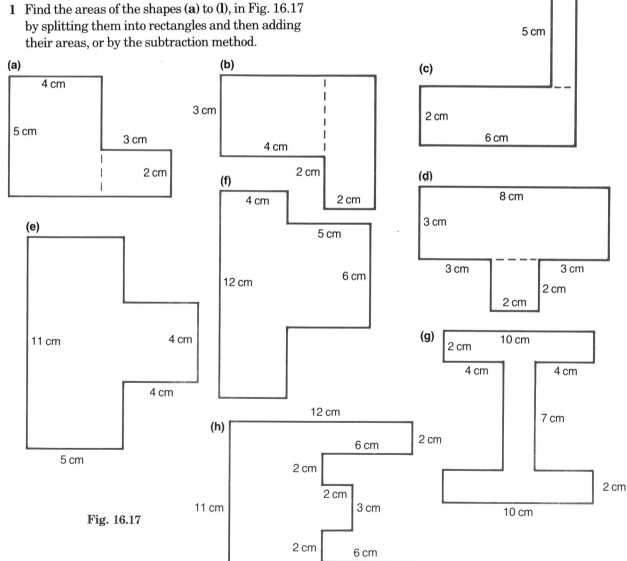

Fig. 16.17

Fig. 16.17 *continued*

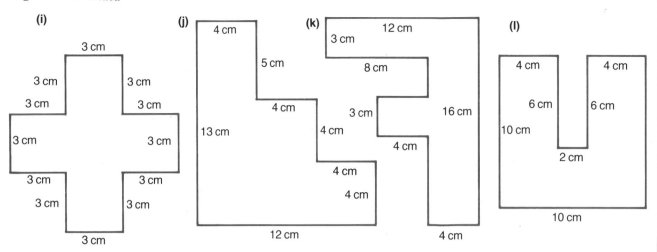

16.4 Area of borders

This is how to find the area of the border surrounding a picture, as in Fig. 16.18.

area of border = (area of frame) − (area of picture)

$$= (6 \times 8) \qquad - (4 \times 6)$$
$$= 48\,\text{cm}^2 \qquad - 24\,\text{cm}^2$$
$$= 24\,\text{cm}^2$$

Fig. 16.18

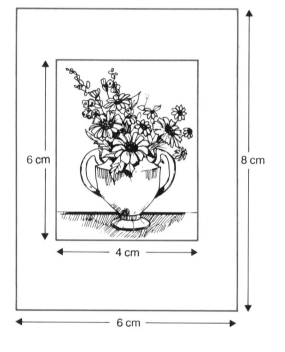

Activities

1 Now, copy and complete Table 16.2.

Frame Size	Frame Area	Picture Size	Picture Area	Area of Border
(a) 12 cm × 10 cm	120 cm²	10 cm × 8 cm	80 cm²	40 cm²
(b) 12 cm × 9 cm		8 cm × 6 cm		
(c) 10 cm × 15 cm		7 cm × 12 cm		
(d) 8 cm × 12 cm		6 cm × 10 cm		
(e) 7 cm × 5 cm		5 cm × 4 cm		
(f) 6 cm × 10 cm		5 cm × 8 cm		

Table 16.2

Conversion of units

1 Express in cm²
   (a) $3\,\text{m}^2$ **(b)** $12\,\text{m}^2$ **(c)** $7.5\,\text{m}^2$ **(d)** $4\frac{1}{4}\,\text{m}^2$

2 Express in mm²
   (a) $9\,\text{cm}^2$ **(b)** $5\,\text{cm}^2$ **(c)** $2.5\,\text{cm}^2$ **(d)** $1\frac{3}{4}\,\text{cm}^2$

3 Express in m²
   (a) $7500\,\text{cm}^2$ **(b)** $220\,000\,\text{cm}^2$ **(c)** $0.5\,\text{km}^2$
   (d) $1\frac{1}{2}\,\text{km}^2$

4 Express 0.050 m² in **(a)** cm²   **(b)** mm²

5 Find **(a)** the area   **(b)** the perimeter of these rectangles, giving your answer in the units indicated:

   (i) length 10 m, width 50 cm,
   area =   cm², perimeter =   m

   (ii) length 4 cm, width 5 mm,
   area =   cm², perimeter =   mm

16.5 Area of a parallelogram

A parallelogram is a 4-sided shape with opposite sides equal in length and parallel to each other. (Obviously, squares and rectangles are special cases of parallelograms with square corners.)

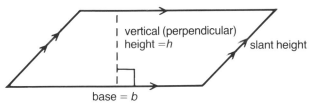

Fig. 16.19

The area of a parallelogram is the base length × vertical height between base and top (sometimes known as the perpendicular height).

$$\text{area} = b \times h$$

Example 1

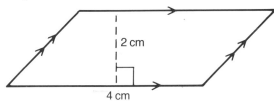

Fig. 16.20

Area = base length × perpendicular height

$= 4 \times 2$

$= 8 \text{ cm}^2$ (square units again, for any area)

Example 2

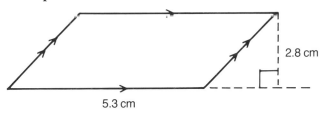

Fig. 16.21

Area = base length × perpendicular height

$= 5.3 \times 2.8$

$= 14.84 \text{ cm}^2$

Example 3

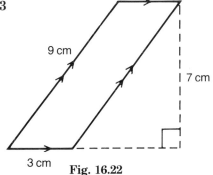

Fig. 16.22

Area of parallelogram $= b \times h$

$= 3 \times 7$

$= 21 \text{ cm}^2$

N.B. If the slant height (i.e., in Fig. 16.22, 9 cm) is given, it must be ignored. We are only interested in the base length and the perpendicular height for the purposes of this calculation.

16.6 Area of a triangle

We have just discovered that the area of a rectangle is its length × its breadth.

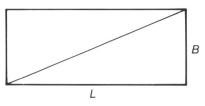

Fig. 16.23

From Fig. 16.23 it is easy to see that if we construct a diagonal line from one corner of the rectangle to the opposite corner, we finish with 2 equal triangles.

Each of these triangles will have an area exactly half of the area of the rectangle.

Example 1 Find the area of the triangle in Fig. 16.24.

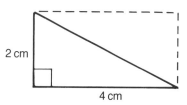

Fig. 16.24

The area of the rectangle would be $L \times B$

$= 4 \times 2 = 8 \text{ cm}^2$

hence, the area of the triangle would be

$\frac{1}{2}$ of $8 \text{ cm}^2 = 4 \text{ cm}^2$

We have also discovered that the area of a parallelogram is its base length × its perpendicular height.

From Fig. 16.25, it is again easy to see that if we construct a diagonal line from one corner of the parallelogram to the opposite corner we obtain 2 equal triangles.

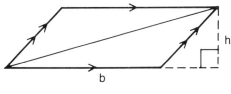

Fig. 16.25

Again, each of these triangles will have an area exactly half of the area of the parallelogram.

Example 2 Find the area of the triangle in Fig. 16.26.

Area of parallelogram would be $b \times h$

$$= 3 \times 4 = 12\,\text{cm}^2$$

hence, the area of the triangle would be
$\frac{1}{2}$ of $12\,\text{cm}^2 = 6\,\text{cm}^2$

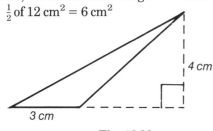

Fig. 16.26

As a general rule, providing we are given the base length of the triangle and its perpendicular height, we can find its area by using the fact that

area of a triangle =
$\frac{1}{2} \times$ base length $\times$ perpendicular height.

Example 3

Area $= \frac{1}{2} \times b \times h$

$= \frac{1}{2} \times 9 \times 7$

$= 31.5\,\text{cm}^2$

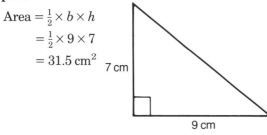

Fig. 16.27

Example 4

(Note that this problem is being worked in m and m^2)

Area $= \frac{1}{2} \times b \times h$

$= \frac{1}{2} \times 14 \times 5$

$= 35\,\text{m}^2$

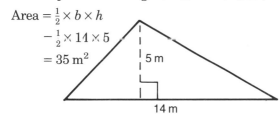

Fig. 16.28

16.7 Area of a trapezium

A trapezium is a 4-sided figure with only one pair of parallel sides as shown in Fig. 16.29.

The lengths of the two parallel sides are a cm and b cm, and the perpendicular distance between them h cm.

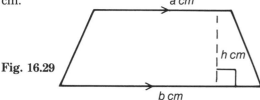

Fig. 16.29

The area of the trapezium is half the sum of the parallel sides $\times$ the perpendicular distance between the parallel sides.

Area of a trapezium $= \frac{1}{2}(a + b) \times h$

Example 1

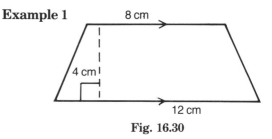

Fig. 16.30

Area of a trapezium $= \frac{1}{2}(a + b) \times h$

$= \frac{1}{2}(8 + 12) \times 4$

$= \frac{1}{2} \times 20 \times 4$

$= 10 \times 4 = 40\,\text{cm}^2$

Example 2

Fig. 16.31

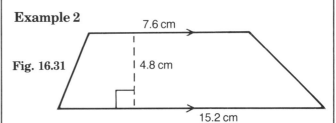

Although this is an odd shape, it is still a trapezium (with one pair of parallel sides).

Area of a trapezium $= \frac{1}{2}(a + b) \times h$

$= \frac{1}{2}(7.6 + 15.2) \times 4.8$

$= \frac{1}{2} \times 22.8 \times 4.8$

$= 11.4 \times 4.8 = 54.72\,\text{cm}^2$

16.8 Area of a kite

Another 4-sided shape which is essentially made up of 2 triangles is a kite (see Fig. 16.32).

To find the area of a kite, it is easiest to split the shape into two triangles. Find the area of each triangle and add them to give the area of the kite.

We note that the base lengths of the 2 triangles are the same but their perpendicular heights h_1 and h_2 will be different.

Area of top triangle $= \frac{1}{2} \times b \times h_1$

Area of bottom triangle $= \frac{1}{2} \times b \times h_2$

Area of kite $= (\frac{1}{2} \times b \times h_1) + (\frac{1}{2} \times b \times h_2)$

Fig. 16.32

Example Find the area of the shape in Fig. 16.33. (It is obviously a kite.)

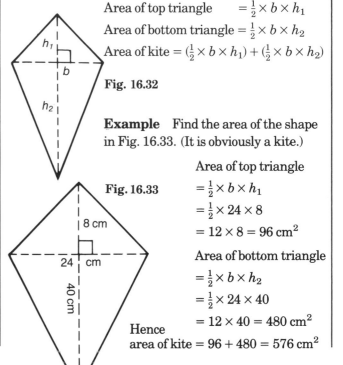

Fig. 16.33

Area of top triangle

$= \frac{1}{2} \times b \times h_1$

$= \frac{1}{2} \times 24 \times 8$

$= 12 \times 8 = 96\,\text{cm}^2$

Area of bottom triangle

$= \frac{1}{2} \times b \times h_2$

$= \frac{1}{2} \times 24 \times 40$

$= 12 \times 40 = 480\,\text{cm}^2$

Hence
area of kite $= 96 + 480 = 576\,\text{cm}^2$

Areas of triangles and quadrilaterals

1 Find the area of each of the shapes in Fig. 16.34.

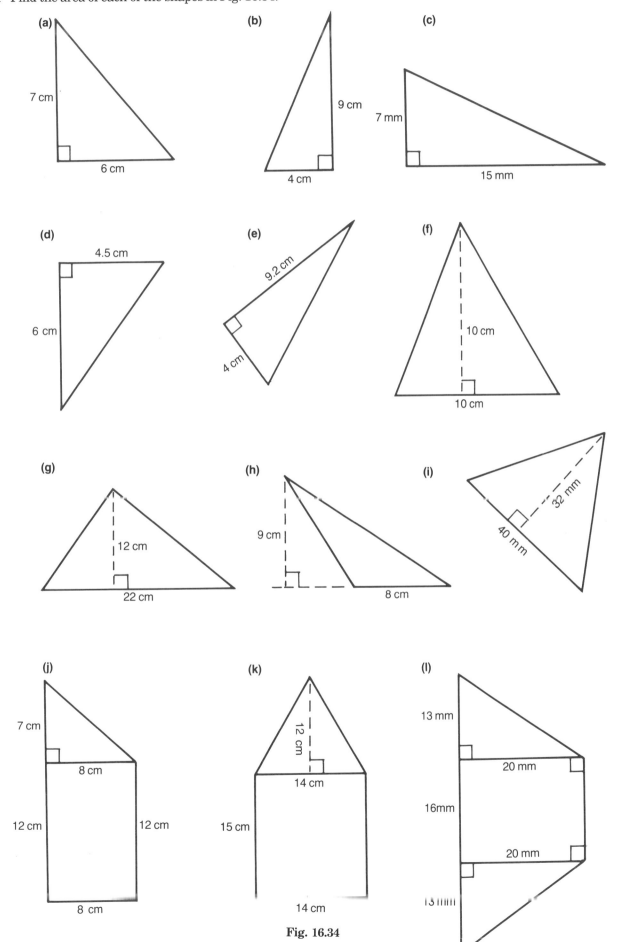

Fig. 16.34

50

2 Calculate the area of each of the parallelograms in Fig. 16.35.

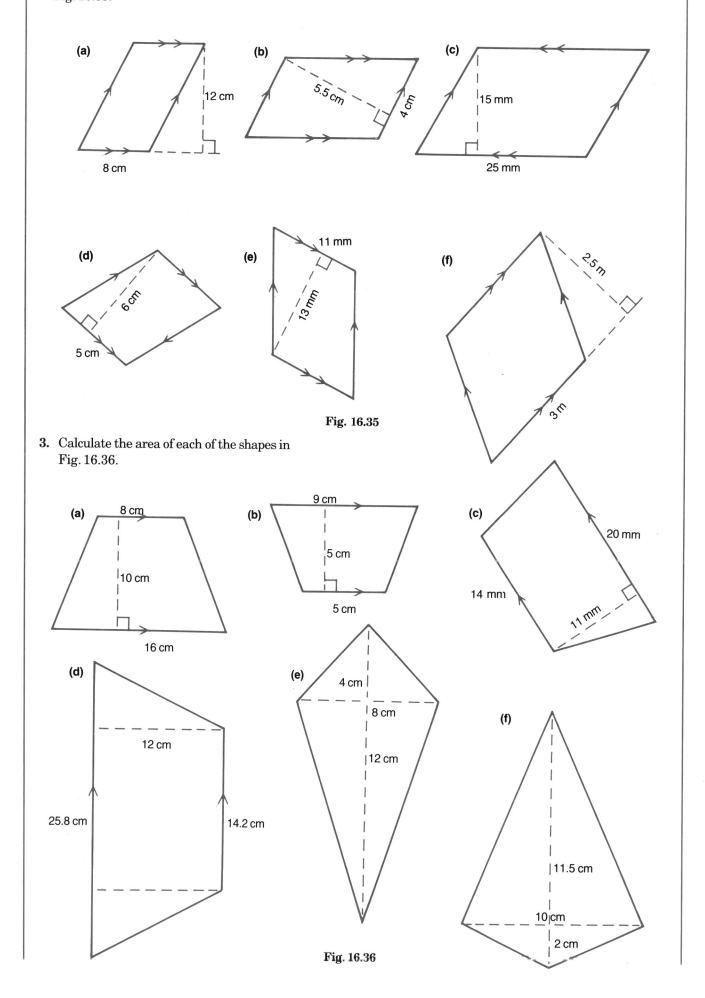

(a) 12 cm, 8 cm

(b) 5.5 cm, 4 cm

(c) 15 mm, 25 mm

(d) 6 cm, 5 cm

(e) 11 mm, 13 mm

(f) 2.5 m, 3 m

Fig. 16.35

3. Calculate the area of each of the shapes in Fig. 16.36.

(a) 8 cm, 10 cm, 16 cm

(b) 9 cm, 5 cm, 5 cm

(c) 20 mm, 14 mm, 11 mm

(d) 12 cm, 25.8 cm, 14.2 cm

(e) 4 cm, 8 cm, 12 cm

(f) 11.5 cm, 10 cm, 2 cm

Fig. 16.36

Problems on area and perimeter

1 The lounge window in a house measures 1.5 m by 3 m and the kitchen window measures 2 m by 2 m. Which is the larger window and by how much?

2 My garden measures 10 m by 8 m. I lay a lawn measuring 6 m by 6 m in the centre of my garden, with a border all around the lawn. What is the area of the border?

3 Find the total area of grass needed to lawn a rectangular area, 7 m by 4.5 m.

4 A trapezium has parallel sides measuring 1.2 m and 3.4 m. If they are 2 m apart, what is the area of the trapezium?

5 Fig. 16.37 is a plan of the downstairs of my house.

(a) What is the area of the lounge?

(b) What is the area of the kitchen?

(c) What is the total area of the downstairs?

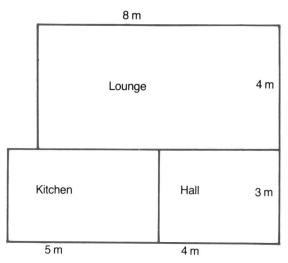

Fig. 16.37

6 Fig. 16.38 shows a flag. All the dimensions are in centimetres. Find:

(a) the area of the red part

(b) the area of the white part

(c) the perimeter of the flag

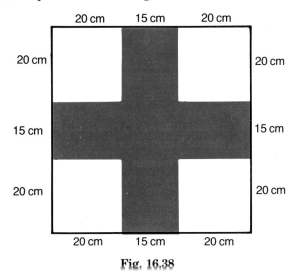

Fig. 16.38

7 Complete Table 16.3 of data about rectangles.

	Length	Breadth	Area	Perimeter
(a)	8 cm	3 cm		
(b)	10 cm		150 cm^2	
(c)	6 mm			20 mm
(d)		11 m	220 m^2	
(e)		5 cm		15 cm

Table 16.3

Composition with Red, Blue and Yellow by Piet Mondrian,
© *DACS 1985*

ALGEBRA

Unit 17

Directed numbers

17.1 Definition

Example 1

Liverpool	80 points + 6
Southampton	77 points + 3
Nottingham Forest	75 points + 1
Manchester United	74 points 0 (zero point)
Q.P.R.	73 points − 1
Arsenal	69 points − 5
Everton	66 points − 8

Table 17.1

Table 17.1 shows the number of points gained at one stage by the top seven clubs in the first division of the football league.

If we compare the other teams with Manchester United, Nottingham Forest has one point more, Southampton has +3 points more but Q.P.R. has one point less and Arsenal has 5 points less.

Compared with Man. Utd., we can then say that Nottingham F. has +1 points, Southampton has +3 points, but Q.P.R. has −1 points and Arsenal has −5 points.

Having chosen Man. Utd. as the starting point, we call this the **zero point**.

If we complete the exercise, then Liverpool has +6 points and Everton has −8 points.

We can see that the + and − signs indicate the directions of the measurements from the zero point, and numbers like +3 (called 'positive 3') and −5 (called 'negative 5') are known as **directed numbers**.

Example 2

In this example, if we take the sea level as the zero point then, in comparison, the kite is 120 m above sea level (i.e. +120 m), the top of the T.V. mast is 110 m above sea level (i.e. +110 m), the cliff is +60 m, the submarine is −20 m and the sea-bed is −50 m.

There would, of course, be nothing to stop us from taking the cliff-top as the zero point, in which case the kite would be +60 m and the sea bed would be −110 m.

To summarize this, we can say that directed numbers are measurements (or numbers) that are more than, or less than, zero.

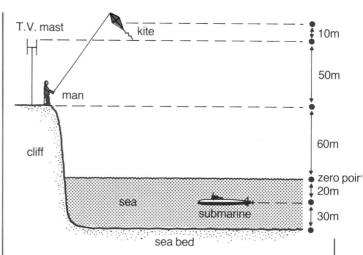

Fig. 17.1

17.2 The number line

So far, we have used a vertical scale as in Fig. 17.2(a), but of course it is just as sensible to use a horizontal number line, like that in Fig. 17.2(b), where numbers to the right of zero are positive (+ve) numbers and numbers to the left of zero are negative (−ve) numbers.

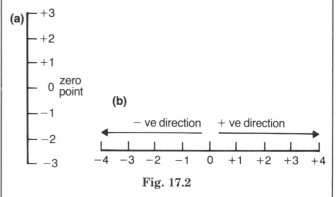

Fig. 17.2

From Fig. 17.3, we can see that the number line travels in two opposite directions, where the line to the right will eventually reach +ve infinity (a very large number that we can never count to) and the line to the left will eventually reach −ve infinity (a very small number that, again, we can never count to).

Fig. 17.3

17.3 'Greater than' and 'less than'

>   this sign means 'greater than'
9 > 3   means 9 is greater than 3
<   this sign means 'less than'
3 < 9   means 3 is less than 9

If we apply the signs to the number line, then we can see that +2 > −4 (plus 2 is greater than negative 4) or −4 < 2 (negative 4 is less than plus 2).

Other examples could be
0 > −1, −1 > −4, −6 < 0 and −8 < −7

17.4 Adding directed numbers

Starting from zero and moving to the right on the number line, is called a positive $(+)$ move.

Moving to the left, is called a negative $(-)$ move.

Example 1 If we start at 0 (zero) on the number line and make a move of $+3$ units (3 units to the right) followed by a move of $+2$ units (2 units to the right), we reach $+5$ (5 units to the right). These moves are equivalent to adding $+2$ to $+3$.

so, $+3 + +2 = +5$ (see Fig. 17.4)

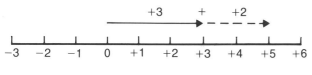

Fig. 17.4

Example 2 Suppose we now consider the addition $-3 + +5$. From 0 (zero) move -3 units (3 units to the left), then add $+5$ units (by moving 5 units to the right).

We end up at $+2$ (see Fig. 17.5).

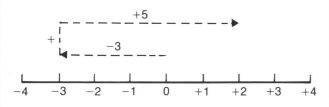

Fig. 17.5

Example 3 $+7 + -3$, we would tackle by going from zero to $+7$. When we add the negative number, the $-$ sign changes the direction, so we add in the opposite direction (see Fig. 17.6).

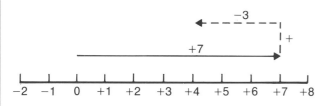

Fig. 17.6

Hence, $+7 + -3 = +4$

17.5 Subtracting directed numbers

Subtraction is finding the difference between 2 amounts. As we saw in Unit 3.3 (Subtraction), the difference between 8 and 15 is $15 - 8$ which is 7.

Example 1 The difference between $+6$ and $+2$ can be $+4$ or -4 depending on which way round we compare the two directed numbers.

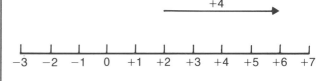

Fig. 17.7

Compared with $+2$, $+6$ is a move of 4 to the right, so $+2 - +6 = +4$ (see Fig. 17.7).

However, compared with $+6$, $+2$ is a move of 4 to the left, so $+2 - +6 = -4$ (see Fig. 17.8).

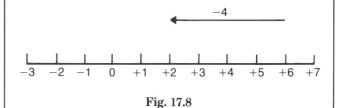

Fig. 17.8

Example 2

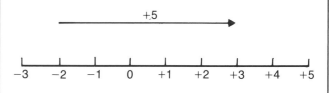

Fig. 17.9

If we consider the situation in Fig. 17.9, we see that, compared with -2, $+3$ is a move of 5 to the right, so $+3 - -2 = +5$.

Example 3

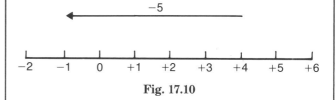

Fig. 17.10

In the situation in Fig. 17.10, we see that, compared with $+4$, -1 is a move of 5 to the left, so
$$-1 - +4 = -5.$$

After a short while, it becomes quite easy to solve the problems without using the number line.

We can see, in Table 17.2, that

$+7 - +2 = +5$
$+5 - -3 = +8$
$-4 - -3 = -1$
$+2 - +5 = -3$
$-4 - +3 = -7$
$-2 - -4 = +2$

Table 17.2

Activities

Negative numbers

> The sign > means **'is greater than'**.
> The sign < means **'is less than'**.

Say whether the following statements are **true** or **false**:

1	$+5 > +2$	**11**	$+8 < -3$
2	$+1 > +6$	**12**	$+7 > \ 0$
3	$+7 < +9$	**13**	$-5 > +3$
4	$+3 < \ 0$	**14**	$-8 < +7$
5	$-4 < -7$	**15**	$-4 < +9$
6	$-5 > -1$	**16**	$0 < -6$
7	$-3 > -9$	**17**	$0 > +4$
8	$-6 > -5$	**18**	$-7 > +2$
9	$+6 < -6$	**19**	$+7 < -7$
10	$+3 > -5$	**20**	$+1 > -2$

Insert either $\oslash$ or $\ominus$ between the pairs of numbers to make the statements true:

21	$+9 \bigcirc +7$	**26**	$+4 \bigcirc -7$
22	$+4 \bigcirc +8$	**27**	$+9 \bigcirc -4$
23	$-5 \bigcirc -3$	**28**	$-6 \bigcirc -4$
24	$-6 \bigcirc +7$	**29**	$0 \bigcirc -5$
25	$-6 \bigcirc -7$	**30**	$-3 \bigcirc \ 0$

Copy the number line in Fig. 17.11.
  Start each problem from 0.
  For positive (+) numbers, move to the right.
  For negative (−) numbers move to the left.
  For $+4 - 7$, start at 0, move to the right 4 and then to the left 7, to reach −3. We say $+4 - 7 = -3$

Work out the following.

31	$+4 - 6$	**41**	$-2 + 6$
32	$+6 - 7$	**42**	$-3 + 8$
33	$+5 - 8$	**43**	$-5 + 9$
34	$+3 - 3$	**44**	$-6 + 5$
35	$+7 - 10$	**45**	$-9 + 4$
36	$+1 - 6$	**46**	$-2 - 4$
37	$+2 - 5$	**47**	$-7 - 1$
38	$+8 - 13$	**48**	$-7 + 7$
39	$+3 - 11$	**49**	$-6 + 11$
40	$+2 + 5$	**50**	$-6 - 3$

Now work out these, but be careful, you need to make three steps.

51	$+4 + 5 - 12$	**56**	$-5 - 2 + 4$
52	$+3 + 5 - 10$	**57**	$-2 - 4 - 1$
53	$+7 - 4 + 6$	**58**	$-3 - 6 + 15$
54	$+2 - 7 + 3$	**59**	$-8 + 2 + 5$
55	$+5 - 2 - 7$	**60**	$-5 + 3 + 6$

Fill in the missing number with the correct sign to make these correct:

61 $\quad +5 \boxed{?} = +8$ $\qquad$ **63** $\quad -5 \boxed{?} = -1$

62 $\quad -3 - 2 \boxed{?} = +1$ $\quad$ **64** $\quad -3 \boxed{?} = +5$

Directed number operations

1 Pete took the temperature outside his house when the weather was very changeable. Fig. 17.12 shows his results. What was the temperature difference on:
(a) Monday and Tuesday?
(b) Wednesday and Friday?
(c) Friday and Saturday?
(d) Thursday and Friday?
(e) Monday and Wednesday?

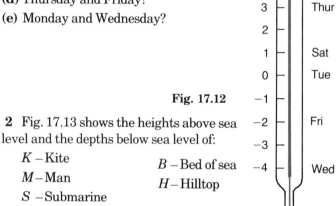

Fig. 17.12

2 Fig. 17.13 shows the heights above sea level and the depths below sea level of:

$\quad K -$ Kite $\qquad\qquad B -$ Bed of sea
$\quad M -$ Man $\qquad\qquad H -$ Hilltop
$\quad S -$ Submarine

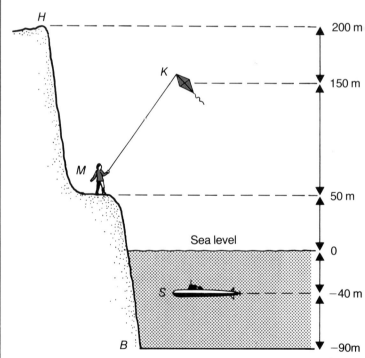

Fig. 17.13

What is the difference in height between
(a) K and S $\qquad$ **(b)** M and B
(c) H and B $\qquad$ **(d)** H and S

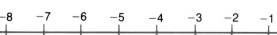

Fig. 17.11

3 At noon, the temperature outside was 2°C. By midnight it had fallen by 5°C. What was the temperature at midnight?

4 The temperature in Moscow was −9°C when it was 3°C in London. What was the temperature difference between the two cities?

5 A submarine is 750 m below sea level and a helicopter is 2000 m above the submarine. How far above sea level is the helicopter?

6 If I drop a coin off a bridge 8 m above the river surface and the river is 4 m deep, how far does the coin fall to reach the river bed?

17.6 Multiplying and dividing directed numbers

Under the operation of multiplication, the directed numbers behave as shown in the following examples.

Example 1 Two positive numbers multiplied together, give a positive product, i.e.

$$+3 \times +6 = +18$$

Example 2 A positive number and a negative number multiplied together, give a negative product, i.e.

$$+5 \times -3 = -15$$
$$\text{or} \quad -6 \times +2 = -12$$

Example 3 Two negative numbers multiplied together, give a positive product, i.e.

$$-4 \times -2 = +8$$

Division of directed numbers follows the same pattern as multiplication, i.e.

$$+35 \div +7 = +5$$
$$+24 \div -6 = -4$$
$$\text{or} \quad -30 \div +5 = -6$$
$$\text{and} \quad -21 \div -7 = +3$$

Summary

$$+ \begin{matrix} \times \\ \div \end{matrix} + = +\text{ve result}$$

$$+ \begin{matrix} \times \\ \div \end{matrix} - = -\text{ve result}$$

$$\text{or} \quad - \begin{matrix} \times \\ \div \end{matrix} + = -\text{ve result}$$

$$\text{and} \quad - \begin{matrix} \times \\ \div \end{matrix} - = +\text{ve result}$$

Table 17.3

More operations with directed numbers

Simplify these:

1	$13 + (-7)$	**11**	$(-13) + (-8)$
2	$8 + (-5)$	**12**	$8 + (-3) + (-7)$
3	$5 + (-8)$	**13**	$9 - (-4) - (-7)$
4	$(-5) + (-6)$	**14**	$5 - (-2) + (-7)$
5	$(-10) + (-3)$	**15**	$10 + (-5) - (-7)$
6	$(-4) + (+6)$	**16**	$(-3) - (-7) + (-1)$
7	$(-5) - (-3)$	**17**	$(-3) + (-6) + (-1)$
8	$3 - (-6)$	**18**	$(-2) - (-5) - (-8)$
9	$(-2) - (-5)$	**19**	$-(-5) - (-8) + (-2)$
10	$8 - (-5)$	**20**	$-(-4) + (-3) - (-5)$

Now, simplify these:

21 $5 \times (-6)$ **28** $\dfrac{-88}{11}$

22 $(-5) \times 7$

23 $(-3) \times (-5)$ **29** $\dfrac{-84}{-12}$

24 $(-10) \times (-4)$

25 $(-16) \div 4$ **30** $\dfrac{36}{-9}$

26 $(-24) \div (-6)$

27 $55 \div (-5)$

Write these in another way:

31 My watch is −5 minutes slow.

32 Your watch is −4 minutes fast.

33 I have −£50 in my bank account.

34 The school population increased by −50 pupils.

35 The party moves −5 kilometres due west.

Unit 18

Collecting like terms

The sum of 3 apples and 9 apples is 12 apples. If, however, 3 apples and 4 bananas are put together, we cannot write the result any more simply than by saying that there are 3 apples and 4 bananas.

In Algebraic terms, only **like terms** can be collected together. Terms which are not the same (unlike terms) cannot be collected together. For instance,

$$3a + 9a = 12a \text{ (like terms)}$$

but $\quad 3a + 4b = 3a + 4b$ (unlike terms)

Note that $3a$ means 3 times a or $3 \times a$.

We can, of course, group together several terms providing that they are all alike. This process is known as **simplifying** the expression.

Example 1 Simplify $4x + 3x + 2x + x$
$$= 10x$$
Note that x means $1x$ (the 1 is not included)

Example 2 Simplify $5m + 3m - 2m + 6m - 8m$

In this particular case, we have both negative ms and positive ms, and the easiest way to deal with this situation is by grouping the positive and negative terms, i.e.

$$5m + 3m + 6m - 2m - 8m$$
$$\text{(positive } m\text{s)} \quad \text{(negative } m\text{s)}$$
$$= 14m - 10m = +4m \text{ (or } 4m)$$

Example 3 Simplify $3a + 8b + 6a + 4b$

In this case, we can group the like terms together, i.e.

$$3a + 6a + 8b + 4b$$
$$a\text{s} \qquad b\text{s}$$
$$= 9a + 12b$$

Example 4 Simplify $7m - 2n + 6 - 5m + 7n + 3$

Grouping once again, we get

$$7m - 5m - 2n + 7n + 6 + 3$$
$$m\text{s} \qquad n\text{s} \qquad \text{numbers}$$
$$= 2m + 5n + 9$$

Bearing in mind what we discovered in directed numbers (in the previous Unit), we can now deal with problems of the following types.

Example 5 Simplify $2y + 9y - 7y - 8y$

Grouping +ve and −ve terms
$$11y - 15y = -4y$$

Example 6 Simplify
$$7a - 3b - 11a + 6c + 9b - 8c$$
Grouping as, bs and cs
$$7a - 11a + 9b - 3b + 6c - 8c$$
$$= -4a + 6b - 2c$$

Example 7 Simplify $3ab + 2bc + 5ba + 3cb$

In this case we must realize that ab is exactly the same as ba, since ab means $a \times b$ and ba means $b \times a$ (which are of course identical – known as commutative) i.e. $3 \times 4 = 4 \times 3 = 12$ (see Unit 19 for full explanation).

Likewise, the same applies to bc and cb.

Hence, grouping like terms
$$3ab + 5ba + 2bc + 3cb$$
$$= 8ab + 5bc$$

Example 8 Simplify $3ab - 8bc - 7ab + 9bc$
Grouping together like terms
$$3ab - 7ab - 8bc + 9bc$$
(Using our directed number knowledge)
$$= -4ab + 1bc \text{ or } -4ab + bc$$

Activities

Simplify:

1

Fig. 18.1

2

Fig. 18.2

3 $\quad 3a + 4a + 5a$

4 $\quad 5b + 2b + 3b$

5 $\quad 6c + 2c + c$

6 $\quad d + 4d + 7d$

7 $\quad 6e + e - 4e$

8 $2f + 6f - 7f$

9 $7g - 2g - 3g$

10 $5h - 3h - 7h$

*Remember – you can only collect **like** terms

11 $2a + 3b + 5a + 4b$

12 $3x + 4y + x + y$

13 $8a + 3y + 5a - y$

14 $5x + 4y - 2x - 3y$

15 $4a + 5b + a - b$

16 $7x + 2y - 6x + 3y$

17 $6m + 9n - m - 9n$

18 $2a + 3b - 2a + 2b$

19 $a + b + a - b$

20 $5f + 10 + 2f + 3$

21 $5a + 2b + a + 3b + 2a + 6b$

22 $3e + 2f + g + g - 2f - g$

23 $2a - b + 3a - 2b$

24 $a + b - a - b + 3c$

25 $2m + n + p - n + 3p$

26 $5x + 2y - z - 5x - 2y + z$

27 $2a + 3b + 5 - a - b - 2$

28 $4p - 2q - r + p - 3q - 2r$

29 $8e + f + 6g - 5g + 3f - 2e$

30 $7a + b - 3c + 2a - 4b - c$

Simplify these: *Remember $ab = ba$

31 $2xy + 5xy + 4xy$

32 $3ab + 2ab + ba$

33 $8pq - 4pq - pq$

34 $xy + yx + x + 2x$

35 $3fg + 5fg + 2gf - f - g$

36 $abc + bac + bca$

37 $efg + 3fge - 2fg$

38 $2pt + 3rt + 3pt + 2rt$

39 $3a + 2b + 5a - b + 2ab$

40 $3yx + 2xy - yx$

First simplify these, then find the value if
$a = 3$, $b = 5$ and $c = 2$.

41 $2a + 3b + 2a + b$

42 $4a + c + 3c + 5a$

43 $2b + 3c + 3b + c$

44 $3c + 4b - 2c - 3b$

45 $2a + 3b + 5b - a$

46 $2a + b + c - a - b - c$

47 $6a + 4b - 3a - b - a$

48 $b + c + 7a - b - c - 5a$

49 $2ab + 5ab + 3ab$

50 $8ac - 3ac - ca$

Unit 19

Laws of equations

19.1 Commutative, Associative and Distributive Laws

If a, b and c represent numbers then,

(a) Commutative Law

$$a + b = b + a \quad \text{(addition is commutative)}$$

$$ab = ba \quad \text{(multiplication is commutative, as described above)}$$

but, $a - b \neq b - a$ (subtraction and division are

and $a \div b \neq b \div a$ obviously non-commutative)

(b) Associative Law

$$(a + b) + c = a + (b + c) \text{ (addition is associative)}$$

$$(ab)c = a(bc) \text{ (multiplication is associative)}$$

(c) Distributive Law

$$a(b + c) = ab + ac$$
$$(b + c)a = ba + ca$$

c + r + i + s + p + s = crisps!!

Unit 20

Simple substitution

A letter used in an algebraic expression may have a numerical value.

Example 1   If $a = 4$ find the value of $3a + 2$

$3a$ means $3 \times 4 = 12$

So, $3a + 2$
$= 12 + 2 = 14$

Example 2   If $a = 5$ find the value of $9a - 5a$

We can simplify, $9a - 5a = 4a$

when $a = 5$, $4a = 4 \times 5 = 20$

Example 3   If $a = 3$ find the value of $3a + 6 - 4a$

Simplify, $3a - 4a + 6$

$= -a + 6$

where $a = 3$,

$= -3 + 6 = 3$

Example 4   If $m = 5$ and $n = 2$, find the value of $2m - 5n$

$2m - 5n = 2 \times 5 - 5 \times 2$

$= 10 - 10 = 0$

Example 5   If $m = 2$, $n = 4$, $u = 1$ and $v = 3$, find the value of

$3m - 2n - u + v$

$= 3 \times 2 - 2 \times 4 - 1 + 3$

$= 6 - 8 - 1 + 3$

$= 6 + 3 - 8 - 1$

$= 9 - 9 = 0$

Example 6   If $x = 3$, $y = 4$, $z = 2$, find the value of

$3xy \div 2z$

$= 3 \times 3 \times 4 \div 2 \times 2$

$= 36 \div 4 = 9$

Activities

Algebraic substitution

If $a = 3$, find the value of:

1	$5a$	**6**	$2a - 1$
2	$8a$	**7**	$3a - 2$
3	$2a + 5$	**8**	$5a - 4$
4	$3a + 4$	**9**	$10a - 7$
5	$5a + 7$	**10**	$\frac{1}{2}a$

If $x = 5$ and $y = 2$, find the value of:

11	$2x + y$	**16**	$5x - 3y$
12	$3x + 2y$	**17**	$2x - 5y$
13	$x + 5y$	**18**	$7x - 3y$
14	$6x + y$	**19**	$10y - 3x$
15	$x + \frac{1}{2}y$	**20**	$3y - x$

If $f = 4$, $g = 6$ and $h = 1$ find the value of:

21	$f + g + h$	**31**	fg
22	$2f + 5g + 3h$	**32**	$2gh$
23	$5f - 4h$	**33**	fgh
24	$3f + g + 2f + 3g$	**34**	$fg + gh$
25	$5h + 8f - 5g$	**35**	$3f \div g$
26	$3f + 5g + 3h - 2f - g - h$	**36**	$2g \div fh$
27	$2f + 6g - 5h - 3f$	**37**	$(2f + 2g) \div g$
28	$\frac{1}{2}g + \frac{1}{4}f$	**38**	$\frac{1}{2}fg$
29	$3f - g - 2h$	**39**	$5fg \div 10$
30	$g - f - 2h$	**40**	$gh - f$

Substitution into formulae

1   The cost (C pence) of putting glass into a window depends on its length (L cm) and height (H cm).
If $C = 2L + H$, find the cost if:
(a) $L = 50$ and $H = 30$
(b) $L = 80$ and $H = 100$

2 The cost (P pence) of framing a picture depends on its length (L cm) and width (W cm).

If $P = 2L + 3W$, find the cost if

(a) $L = 60$ and $W = 40$

(b) $L = 25$ and $W = 20$

3 Mrs Jones decides that she will buy x cakes for her son's party. If there are B boys and G girls, then $x = 3B + G$.

How many cakes will she buy if:

(a) $B = 5$ and $G = 3$

(b) $B = 10$ and $G = 6$

4 The number of lollipops (L) that a shop sells depends upon the number of hours (H) that the shop is open and (S) the number of hours of sunshine in the day.

Now $L = 3HS + H$. How many lollipops does the shop sell if:

(a) $H = 8$ and $S = 5$ **(b)** $H = 6$ and $S = 3$

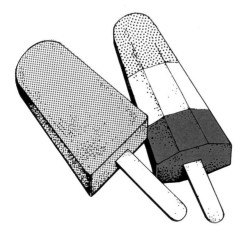

Unit 21

Solving simple equations

$2 + 4 = 6$ is called an **arithmetic equation**.

I think of a number and call it x and add 2. My answer is 6.

Then $x + 2 = 6$. This is called an algebraic equation in which x has only one value, i.e. $x = 4$.

Example 1   Consider the algebraic equation
$$2x - 4 = 10$$

The solution of this equation (i.e. the value of x which satisfies the situation) is best found by using the balance method.

If we imagine the $=$ sign to be the pivot of the balance, then we can represent the equation as a balance (see Fig. 21.1).

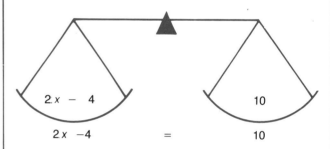

$$2x - 4 \qquad = \qquad 10$$

Fig. 21.1

In order to solve the equation, we must always remember that whatever we do to one side of the balance, we must do exactly the same to the other side, in order to maintain the state of balance.

Suppose we add 4 to each side, we would then have the situation in Fig. 21.2.

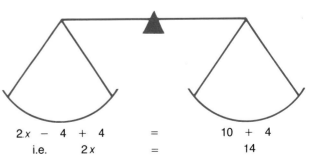

$$2x - 4 + 4 \qquad = \qquad 10 + 4$$
$$\text{i.e.} \qquad 2x \qquad = \qquad 14$$

Fig. 21.2

We now know that $2x = 14$, but we require the value of x. In order to find this, we must divide both sides of the equation by 2 (see Fig. 21.3).

60

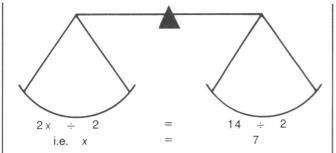

$$2x \div 2 \qquad = \qquad 14 \div 2$$
$$\text{i.e.} \quad x \qquad = \qquad 7$$

Fig. 21.3

We can summarize the above as follows:

$$2x - 4 = 10$$

Add 4 to each side, $\quad 2x = 14$

Divide each side by 2, $x = 7$

Example 2 When x appears on both sides of the equation, we must first of all collect all the xs together on the same side, before using the balance method, i.e.

Solve $7x - 7 = 3x + 9$

Firstly, we will subtract $3x$ from each side (see Fig. 21.4).

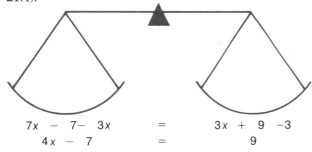

$$7x - 7 - 3x \qquad = \qquad 3x + 9 - 3$$
$$4x - 7 \qquad = \qquad 9$$

Fig. 21.4

We then proceed as in Example 1, by adding 7 to each side of the equation (see Fig. 21.5).

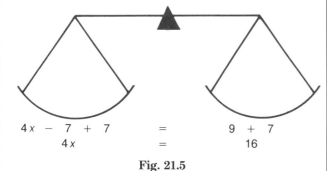

$$4x - 7 + 7 \qquad = \qquad 9 + 7$$
$$4x \qquad = \qquad 16$$

Fig. 21.5

Finally, to find the value of x, we divide both sides of the equation by 4 (see Fig. 21.6).

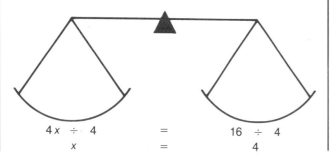

$$4x \div 4 \qquad = \qquad 16 \div 4$$
$$x \qquad = \qquad 4$$

Fig. 21.6

Summary

$$7x - 7 = 3x + 9$$

Subtract $3x$ from each side	$4x - 7 = 9$
Add 7 to each side	$4x = 16$
Divide each side by 4	$x = 4$

Activities

Write these statements in **algebraic form**

A I think of a number, I call it x,
   I double it and add 3.

B I think of a number, I call it y,
   I double it and subtract 5.

C I think of a number, I call it b,
   I treble it and add 7.

D I think of a number, I call it q,
   I multiply it by 5 and add 11 to the result.

E I think of a number, I call it x,
   I add 7 and my answer is 13.

F I think of a number, I call it y,
   I subtract 5 and my answer is 4.

Solve the following equations by taking the same number from both sides:

1	$x + 7 = 15$		**6**	$c + 2 = 3$
2	$x + 6 = 11$		**7**	$7 + c = 10$
3	$x + 4 = 21$		**8**	$a + 8 = 15$
4	$x + 5 = 16$		**9**	$1 + a = 6$
5	$9 + x = 12$		**10**	$y + 4 = 9$

Solve the following equations by adding the same number to both sides:

11	$x - 6 = 4$		**16**	$10 = a - 1$
12	$x - 5 = 9$		**17**	$4 = c - 7$
13	$x - 3 = 11$		**18**	$e - 25 = 5$
14	$x - 9 = 3$		**19**	$g - 2 = 2$
15	$x - 1 = 2$		**20**	$13 = g - 2$

Solve this mixed bag:

21	$4x = 20$		**26**	$x + 8 = 17$
22	$3x = 12$		**27**	$x - 5 = 4$
23	$2x = 40$		**28**	$6 + x = 8$
24	$10x = 50$		**29**	$11 = x - 2$
25	$8x = 32$		**30**	$x - 7 = 20$

Unit 22

Simple set theory

22.1 Description of a set

A set is simply a collection of objects. We are only really interested in the distinct objects in a set – identical objects are not counted.

The objects in a set are called the members or elements of the set.

Examples: the members of your class; a set of golf clubs; a set of postage stamps; the set of even numbers etc.

When it is possible to list the members of the set, we write down the list in curly brackets, separating the members by commas.

For example

$\{a, e, i, o, u\}$ is the set of vowels in the alphabet.

$\{2, 4, 6, 8\}$ is the set of the first four even numbers.

A set is usually described by a capital letter, such as V.

i.e. $V = \{a, e, i, o\ u\}$ which means that 'V is the set containing the elements a, e, i, o, u'

To illustrate this description and listing of sets we will consider the following:

$A = \{\text{months whose names begin with } J\}$

i.e., $A = \{\text{January}, \text{June}, \text{July}\}$

$W = \{\text{the set of whole numbers}\}$

i.e., $W = \{1, 2, 3, 4, 5, ----\}$

$P = \{\text{the set of prime numbers}\}$

i.e., $P = \{2, 3, 5, 7, 11, 13, -----\}$

In the last two cases, the dashes mean that the list goes on and on (it is called **infinite** set).

Sets which have a definite number of members such as $A = \{\text{January}, \text{June}, \text{July}\}$ as above are known as **finite** sets.

22.2 Members of a set

The symbol $\in$ means 'is a member of' or 'is an element of'.

For example, $4 \in$ the set of whole numbers between 1 and 10.

We must also know that $\notin$ means 'is not a member of' etc.

i.e. $6 \notin$ the set of prime members.

Suppose we consider the following statements and say which are true and which are false.

(a) cotton $\in \{\text{man-made fibres}\}$ false

(b)   17 $\in \{\text{whole numbers} < 20\}$ true

(c)   6 $\notin \{\text{odd numbers}\}$ true

(d)   5 $\notin \{\text{prime numbers}\}$ false

22.3 The empty set

The empty set is the set which contains no elements or has no members. Its symbol is φ or $\{\ \}$.

Examples of the empty set are:

(a) The set of odd numbers which are divisible by 2.

(b) The set of months that have more than 31 days.

(c) The set of prime numbers between 32 and 36.

(d) The set of people over 500 years of age.

22.4 Equal sets

Equal sets have the same members. The order of listing the members does not matter, for example

(a) $\{p, q, r, s\} = \{s, p, r, q\}$

(b) $\{1, 2, 3, 4\} = \{2, 4, 3, 1\}$

(c) $D = \{\square, *, \triangle, \bigcirc\}$ $E = \{\triangle, \square, \bigcirc, *\}$

Hence $D = E$

22.5 Subsets

These are what we call sets within sets.

Set B is a subset of set A if every member of B is a member of A.

We write $B \subset A$ which means

$\quad\quad$ 'B is a subset of A'

or $\quad$ 'B is contained in A'

Among the subsets of a set, we must include the set itself and also the empty set.

Example 1 List all the subsets of $\{a, b\}$

The subsets will be $\{a\}, \{b\}, \{a, b\}, \varphi$

Example 2 List all the subsets of $\{1, 2, 3\}$

$\quad$ $\{1\}, \{2\}, \{3\}, \{1, 2\}, \{1, 3\}, \{2, 3\}, \{1, 2, 3\}$
$\quad$ and φ

Example 3 $A = \{1, 3, 5, 7, 9\}$. List the subset T of numbers $\in A$ which are divisible by 3.

$\quad$ $T = \{3, 9\}$

$\quad$ i.e. $T \subset A$

22.6 The universal set

A universal set contains all the elements being discussed. It has a symbol $\mathscr{E}$, E or $\mathcal{U}$. All other sets in the discussion will of course be subsets of E.

Listed below are a few examples of universal sets and some of their possible subsets.

Example 1 $E = \{$the letters of the alphabet$\}$
$\quad\quad\quad$ i.e. $\{a, b, -----x, y, z\}$
$A = \{a, b, c, d\}$ which is a subset of E.

It is in fact the set of the first four letters of the alphabet.

Another might be $V = \{a, e, i, o, u\}$ which again is a subset of E, which we know to be the set of vowels of the alphabet.

Example 2 $E = \{$the countries of Europe$\}$

$C = \{$Spain, France, Holland$\}$ is a subset of this universal set.

Example 3 $E = \{1, 2, 3, 4, 5, 6, 7, 8, 9, 10\}$

The universal set is, in this case, the set of whole numbers from 1 to 10 inclusive.

$T = \{3, 6, 9\}$ is a subset, which is a set of multiples of 3 within this universal set.

$O = \{1, 3, 5, 7, 9\}$ is another subset which is the set of odd numbers within the universal set.

$X = \{1, 5, 6, 8\}$ is another subset of E with no particular description.

22.7 Combining sets

Having discovered what a set actually is, we now want to know what we can actually do with them.

Suppose we have 2 sets, i.e.

$$A = \{1, 2, 3, 4\}$$
$$\text{and}\ \ B = \{5, 6, 7\}$$

We can combine set A and set B together to form a new set. All the elements of A and B together make the set

$$\{1, 2, 3, 4, 5, 6, 7\}$$

This operation is called the **union** of A and B and is written as $A \cup B$ – we say 'A union B'.

Another example could consist of 3 sets, i.e.

$\quad$ $X = \{$Fred, Pete, John, Sam$\}$
$\quad$ $Y = \{$Bill, Keith, Sam$\}$
$\quad$ $Z = \{$Charlie, Ted, Sam, Fred$\}$

We can union all three sets together,

$X \cup Y \cup Z = \{$Fred, Pete, John, Sam, Bill, Keith,
$\quad\quad\quad\quad\quad\quad\quad\quad\quad$ Charlie, Ted$\}$

Notice that Sam is a member of X and Y and Z and Fred is a member of X and Z, but they are included in the union only once.

N.B. Elements of a set are distinct and must never be repeated.

Another way of combining sets is to look for an overlap or **intersection** of the sets. Here we look for elements which belong to more than one set.

If we look again at the example above,

$\quad\quad$ $X = \{$Fred, Pete, John, Sam$\}$
$\quad\quad$ $Y = \{$Bill, Keith, Sam$\}$
$\quad\quad$ $Z = \{$Charlie, Ted, Sam, Fred$\}$

we can immediately see that Fred is a member of both sets X and Z and so we can say the intersection set of sets X and Z is another set containing Fred.

We write this as $X \cap Z = \{$Fred$\}$ and we say 'X intersected with Z' = $\{$Fred$\}$.

So, $\cup$ means union (or joined together)
and $\cap$ means intersection (or overlap)

In the same example of course, Sam is a member of all three sets X, Y and Z and so we can write

$$X \cap Y \cap Z = \{Sam\}$$

It is of course possible to have an empty intersection set as we can see from the following example:

$$M = \{1,2,3,4,5\} \quad N = \{a,b,c,d\}$$

If we union the two sets then

$$M \cup N = \{1,2,3,4,5,a,b,c,d\}$$

But if we intersect the two sets, then $M \cap N = \emptyset$ or $\{\ \}$ since there are no overlapping elements in sets M and N.

22.8 Complement sets

Suppose we have a universal set

$$E = \{1, 2, 3, 4, 5, 6, 7, 8, 9, 10\}$$

If set $A = \{2, 3, 5, 6, 9\}$ then the elements which belong to the universal set E but are not members of set A, are said to be elements of the complement set A. The symbol used for a complement, is a dash i.e. A' (we say 'A dash') and in this case

$$A' = \{1, 4, 7, 8, 10\}$$

Hence a complement of a set contains elements of the universal set which are not members of the original set.

Another example might be as follows:

$$E = \{a, b, c, d, e, f\}$$
$$M = \{a, c\ e\} \qquad N = \{d, e, f\}$$

Then, $M' = \{b, d, f\}$ and $N' = \{a, b, c\}$

We can of course union and intersect complement sets and, considering the example above, we can look at several possibilities, i.e. as in Table 22.1.

$M \cup N$	$= \{a, c, d, e, f\}$
$M \cap N$	$= \{e\}$
$M' \cup N$	$= \{b, d, e, f\}$
$M \cup N'$	$= \{a, b, c, e\}$
$M' \cup N'$	$= \{a, b, c, d, f\}$
$M' \cap N'$	$= \{b\}$
$M' \cap N$	$= \{d, f\}$
$M \cap N'$	$= \{a, c\}$

Table 22.1

If we then consider $(M \cup N)'$, this is asking us for the complement of the set $M \cup N$.

Since $M \cup N = \{a, c, d, e, f\}$ (shown in Table 22.1) then $(M \cup N)' = \{b\}$ i.e. the complement of $M \cup N$.

But notice that this is also the same as $M' \cap N'$ (shown in Table 22.1).

Likewise, consider $(M \cap N)'$. This is asking for the complement of $M \cap N$.

Since $M \cap N = \{e\}$ (shown in Table 22.1)

then $(M \cap N)' = \{a, b, c, d, f\}$
i.e. the complement of $M \cap N$

Again, notice that this is also the same as $M' \cup N'$ (shown in Table 22.1).

This gives us two very important results namely:

$$(A \cup B)' = A' \cap B'$$

i.e. the complement of the union of two sets is the same as the intersection of the complements of the same two sets.

and, $(A \cap B)' = A' \cup B'$

i.e. the complement of the intersection of two sets is the same as the union of the complements of the same two sets.

22.9 The number of elements in a set

Suppose we have set $A = \{w, x, y, z\}$

This set has four elements and so we say the number of elements in this set is 4 and we write it as

$$n(A) = 4$$

(number of elements in A = 4)

Another example could be

$$B = \{1, 7, 15, 19, 23, 24\}$$
$$C = \{2, 6, 7, 14, 19, 24, 25\}$$

Then $n(B) = 6$ (since there are 6 elements in set B) and $n(C) = 7$ (since there are 7 elements in set C)

N.B. We use rounded brackets when we talk about the number of elements in a set.

In the above example, suppose we were asked for $n(B \cup C)$ and also $n(B \cap C)$

To enable us to do this we would firstly work out

$$B \cup C = \{1, 2, 6, 7, 14, 15, 19, 23, 24, 25\}$$

then count the elements, i.e. $n(B \cup C) = 10$

and $B \cap C = \{7, 19, 24\}$

then count the elements, i.e. $n(B \cap C) = 3$

Activities

Describing sets

Example

Description	Listing
V = Vowels in the alphabet	$A = \{a, e, i, o, u\}$

1 List these sets, using curly brackets, $\{\ \}$

A = the set of the first five letters of the English alphabet

B = the set of days in the week

C = the set of English coins

D = the set of months with 30 days

E = the set of odd numbers less than 10

F = the set of even numbers between 9 and 25

G = the set of square numbers less than 50

H = the set of multiples of 8 less than 50

I = the set of seasons

J = the set of prime numbers between 10 and 30

K = the set of the last five letters in the English alphabet

L = the set of numbers that divide exactly into 20

Describe these sets in words:

2 {red, orange, yellow, green, blue, indigo, violet}

3 {apple, orange, pear, peach, banana}

4 {January, June, July}

5 {2, 4, 6, 8, 10}

6 {circle, square, triangle, rectangle}

7 {5, 10, 15, 20, 25, 30, 35, 40}

8 {11, 13, 15, 17, 19}

9 {kilometre, metre, centimetre, millimetre}

10 {rose, tulip, daffodil, pansy}

11 {+, −, ×, ÷}

Members of sets

Use the symbol ∈ (is a member) to link the following objects to their sets, e.g. lorry ∈ {vehicles}.

1 objects: cycle, oak, desk, elm, apple, soccer, car, tennis, fir, chair, table, banana, cricket, van, golf

  sets: {sports} {furniture} {fruit} {vehicles} {trees}

2 State whether the following are true (t) or false (f):

(a) 8 ∈ {odd numbers}

(b) 9 ∈ {prime numbers}

(c) litre ∈ {metric units}

(d) 144 ∉ {square numbers}

(e) John ∉ {girls names}

(f) cod ∈ {fish}

(g) 70 ∉ {multiples of 10}

(h) 9 ∉ {factors of 30}

(i) $\frac{3}{8}$ ∈ {fractions greater than $\frac{1}{2}$}

(j) £10 note ∉ {percentages}

3 Which of the following sets are equal:

  A = {2, 4, 6, 8}

  B = {numbers on a die}

  C = {whole numbers from 1 to 6 inclusively}

  D = {6, 12, 18}

  E = {even numbers less than 9}

  F = {multiples of 6 less than 20}

  G = {first five numbers}

Special sets

Empty set φ or { }

1 Which of the following are examples of empty sets?

(a) {pigs that can fly}

(b) {green elephants}

(c) {men who have been on the Moon}

(d) {people over 200 years old}

(e) {odd numbers exactly divisible by 2}

2 List these sets, using φ when necessary:

(a) {prime numbers between 24 and 28}

(b) {months beginning with the letter S}

(c) {whole numbers between $\frac{1}{4}$ and $\frac{7}{8}$}

(d) {days beginning with the letter D}

(e) {prime numbers that are also even numbers}

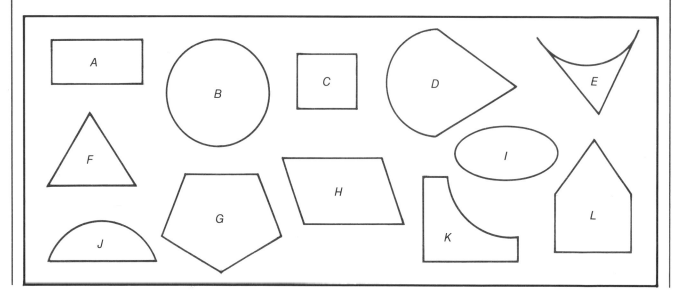

Fig. 22.1

Subsets

1 Fig. 22.1 shows a set S of shapes. Use the letters to list the members of the following subsets of S:

(a) the subset of S with 4 straight lines

(b) the subset of S with no straight lines

(c) the subset of S with straight sides only

(d) the subset of S with more than 4 straight sides

(e) the subset of S with straight and curved lines in the same shape.

2 Say whether each of the following statements is true (t) or false (f):

(a) $\{2, 3\} \quad \subset \{2, 3, 4, 5\}$

(b) $\{a, b, c\} \subset \{alphabet\}$

(c) $\{2, 3, 4\} \subset \{even\ numbers\}$

(d) $\{red, green\} \subset \{colours\}$

(e) $\{Pete, Joan\} \subset \{boys\ names\}$

3 If the set $N = \{2, 3, 4, 5, 6, 7, 8\}$ which of the following are proper subsets of the set N:

(a) $\{odd\ numbers\ less\ than\ 8\}$

(b) $\{even\ numbers\ less\ than\ 7\}$

(c) $\{prime\ numbers\ between\ 2\ and\ 10\}$

(d) $\{numbers\ that\ appear\ on\ a\ die\}$

(e) $\{the\ first\ two\ multiples\ of\ 3\}$

Universal sets

1 Suggest a suitable universal set for the following:

(a) $\{France, Germany, Spain\}$

(b) $\{Fiat, Chrysler, Ford, Rover\}$

(c) $\{golf, tennis, football, rugby\}$

(d) $\{vowels\}$

(e) $\{3, 6, 9, 12\}$

2 Make up sets with four members that belong to the following universal sets:

(a) $\mathscr{E} = \{capital\ cities\}$

(b) $\mathscr{E} = \{even\ numbers\}$

(c) $\mathscr{E} = \{school\ subjects\}$

(d) $\mathscr{E} = \{shapes\ made\ up\ with\ straight\ lines\}$

(e) $\mathscr{E} = \{pets\}$

Unit 23

Venn diagrams

23.1 Pictures of sets

An English Mathematician, John Venn, who lived in the nineteenth century, provided us with a useful method of representing sets by a picture.

He used a rectangle to represent the universal set and circles to represent sets within (subsets of) the universal set.

Example 1 $E = \{1, 2, 3, 4, 5, 6, 7, 8, 9\}$

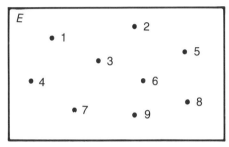

Fig. 23.1

If we consider a subset $A = \{3, 4, 7\}$ in the situation in Fig. 23.1 then the Venn diagram would look like Fig. 23.2.

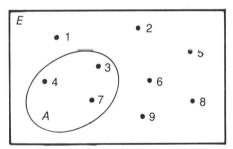

Fig. 23.2

If we then consider a subset $B = \{3, 7\}$ in the same situation, then the Venn diagram would look like Fig. 23.3.

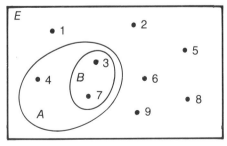

Fig. 23.3

In fact, this shows what we already know,

i.e., $B \subset A$ (B is a subset of A).

Example 2 $E = \{a, b, c, d, e, f, g\}$

$\qquad A = \{a, b, c, d\} \qquad B = \{c, d, e, f, g\}$

Draw the Venn diagram to illustrate the information.

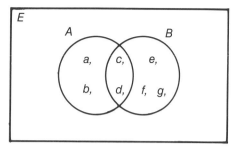

Fig. 23.4

Notice from the diagram in Fig. 23.4 that we can immediately pick up the intersection set as being the overlap of the two circles. Hence,

$\qquad A \cap B = \{c, d\}$

Looking at the diagram, it is obvious too that both elements c and d belong to both sets A and B. This is very important.

We can also easily find complement sets from Venn diagrams. If we want B', then simply cover the whole of set B – what is left showing? Just a and b. Hence,

$\qquad B' = \{a, b\}$

Likewise,

$\qquad A' = \{e, f, g\}$ (with all of A covered).

Example 3 $E = \{p, q, r, s, t, u, v, w, x, y, z\}$
$\qquad C = \{p, q, r\} \qquad D = \{s, t, u, v\}$

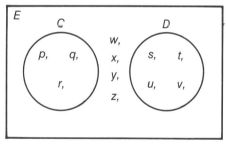

Fig. 23.5

Sets C and D have no intersection (see Fig. 23.5) i.e. $C \cap D = \varphi$ and so are called **distinct** sets.

The elements w, x, y, z belong to neither set C nor set D and are, as a result, positioned on the outside of sets C and D and yet are still enclosed within the universal set.

23.2 Shading Venn diagrams

In Venn diagrams, by using careful shading, we can show a whole variety of sets. For instance as in Fig. 23.6. Shaded area represents A'.

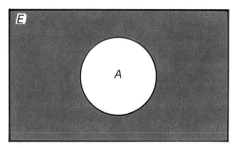

Fig. 23.6

From a diagram such as this, we can see that

$\qquad A' \cup A = E$

and $\quad A' \cap A = \varphi$

These results will always hold because, obviously, A and A' are two completely distinct sets.

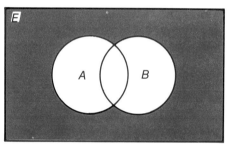

Fig. 23.7

In Fig. 23.7, the shaded area represents, the complement of $A \cup B$, i.e. $(A \cup B)'$

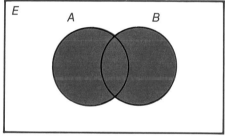

Fig. 23.8

In Fig. 23.8, the shaded area represents the union of A and B, i.e. $A \cup B$

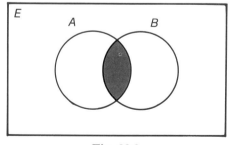

Fig. 23.9

In Fig. 23.9, the shaded area represents the overlap (intersection) of sets A and B, i.e. $A \cap B$.

More complicated situations can be seen more clearly with the help of a Venn diagram.

Example If E is the set of all cars, S is the set of all sports cars and F is the set of all cars with 4 doors, draw on a Venn diagram the set of all sports cars which do not have four doors.

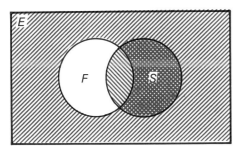

Fig. 23.10

In Fig. 23.10, vertical lines indicate sports cars i.e. (S); horizontal lines indicate cars without 4 doors i.e. (F').

What we are, in fact, trying to find is $S \cap F'$ and this is shown on the Venn diagram as the area with both horizontal and vertical lines giving a criss-cross effect.

23.3 Three subsets in a universal set

Situations involving universal sets having 3 subsets can also be handled very well using Venn diagrams. More than 3 subsets can be difficult to draw but, generally speaking, we do not come across this type of situation in our studies of this topic.

Example Consider

$$E = \{1, 2, 3, 4, 5, 6, 7, 8, 9, 10, 11, 12\}$$
$$A = \{1, 3, 5, 7\} \quad B = \{3, 5, 8, 11\} \quad C = \{3, 8, 12\}$$

The Venn diagram of this situation will look as shown in Fig. 23.11.

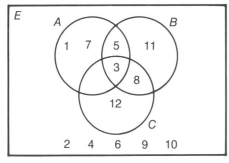

Fig. 23.11

3 is an element of all three sets, so

$$A \cap B \cap C = \{3\}$$

Other interesting combinations that we can easily pick out are:

$$A \cap B = \{3, 5\}$$
$$A \cap C = \{3\}$$
$$B \cap C = \{3, 8\}$$
$$A \cup B \cup C = \{1, 3, 5, 7, 8, 11, 12\}$$
$$(A \cup B \cup C)' = \{2, 4, 6, 9, 10\} \quad \text{These elements are}$$
shown in the outer sector of the rectangle.

$$A \cup B = \{1, 3, 5, 7, 8, 11\}$$
$$B \cup C = \{3, 5, 8, 11, 12\}$$
$$A \cup C = \{1, 3, 5, 7, 8, 12\}$$

Also, $n(A) = 4$, $n(B) = 4$, $n(C) = 3$

$n(A \cup B \cup C)' = 5$, $n(A \cup B) = 6$, $n(A \cup B)' = 6$

See if you can find the number of elements in some of the remaining set combinations, i.e. $n(A \cap C)$ etc.

Summary

(a)

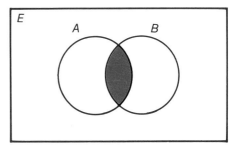

Fig. 23.12

Fig. 23.12: $A \cap B$ (the intersection of sets A and B)

(b)

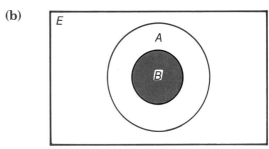

Fig. 23.13

Fig. 23.13: $B \subset A$ (set B is a subset of A)

(c)

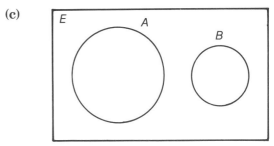

Fig. 23.14

Fig. 23.14: $A \cap B = \varphi$ (disjoint sets)

(d)

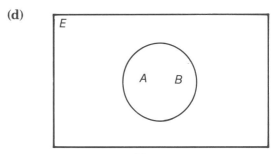

Fig. 23.15

Fig. 23.15: $A = B$ (equal sets)

68

(e)

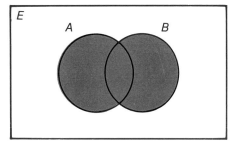

Fig. 23.16

Fig. 23.16: $A \cup B$ (shaded area, the union of sets A and B)

(f)

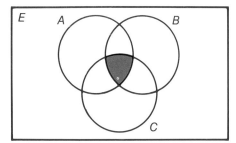

Fig. 23.17

Fig. 23.17: $A \cap B \cap C$ (shaded area, the intersection of all 3 sets)

(g)

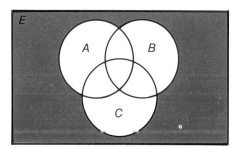

Fig. 23.18

Fig. 23.18: $(A \cup B \cup C)'$ (shaded area, the complement of the union of sets A, B and C, i.e. elements outside the sets A, B and C)

Activities

Pictures of sets

1 Draw Venn diagrams to show each of the following:
(a) $\mathscr{E} = \{1, 2, 3, 4, 5, 6, 7, 8\}$ $A = \{2, 3, 4\}$
(b) $\mathscr{E} = \{a, b, c, d, e, f, g, h\}$ $B = \{a, e\}$
(c) $\mathscr{E} = \{$whole numbers from 1 to 11$\}$
  $C = \{$even numbers from 1 to 11$\}$

2 Copy the diagrams in Figs. 23.19, 23.20 and 23.21 and put the members of the given sets in the correct position:
(a) $\mathscr{E} = \{1, 2, 3, 4, 5, 6, 7, 8\}$
  $A = \{2, 3, 4\}$
  $B = \{5, 6, 7\}$

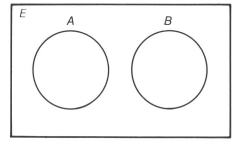

Fig. 23.19

(b) $\mathscr{E} = \{a, b, c, d, e, f, g, h\}$
  $X = \{a, b, c, d\}$
  $Y = \{c, d, e, f\}$

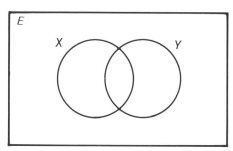

Fig. 23.20

(c) $\mathscr{E} = \{m, n, o, p, q, r, s, t\}$
  $G = \{p, q, r, s\}$
  $H = \{p, q\}$

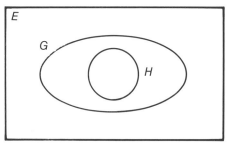

Fig. 23.21

3 The Venn diagram in Fig. 23.22 shows whether or not a group of children enjoyed Tea and Coffee.
(a) How many liked Tea?
(b) How many liked Coffee?
(c) How many liked both Tea and Coffee?
(d) How many liked Tea but not Coffee?
(e) How many liked Coffee but not Tea?
(f) How many liked neither?

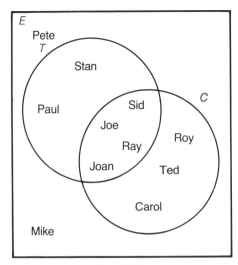

Fig. 23.22

Union of sets ∪

Find the union of the two given sets in the following:

1. $A = \{\text{Roy, Mike, Andy}\}$ $B = \{\text{Matt, Sid, Frank}\}$
2. $F = \{2, 4, 6, 8\}$ $G = \{5, 6, 7, 8\}$
3. $P = \{a, e, i, o, u\}$ $Q = \{a, b, c, d, e\}$
4. $X = \{p, q, r\}$ $Y = \{s, t, u\}$
5. $A = \{1, 2, 3, 4, 5, 6\}$ $B = \{2, 4, 6\}$
6. $L = \{2, 3, 5, 7\}$ $M = \{2, 3, 5, 8\}$

7. $P = \{\text{whole numbers that divide exactly into 8}\}$
    $Q = \{\text{whole numbers that divide exactly into 12}\}$

8. $X = \{\text{letters in the word 'missile'}\}$
    $Y = \{\text{letters in the word 'smiling'}\}$

9. $A = \{\text{letters in the word 'write'}\}$
    $B = \{\text{letters in the word 'pretty'}\}$

10. $X = \{\text{letters in the word 'pencil'}\}$
    $Y = \{\text{letters in the word 'pen'}\}$

*Remember,

$$P = \{2, 3, 4, 5\}$$
$$Q = \{2, 4, 6, 8\}$$
$$P \cup Q = \{2, 3, 4, 5, 6, 8\}$$

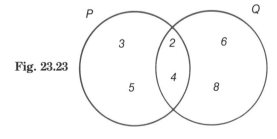

Fig. 23.23

Draw suitable Venn diagrams to show the union of the following sets:

11. $A = \{d, e, f, g\}$ $B = \{f, g, h, i\}$

12. $X = \{\text{months beginning with the letter 'J'}\}$
    $Y = \{\text{months ending with the letter 'Y'}\}$

13. $P = \{\text{odd numbers from 2 to 10}\}$
    $Q = \{\text{prime numbers from 2 to 10}\}$

Intersection of sets ∩

If $A = \{\text{set of people who wear specs}\}$
  $B = \{\text{set of people who wear a wristwatch}\}$
then we can say,

  $A \cap B = \{\text{set of people who wear both specs and a wristwatch}\}$

Describe the intersection of these two sets:

1. $A = \{\text{boys in your class who like football}\}$
    $B = \{\text{boys in your class who like cricket}\}$

2. $X = \{\text{people in your family who like tea}\}$
    $Y = \{\text{people in your family who like coffee}\}$

3. $P = \{\text{four-minute milers}\}$
    $Q = \{\text{athletes}\}$

Now try the following:

4. $A = \{2, 4, 6, 8\}$ $B = \{4, 5, 6, 7\}$ $C = \{5, 6, 7\}$
(a) List $A \cap B$ **(b)** List $A \cap C$ **(c)** List $B \cap C$

5. $X = \{\text{Bob, Alice, Fred, Sue}\}$
    $Y = \{\text{Fred, Bob, Roy, Jim}\}$
List the members of $X \cap Y$.

6. $M = \{\text{prime numbers less than 15}\}$
    $N = \{\text{odd numbers less than 16}\}$
List $M \cap N$.

7. $X = \{\text{letters in the word 'soil'}\}$
    $Y = \{\text{letters in the word 'lost'}\}$
List the set $X \cap Y$.

8. In a certain class, these girls studied French, {Joy, Joan, Val, Sue} and these studied Latin, {Joan, Linda, Sue, Jane}.
(a) Illustrate these facts on a Venn diagram.
(b) Shade in the area which shows the girls who studied both Latin and French.

Complement of a set

Describe the complements of the following sets:

1. {odd numbers}
2. {girls}
3. {people older than yourself}
4. {left-handed people}
5. {weekdays}

6. If $\mathscr{E} = \{\text{the first ten letters of the alphabet}\}$
      $A = \{a, b, c, d, e\}$ and $B = \{a, e, i\}$
List **(a)** A' **(b)** B' **(c)** $A \cup B$ **(d)** $A \cap B$

7. $\mathscr{E} = \{\text{numbers between 5 and 25}\}$
    $A = \{\text{multiples of 3}\}$
    $B = \{\text{multiples of 10}\}$ $C = \{\text{even numbers}\}$
List the members of the sets:
    (a) A' **(b)** B' **(c)** C' **(d)** $A \cap C$

8 $\mathscr{E} = \{$numbers from 10 to 20 inclusive$\}$
$A = \{11, 13, 15, 17, 19\}$ $B = \{12, 15, 18\}$
$C = \{12, 16, 20\}$ $D = \{10, 15, 20\}$

List the members in the sets:

(a) A' (b) B' (c) C' (d) D'

9 $\mathscr{E} = \{$letters in the word 'relations'$\}$
$A = \{$letters in the word 'slate'$\}$
$B = \{$letters in the word 'rails'$\}$

List the members in the sets:

(a) A' (b) B' (c) $A \cup B$ (d) $(A \cup B)'$

10 $\mathscr{E} = \{$the first 20 natural numbers$\}$
$A = \{$multiples of 5$\}$ $B = \{$multiples of 4$\}$
$C = \{8, 9, 10, 11, 12\}$

List the members of the sets:

(a) $A \cup B'$ (b) $A' \cup B'$ (c) $A \cap B'$ (d) $C' \cap B$
(e) $C \cap A'$

How many in the set?

1 How many members are there in the following sets?

(a) set $A = \{$months in the year$\}$

(b) set $B = \{$days in the week$\}$

(c) set $C = \{$whole numbers between 1 and 10 inclusive$\}$

(d) set $D = \{$letters of the alphabet$\}$

(e) set $E = \{$vowels$\}$

Hint: Answer the question like this: (a) $n(A) = ?$

2 Examine the Venn Diagram in Fig. 23.24 and answer the following.

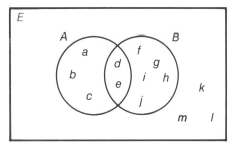

Fig. 23.24

Write down, (a) $n(A)$ (b) $n(B)$ (c) $n(A \cap B)$
         (d) $n(A \cup B)$ (e) $n(A \cup B)'$

3 If $\mathscr{E} = \{1, 2, 3, 4, 5, 6, 7, 8, 9, 10\}$
$X = \{2, 3, 4, 5, 6\}$ and $Y = \{5, 6, 7, 8\}$
draw a Venn diagram and answer the following.

List, (a) $X \cup Y$ (b) $X \cap Y$ (c) $n(X)$ (d) $n(Y)$
     (e) $n(X \cup Y)$ (f) $n(X \cap Y)$ (g) $n(X)'$ (h) $n(Y)'$

4 Study the Venn diagram in Fig. 23.25 and list the following:

(a) $A \cap B$ (b) $A \cap C$ (c) $B \cap C$ (d) $n(A)$
(e) $n(B)$ (f) $n(C)$ (g) $A \cup B \cup C$ (h) $A \cap B \cap C$
(i) $n(A \cup B \cup C)$ (j) $n(A \cap B \cap C)$

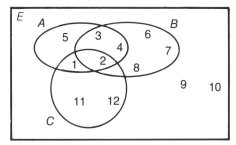

Fig. 23.25

Shading sets

1 Copy the Venn diagram in Fig. 23.26 for each part of the question and shade in the area indicated.

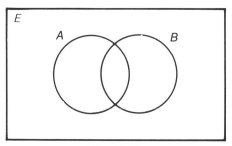

Fig. 23.26

(a) $A \cup B$ (b) $A \cap B$
(c) $(A \cup B)'$ (d) $(A \cap B)'$
(e) A' (f) $A' \cap B$
(g) $B' \cap A$ (h) $A \cup B'$

2 Describe using set notation, the shaded areas in Figs. 23.27 to 23.30.

(a)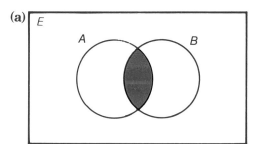

Fig. 23.27

(b)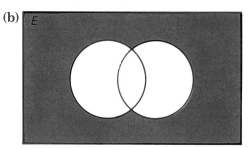

Fig. 23.28

(c)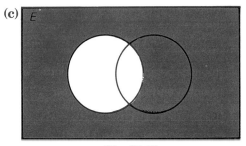

Fig. 23.29

(d)

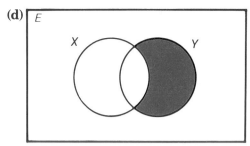

Fig. 23.30

3 Copy the Venn diagram in Fig. 23.31 and shade in the area indicated.

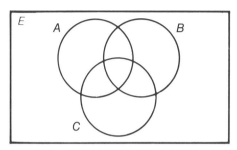

Fig. 23.31

(a) $A \cap B \cap C$ **(b)** $(A \cup B \cup C)'$ **(c)** $(A \cap B) \cup C$

GEOMETRY

Unit 24

Straight lines

24.1 Definition

A straight line is the shortest distance between two points.

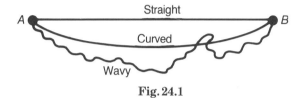

Fig. 24.1

Obviously the direct (straight) line from Point A to Point B, in Fig. 24.1, is the shortest.

24.2 Vertical and horizontal lines

A line which is 'straight up and down' is **vertical**.

A plumb line is often used to draw a vertical line on a wall before hanging the first piece of wallpaper.

Horizontal lines are level like the horizon.

A bricklayer uses a spirit level to check that the top of a wall is horizontal.

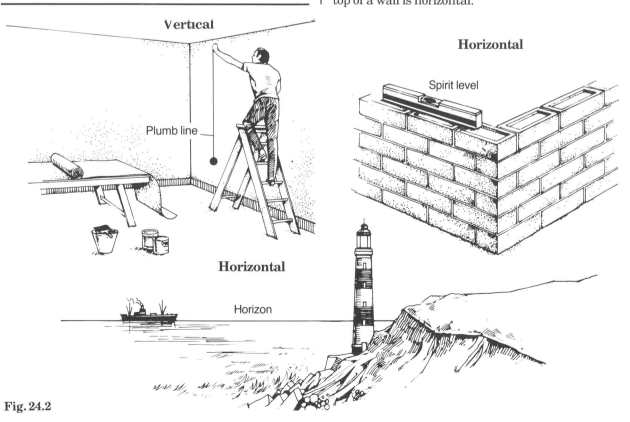

Fig. 24.2

If we look at Fig. 24.3 we can pick out the **vertical** and **horizontal** lines that it contains.

Fig. 24.3

Fig. 24.4

In the drawing, vertical lines can be found in such things as the curtains, table-legs, candle, light flex, street lamp, the line where the two walls meet and some others.

Horizontal lines can be found in such things as the curtain-rail, the top of the table, the skirting board, the window-sill and some others.

24.3 Parallel lines

If we look at the photograph of railway tracks shown in Fig. 24.4, it is obvious that the rails on which the trains run are always the same distance apart. In this country, that distance is 4 feet and $8\frac{1}{2}$ inches (approximately 144 cm).

Such lines, which are always the same distance apart, are said to be **parallel**.

If we look at the items of furniture shown in Fig. 24.5, we can easily pick out pairs of horizontal and vertical parallel lines.

If we consider the diagram in Fig. 24.6, we can discover several sets of parallel lines.

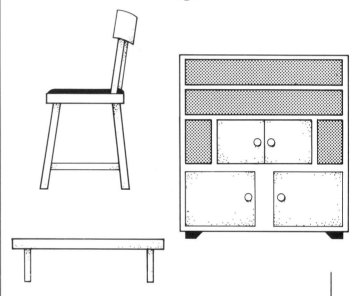

Fig. 24.5

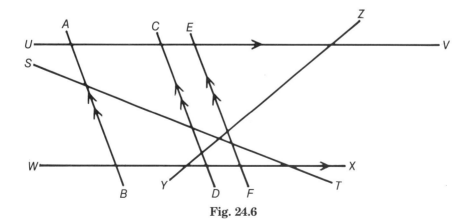

Fig. 24.6

Obviously, the line UV is parallel to the line WX (we can show this by a single arrow along each of the two lines).

Also, AB is parallel to both CD and EF (to show this we can use double arrows as shown in the diagram).

Activities

Straight lines

1 Try to copy the straight line drawings in Fig. 24.7.

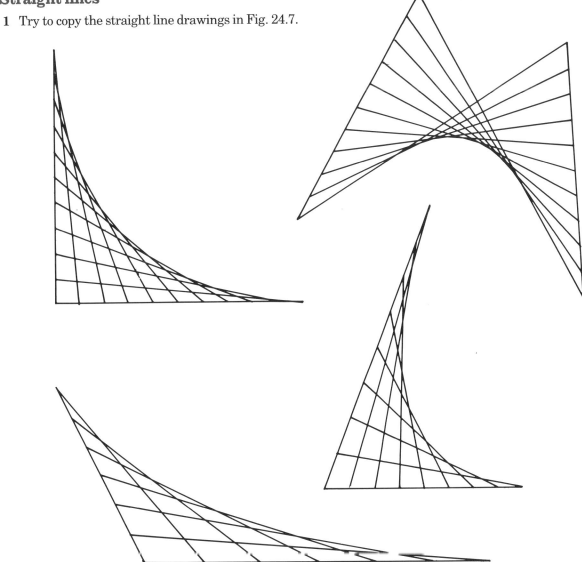

Fig. 24.7

Can you make up some patterns
using straight lines only?

2

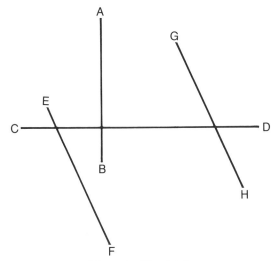

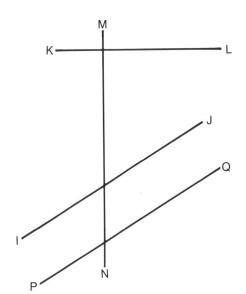

Fig. 24.8

(a) List the horizontal lines in Fig. 24.8.
(b) List the vertical lines.
(c) List the lines which are parallel to each other.

Unit 25

Angles

25.1 Degrees and right angles

The mathematical name for a turn is a **rotation**.

Angle is a measure of rotation and the units we measure this in are known as **degrees**.

Look at the dials in Fig. 25.1.

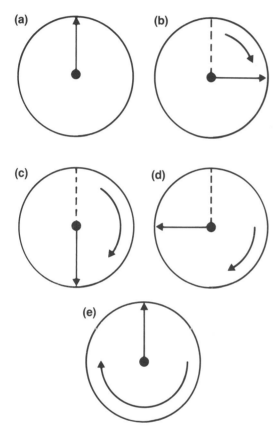

Fig. 25.1

The pointer has completed a quarter of a turn (**b**), half a turn (**c**), three-quarters of a turn (**d**) and a full turn (**e**) or back to the starting-point (**a**).

When a line is rotated through a quarter of a turn, the angle formed is called a **right angle**. The symbol for a right angle is a square as shown in Fig. 25.2.

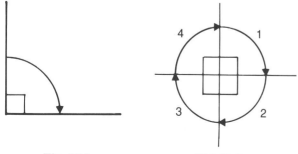

Fig. 25.2   Fig. 25.3

We can then see, from Fig. 25.3, that four of these right angles make a complete turn.

25.2 Other types of angle

Angles that are smaller than one right angle are called **acute** angles.

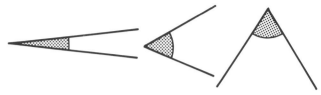

Fig. 25.4

All the angles in Fig. 25.4 are less than one right angle and hence are **acute** angles.

Angles that are greater than one right angle, but smaller than two right angles, are called **obtuse** angles.

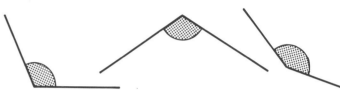

Fig. 25.5

All the angles in Fig. 25.5 are less than two right angles, but are greater than one right angle and hence are **obtuse** angles.

Angles that are greater than two right angles, but smaller than four right angles are called **reflex** angles.

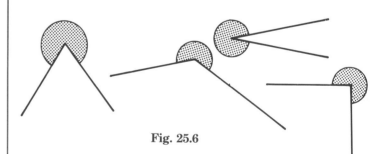

Fig. 25.6

All the angles in Fig. 25.6 are greater than two right angles but less than four right angles, and hence are known as **reflex** angles.

N.B. At this point we can see another way of describing a straight line (see Fig. 25.7).

Fig. 25.7

It is of course a line of two quarter-turns (or two right angles) exactly.

25.3 Units

As mentioned earlier, we measure angles in degrees.

This came from a system invented by the Babylonians. They divided a complete turn (rotation) into 360 equal parts. Each one of these small parts of the rotation they called a **degree**.

One complete turn represents 360 degrees which we write as 360°. A quarter turn (a right angle) therefore measures 90°.

In terms of measurement then:

Acute angle < 90° < Obtuse angle < 180° <Reflex angle < 360°

It is interesting to note that angles are formed whenever two or more lines meet or cross. So, from Fig. 25.8, we can say that

$$a° + b° + c° + d° = 360°$$

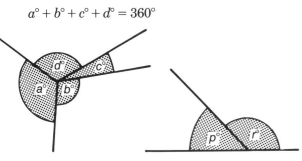

Fig. 25.8   **Fig. 25.9**

Also, angles which are on the same straight line together make a half turn. So, from Fig. 25.9

$$p° + r° = 180°$$

Example   If $p = 45°$ then $r = 135°$, etc.

Such angles which add up to 180° are called **supplementary** angles.

Finally, two angles which add up to 90° are called **complementary** angles. So, from Fig. 25.10,

$$m° + n° = 90°$$

Example   If $m = 60°$ then $n = 30°$, etc.

Hence, m and n are **complementary** angles.

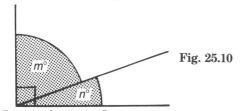

Fig. 25.10

25.4 Measuring angles

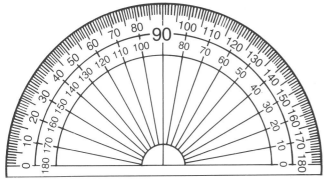

Fig. 25.11 Semi-circular protractor

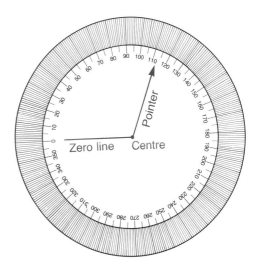

Fig. 25.12 Complete circular protractor

The instrument we use to measure angles is called a **protractor**. The diagrams in Figs. 25.11 and 25.12 show two different types of protractor.

They are usually made of a transparent plastic material with the degrees marked on the outside edge. We name angles using letters, as seen in Fig. 25.13.

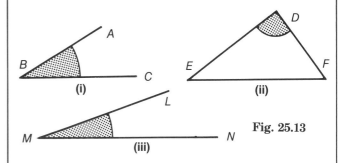

Fig. 25.13

The shaded angle in (i) is called angle ABC, written as $A\hat{B}C$ or $\angle ABC$.

In (ii), the shaded angle is written as $E\hat{D}F$ or $\angle EDF$. We could also write it as $F\hat{D}E$ or $\angle FDE$.

To measure angle LMN ($L\hat{M}N$) in (iii), we must first decide whether it is **acute**, **obtuse** or **reflex**.

In this case the angle is obviously **acute**.

Using the **semi-circular protractor** – the centre of the protractor must be on the point M and the zero line along the line MN (see Fig. 25.14).

We find where the line ML cuts the scales.

There appear to be two values for $L\hat{M}N$: 18° on the **inner** scale and 162° on the outer scale. Since $L\hat{M}N$ is an acute angle, 18° must be its value.

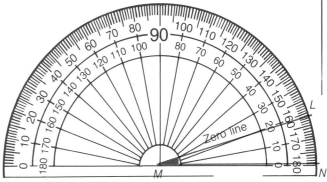

Fig. 25.14

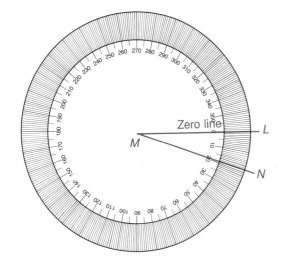

Fig. 25.15

Using the **circular protractor** – we place the centre of the protractor on M, and the zero line along ML. We then read the angle where MN cuts the scale (see Fig. 25.15).

Types of angle

1 Say whether each of the angles in Fig. 25.16 is less than or greater than a **right angle**.

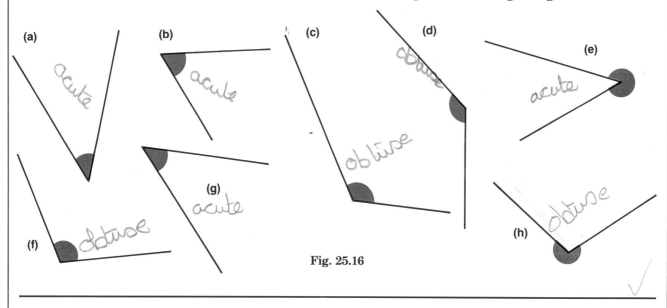

Fig. 25.16

2 Say whether each of the angles in Fig. 25.17 is an acute angle, an obtuse angle, a reflex angle, a right angle or a straight angle.

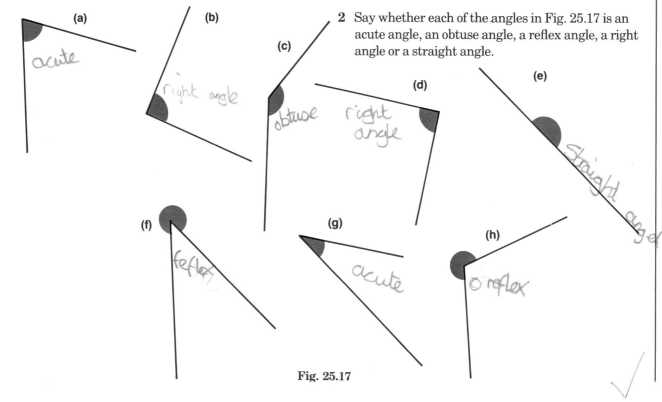

Fig. 25.17

Measuring angles

1 Make a guess as to how many degrees there are in
the angles shown in Fig. 25.18. (Before guessing,
ask yourself, 'Is it less than, or greater than, 90°?')

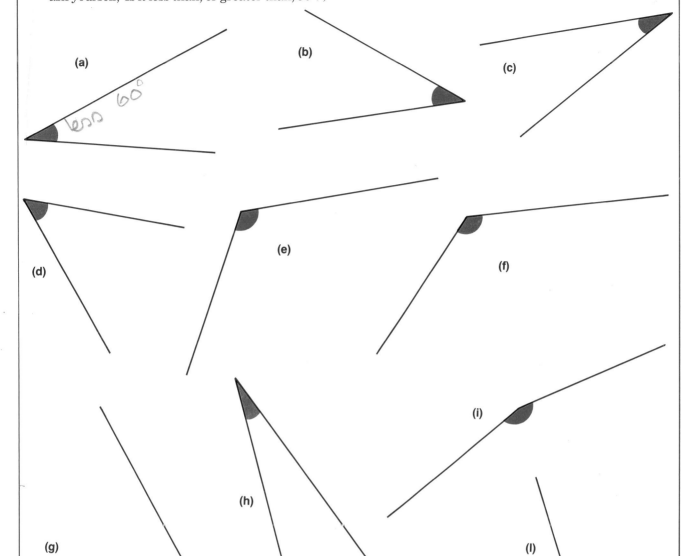

Fig. 25.18

2 Take your protractor and measure these angles
accurately. How accurate were your guesses?

3 Now, use your protractor to construct angles of the
following sizes:

(a) 30°   (b) 60°   (c) 125°   (d) 154°   (e) 97°

Right angles

1 How many degrees are there in:

(a) 1 right angle   (b) 2 right angles

(c) 3 right angles   (d) 4 right angles

(e) 6 right angles   (f) 8 right angles

2 How many degrees are there in:

(a) $\frac{1}{2}$ turn   (b) $\frac{1}{4}$ turn

(c) $\frac{3}{4}$ turn   (d) $\frac{2}{3}$ turn

(e) $\frac{1}{3}$ turn   (f) $\frac{1}{8}$ turn

(g) $\frac{1}{10}$ turn   (h) $\frac{1}{12}$ turn

3 How many **right angles** are there in:

(a) $\frac{3}{4}$ turn   (b) $1\frac{1}{2}$ turns

(c) $2\frac{1}{4}$ turns   (d) $1\frac{3}{4}$ turns

(e) 5 turns   (f) $3\frac{1}{2}$ turns

(g) 3 turns   (h) 10 turns

4 Calculate the missing angles in Fig. 25.19. (Do not try to find the answers by measuring; these sketches are not drawn to true size.)

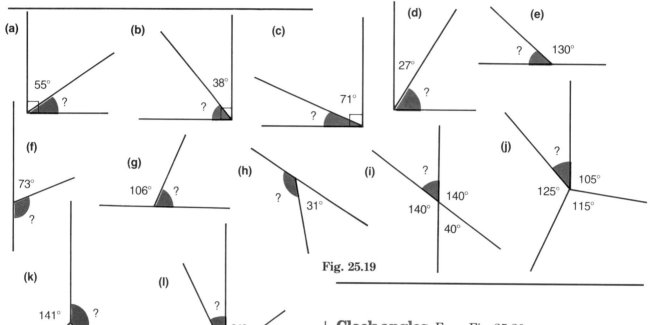

Fig. 25.19

Clock angles From Fig. 25.20,

1 How much time has passed if the **hour** hand on the clock turns through,

(a) 90°   (b) 60°   (c) 120°   (d) 210°   (e) 300°

2 How much time has passed when the **minute** hand of the clock turns through,

(a) 30°   (b) 180°   (c) 240°   (d) 150°   (e) 330°

3 Through how many degrees does the **hour** hand turn in going from,

(a) 1.00 to 5.00   (b) 6.00 to 12.00   (c) 2.00 to 11.00

(d) 3.00 to 5.30   (e) 4.30 to 7.00   (f) 6.20 to 8.50

4 Through how many degrees does the **minute** hand turn between

(a) 12.00 and 12.15   (d) 9.25 and 10.10

(b) 2.25 and 2.50   (e) 1.05 and 2.15

(c) 4.05 and 4.40   (f) 5.10 and 5.50

5 How many degrees are there between the hour hand and the minute hand at these times? (Always give the smallest angle.)

(a) 8.00   (b) 5.00   (c) 2.00   (d) 11.00

(e) 9.30   (f) 4.30   (g) 6.20   (h) 8.40

Fig. 25.20

Unit 26

Shapes

26.1 Triangles

A triangle is a shape with three straight sides.

Inside any triangle there are three angles (see Fig. 26.1).

Fig. 26.1

26.2 Types of triangle

There are several types of triangle.

(a) **Scalene triangle** – this is a triangle with all three sides of different length and all three angles different from one another, as in Fig. 26.2.

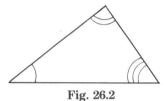

Fig. 26.2

(b) **Isosceles triangle** – this is a triangle which has two sides of equal length and two of its angles equal, as in Fig. 26.3.

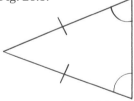

Fig. 26.3

(c) **Equilateral triangle** – this is a triangle which has all three sides equal in length and all three angles equal, as in Fig. 26.4.

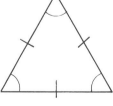

Fig. 26.4

N.B. Bars on the line, mean the lines are of the same length.

(d) **Right-angled triangle** – this is a triangle in which one of the angles is a right angle, as we can see in the two examples in Fig. 26.5.

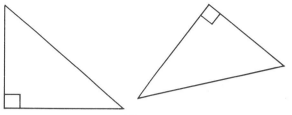

Fig. 26.5

A very interesting observation which we must be aware of is that, if we take a triangle and cut off each of the angles, and then rearrange them as shown in Fig. 26.6, they make a straight line.

This shows that the sum of the angles of the triangle is 180°.

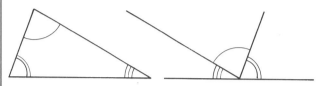

Fig. 26.6

So we can say that for any triangle the angles total 180°.

In the case of an equilateral triangle, each angle will, of course, be 60°.

Activities

Triangles

1 Describe the triangles in Fig. 26.7 as accurately as you can.

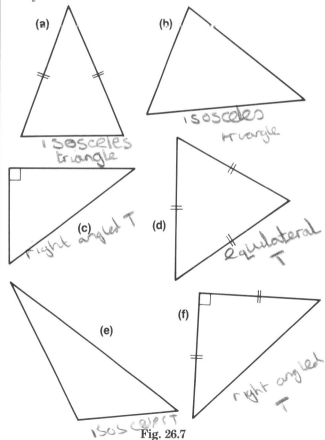

Fig. 26.7

2 Calculate the missing angle in each of the triangles sketched in Fig. 26.8.

*Remember, the angles of a triangle add up to 180°.

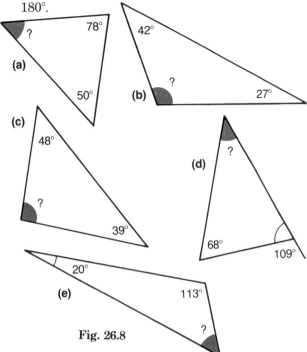

Fig. 26.8

3 Two of the angles of a triangle are 30° and 55°. Find the third angle.

4 Two angles of a triangle are 123° and 39°. Find the third angle.

Special triangles

1 Calculate the missing angles in the triangles sketched in Fig. 26.9.

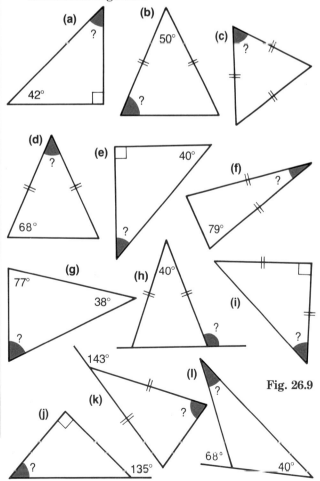

Fig. 26.9

2 One of the angles of an isosceles triangle was 110°. What was the size of the other angles?

3 A ladder leans against a vertical wall and makes an angle of 18° with the wall. What angle does the ladder make with the horizontal ground?

26.3 Quadrilaterals

A **quadrilateral** is a shape with four sides.

Inside any **quadrilateral** there are four angles and the sum of these four angles totals 360° (we can show this in a similar manner to the method shown for the triangle above).

26.4 Types of quadrilateral

There are several types of quadrilateral.

(a) The **general quadrilateral** – this is a figure which has four sides of different lengths and four **unequal** angles (see Fig. 26.10).

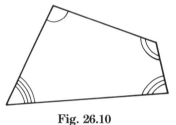

Fig. 26.10

(b) The **parallelogram** (see Fig. 26.11).

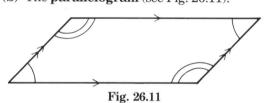

Fig. 26.11

A parallelogram is a four-sided figure with opposite sides equal in length and parallel to each other and diagonally opposite angles equal to each other.

Diagonal lines

At this point, we can say that a diagonal line always joins two corners of a shape and any quadrilateral has two diagonals.

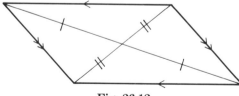

Fig. 26.12

In the case of a parallelogram the diagonals bisect (divide equally) each other, but they are not of the same length (see Fig. 26.12).

(c) The **rectangle** or **oblong** (see Fig. 26.13)

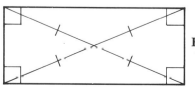

Fig. 26.13

A rectangle is a four-sided figure with opposite sides equal in length. The four angles of the rectangle are all right angles. Its diagonals are equal in length and they bisect each other.

(d) The **rhombus** (see Fig. 26.14)

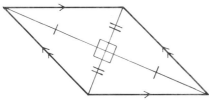

Fig. 26.14

A rhombus is a four-sided figure with opposite sides parallel and all sides of equal length. The diagonals bisect each other at right angles and also bisect the corner angles. As with the parallelogram, the rhombus has equal diagonally opposite angles.

We sometimes call this shape the diamond.

(e) The **square** (see Fig. 26.15)

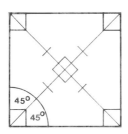

Fig. 26.15

The square is a four-sided figure with all sides of equal length. The four angles of the square are all right angles. The diagonals bisect each other at right angles and also bisect the corner angles (45°).

(f) The **trapezium** (see Fig. 26.16)

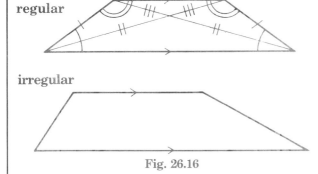

Fig. 26.16

A trapezium is a four-sided figure with only one pair of parallel sides of unequal lengths.

In the case of the **regular** trapezium, the base angles are equal as are the lengths of the non-parallel sides. The diagonals do not bisect each other.

However, for the **irregular** trapezium, we can only say that it has one pair of parallel sides of unequal lengths.

(g) The **kite** (see Fig. 26.17)

Fig. 26.17

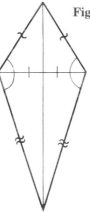

This four-sided shape is basically made up of two different isosceles triangles with the same base lengths. The diagonals do not, in this shape, bisect each other.

Activities

Properties of quadrilaterals

1 The **rectangle** (Fig. 26.18)
Copy and complete:
(a) $AB = ?$ **(b)** $BC = ?$
(c) $AX = ? = ? = ?$ **(d)** $AC = ?$
(e) angle AXC = angle ?
(f) angle AXB = angle ?

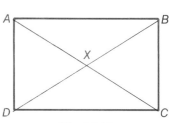

Fig. 26.18

2 The **square** (Fig. 26.19)
(a) $EF = ? = ? = ?$
(b) $EX = ? = ? = ?$
(c) $EG = ?$
(d) EG is perpendicular to ?
(e) angle $EXF = ?$ °

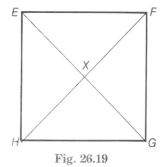

Fig. 26.19

3 The **parallelogram** (Fig. 26.20)

(a) $JK = ?$ **(b)** $KL = ?$
(c) $JX = ?$ **(d)** $KX = ?$
(e) angle KJX = angle ?
(f) angle KMJ = angle ?

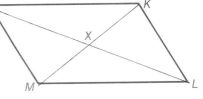

Fig. 26.20

4 The **kite** (Fig. 26.21)
(a) $PQ = ?$ **(b)** $PS = ?$
(c) $PX = ?$ **(d)** angle $QXR = ?$ °
(e) angle PQX = angle ?
(f) angle PSX = angle ?

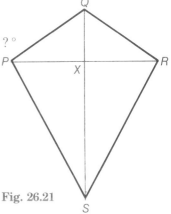

Fig. 26.21

Diagonals

1 Which pairs of diagonals, in Fig. 26.22, belong to a square?

(a)  **(b)**  **(c)**

Fig. 26.22

2 Which pairs of diagonals, in Fig. 26.23, belong to a rectangle?

(a)  **(b)** 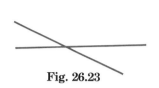 **(c)**

Fig. 26.23

3 Which pairs of diagonals, in Fig. 26.24, belong to a kite?

(a)  **(b)** 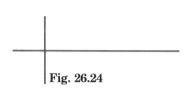 **(c)**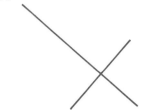

Fig. 26.24

4 Which pairs, in Fig. 26.25, belong to a parallelogram?

(a)  **(b)** 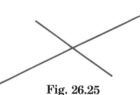 **(c)**

Fig. 26.25

5 Which pairs, in Fig. 26.26, belong to a rhombus?

(a) **(b)**

(c)

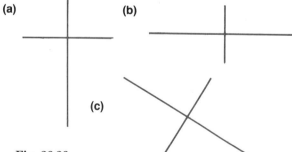

Fig. 26.26

Meet the referee

The referee, in Fig. 26.27, is made up of various shapes. Let's see how many you can recognize.

What is the shape of:

1 his body?   square   7 the ball? hex
2 his head?   rectangle   8 his arms? Parrel
3 his eyes?   circle   9 his right hand? right.
4 his legs?   kite   10 his left hand? halt circle
5 his hat?   Parrel   11 his neck? equilateral
6 his feet?   Parrel   12 his mouth?

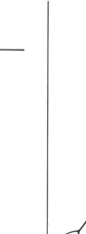

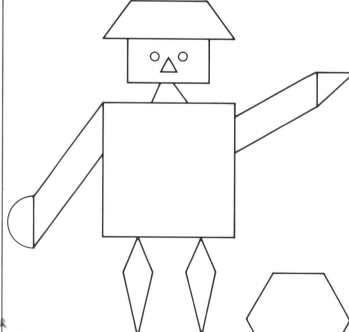

Fig. 26.27

Unit 27

Simple construction

We may find the following constructions useful in our study of shapes.

27.1 To draw a triangle with sides of given lengths

Suppose we have to draw a triangle with lengths of the sides as 10.5 cm, 6.8 cm and 9.7 cm respectively. Taking the longest side (i.e. 10.5 cm) as the base, draw a straight line AB of length 10.5 cm.

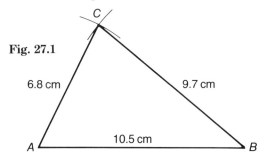

Fig. 27.1

Open the compasses to 9.7 cm, place the point of the compasses on the point B and draw an arc. Then every point on this arc will be at a distance of 9.7 cm from B.

Open the compasses to 6.8 cm, place the point of the compasses on the point A and draw an arc. Then every point on this arc will be at a distance of 6.8 cm from A.

If the two arcs intersect at C as shown in Fig. 27.1, then C will be 6.8 cm from A and 9.7 cm from B. To complete the triangle, we simply draw in the lines AC and BC, and the triangle ABC then formed, will be the triangle we require.

27.2 To bisect an angle

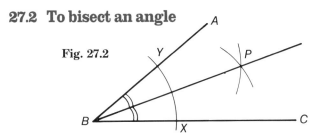

Fig. 27.2

To bisect the angle $A\hat{B}C$, we place the point of the compasses on B and draw an arc of any radius, which cuts BC at X and BA at Y, as in Fig. 27.2.

We then place the point of the compasses on X and draw an arc, repeating the operation on Y with an arc of the same radius. From where the two arcs intersect, i.e. at the point P, we then draw in the line PB which then bisects the angle ABC.

Hence, $\angle ABP = \angle PBC$.

27.3 To construct a right angle

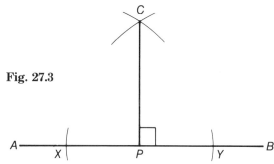

Fig. 27.3

To construct a right angle at the point P to the line AB, place the point of the compasses on P and draw arcs (of any equal radii) cutting AB at X and Y (see Fig. 27.3). Then, placing the point of the compasses on X and Y in turn and with equal radii greater than XP, draw arcs to meet at C. The line CP is then drawn and is at right angles to AB.

Hence, we can see that $C\hat{P}B = 90°$ and, of course, $C\hat{P}A$ is also $90°$.

27.4 To construct an angle of 45°

In order to do this, we can construct an angle of 90° (as in the previous case) and then bisect it by means of the method shown previously (see Fig. 27.4).

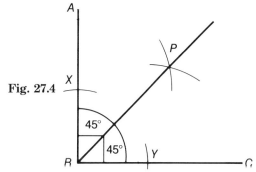

Fig. 27.4

The line BP bisects the right angle.
Hence, $\angle ABP = \angle PBC = 45°$.

27.5 To construct an angle of 60°

We described an equilateral triangle, earlier, in the unit as having equal sides and all three angles of 60°.

So, to construct a 60° angle, we can perform this easily by drawing just two sides of any equilateral triangle, as in Fig. 27.5.

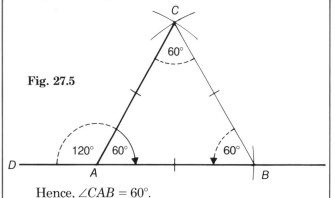

Fig. 27.5

Hence, $\angle CAB = 60°$.

N.B. Only one angle is required. To achieve this, only 2 sides of the triangle need be drawn.

If an angle of 120° was required, we could do this by taking the obtuse angle CAD as the supplementary angle of $\angle CAB$.

27.6 To construct an angle of 30°

We simply construct the 60° angle as described previously and bisect it in the now familiar manner, as in Fig. 27.6.

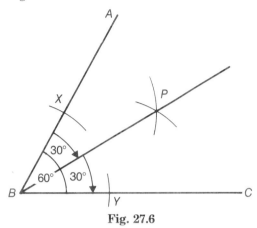

Fig. 27.6

Hence, $A\hat{B}P = P\hat{B}C = 30°$.

27.7 Regular shapes

A regular shape has:

(i) All its sides equal,

(ii) All its angles equal.

We have already noticed that a **regular triangle** will be the equilateral triangle, and that a **regular quadrilateral** will be a square.

Constructing triangles

1 Using a pencil, ruler and compasses, construct the following triangles (see Fig. 27.7).

  (a) $AB = 6$ cm $BC = 5$ cm $AC = 4$ cm

  (b) $AB = 5$ cm $BC = 4$ cm $AC = 3$ cm

  (c) $AB = 10$ cm $BC = 6$ cm $AC = 8$ cm

  (d) $AB = 9$ cm $BC = 7$ cm $AC = 6$ cm

  (e) $AB = 8.5$ cm $BC = 6.5$ cm $AC = 7.5$ cm

  (f) $AB = 11.3$ cm $BC = 7.9$ cm $AC = 10.6$ cm

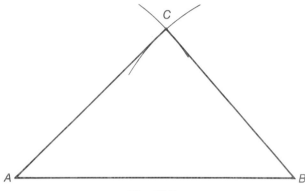

Fig. 27.7

2 For practice, use a protractor to measure the three angles of each of the triangles you have constructed.

3 Using your pencil, ruler and compasses **only**, construct the following:

  (a) a right angle

  (b) a 45° angle

  (c) a 60° angle

  (d) a 30° angle

  (e) an equilateral triangle (all angles are 60°)

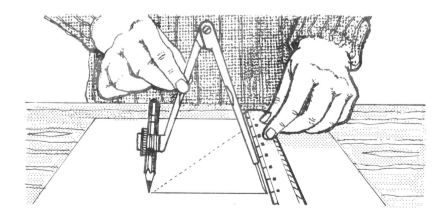

Unit 28

Polygons

28.1 Introduction

Shapes which have three or more sides are called by a general name – **polygons**.

The triangle is a three-sided polygon.

The quadrilateral is a four-sided polygon.

Following these we have the polygons in Table 28.1 (and more, with which we are unlikely to have to deal).

5 sides —— the **pentagon**
6 sides —— the **hexagon**
7 sides —— the **heptagon**
8 sides —— the **octagon**
9 sides —— the **nonagon**
10 sides —— the **decagon**

Table 28.1

A **pentagon**
(5 sides, 5 angles)

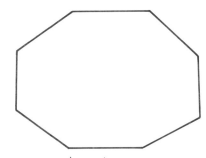

An **octagon**
(8 sides, 8 angles)

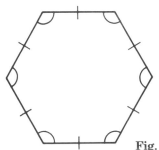

A **regular hexagon**
(6 equal sides and
6 equal interior
angles)

Fig. 28.1

28.2 The sum of the interior angles of a polygon

To find the sum of the interior angles of a **polygon** having n sides, consider the quadrilateral (**a**), the pentagon (**b**), and the hexagon (**c**), shown in Fig. 28.2, in each of which one vertex (corner) is joined to all the other vertices.

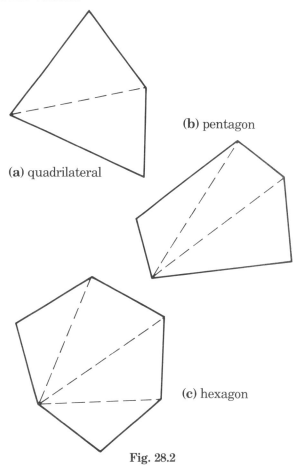

(**b**) pentagon

(**a**) quadrilateral

(**c**) hexagon

Fig. 28.2

The quadrilateral has 4 sides,

there are 2 triangles.

The pentagon has 5 sides,

there are 3 triangles.

The hexagon has 6 sides,

there are 4 triangles.

It is easy for us to see that, whatever the number of sides the polygon has, there will be two fewer triangles than sides.

In the case of a polygon with n sides, there will be n minus 2 i.e. $(n-2)$, triangles.

But we already know that the sum of the interior angles of a triangle is 180° or 2 right angles.

And so the sum of the angles of an n-sided polygon is $2(n-2)$ right angles, which we normally quote as $2n-4$ right angles.

In the case of (**a**), the quadrilateral, $n = 4$ and so the sum of the interior angles of the quadrilateral is $2n-4$ right angles.

Since $n = 4$,
this is $2 \times 4 - 4$
$= 8 - 4 = 4$ right angles,

which is, of course, 360° (something we have already discovered).

In the case of **(b)**, the pentagon, $n = 5$ and so the sum of the interior angles of the pentagon is $2n - 4$ right angles.

$$\text{Since } n = 5,$$
$$\text{this is } \quad 2 \times 5 - 4$$
$$= 10 - 4 = 6 \text{ right angles, or } 540°.$$

Similarly for **(c)**, the hexagon, we find that the sum of the interior angles of the hexagon is 8 right angles, or 720°.

For any regular polygon we can, of course, calculate exactly the value of any one interior angle, since they are all identical.

Example Find the size of an interior angle of a **regular octagon**.

Regular octagon has 8 equal sides and 8 equal interior angles.

Hence, $n = 8$ and the sum of the interior angles is $2n - 4$ right angles

$$\text{i.e. } 2 \times 8 - 4 = 16 - 4$$
$$= 12 \text{ right angles}$$
$$\text{or, } 12 \times 90° = 1080°.$$

Since all the interior angles are equal, then each interior angle will be

$$\frac{1080°}{8} = 135°.$$

28.3 The sum of the exterior angles of a polygon

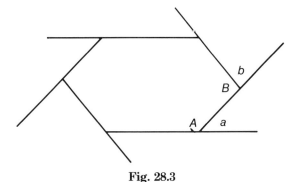

Fig. 28.3

Suppose we consider a six-sided polygon, as in Fig. 28.3, with each side produced (extended).

If we call the interior angles A, B, C etc. and the exterior angles a, b, c etc. then,

$$A + a = 180° \text{ (2 right angles)}$$
$$B + b = 180° \text{ (2 right angles)}$$
$$C + c = 180° \text{ (2 right angles)} \ldots \text{ and so on.}$$

Since there are 6 sides and 6 vertices,
$$A + a + B + b + \ldots = 12 \text{ right angles}$$

But we also know that
$$A + B + C + \ldots = 8 \text{ right angles}$$
(using $2n - 4$, with $n = 6$)

$$\therefore a + b + c + \ldots = 4 \text{ right angles}$$

And so the sum of the exterior angles of the hexagon is 4 right angles, or 360°.

If we were to perform the same operation for any other polygon we would reach the same conclusion as above, telling us that for **any** polygon, the sum of the exterior angles is always 4 right angles, or 360°.

Since the interior and exterior angles of any polygon are supplementary, in the case of a regular polygon we now have another method for finding the size of an interior angle.

Example Consider the **regular pentagon**.
This has 5 equal exterior angles as well as 5 equal interior angles.

Since the exterior angles of any polygon total 360°, then one such exterior angle of a regular pentagon will be

$$\frac{360°}{5} = 72°$$

Hence, the interior angle size will be

$$180° - 72° = 108°.$$

Check by interior angle method.
Sum of the angles $= 2n - 4$ right angles, where $n = 5$.
Sum of the angles $= 2 \times 5 - 4 = 6$ right angles,
$$\text{i.e. } 540°.$$

For a regular pentagon, each interior angle will be

$$\frac{540°}{5} = 108°,$$

thus confirming the above result.

Construction of quadrilaterals

1 Construct quadrilaterals from the information given in Fig. 28.4 (not drawn here to true size).

(a)
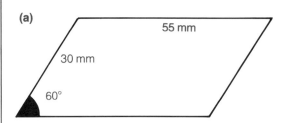

(b)
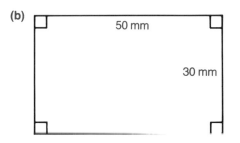

Fig. 28.4

continued on next page

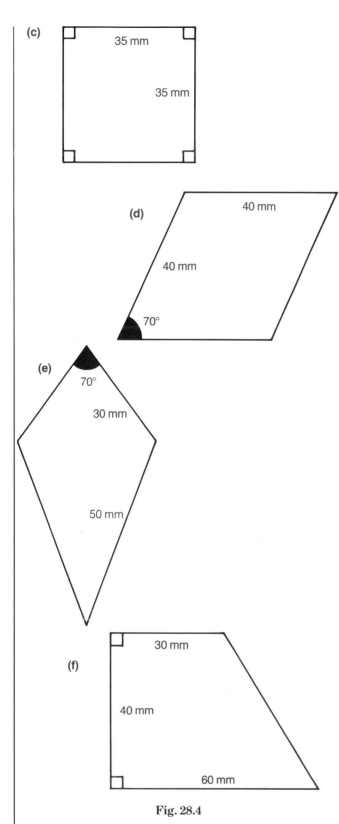

Fig. 28.4

2 Construct a square of side length 6 cm.

3 Construct a rectangle of length 9 cm and width 7 cm.

4 Construct a rhombus whose sides are 7 cm and one of whose angles is 75°.

5 Construct a parallelogram *ABCD* with *AB* = 8 cm *BC* = 6 cm and angle *ABC* = 120°.

6 Construct a kite with sides of 30 mm and 65 mm with the angle between these sides, 110°.

Regular polygon exercises

Draw a circle of radius 5 cm. Locate the centre spot and make six equal angles of 60° (see Fig. 28.5). Pencil lines should be feint. Join up the points on the circumference to make a regular hexagon.

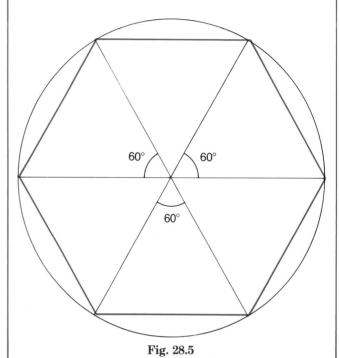

Fig. 28.5

Repeat the exercise with centre angles of 45° (see Fig. 28.6), to make a regular octagon.

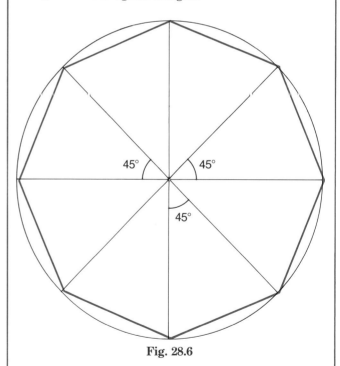

Fig. 28.6

Polygon exercises

1 Repeat the excercises in the previous section, but drawing the angles at the centre:

   (a) 72° (regular pentagon)

   (b) 40° (regular nonagon)

   (c) 36° (regular decagon)

2 Calculate the interior angles of the following regular polygons:

   (a) pentagon   **(b)** octagon   **(c)** hexagon

   (d) decagon   **(e)** nonagon

3 Now repeat Question 2, but this time calculate the exterior angles.

4 Look at the polygons in Fig. 28.7.

(a)

(b)

(c)

(d)

(e)

(f)

(g)

(h)

Fig. 28.7

   (i) Which are quadrilaterals?

   (ii) Which are rectangles?

   (iii) Which are regular polygons?

5 Copy and complete Table 28.2.

Regular Polygon	Number of sides (n)	Number of triangles	$(2n - 4)$ Rt. Angles	Interior Angle	Exterior Angle
Triangle	3	1	2	60°	120°
Square	4	2	4		
Pentagon					
Hexagon					
Heptagon	7	5	10	$128\frac{4}{7}^\circ$	$51\frac{3}{7}^\circ$
Octagon					
Nonagon					
Decagon					
Dodecagon	12				

Table 28.2

6 Draw all possible diagonals from **one** vertex only in the shapes shown in Fig. 28.8, and decide whether or not there is a relationship between the number of triangles formed and the number of sides to the shape.

The first two shapes have been completed, to help you.

   (a) quadrilaterial   **(b)** pentagon   **(c)** hexagon   **(d)** octagon

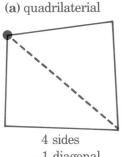

4 sides
—1 diagonal
—2 triangles

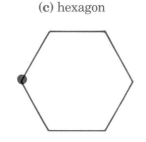

5 sides
—2 diagonals
—3 triangles

Fig. 28.8

STATISTICS

Unit 29

Collecting information

Collecting accurate information is probably the most difficult task facing the statistician. Some information (data) is easily obtained whilst other data is not accurate, is incomplete and sometimes quite unreliable.

Newspaper articles and television programmes provide us with a great deal of statistical information as shown in the following graphs taken from a daily newspaper.

Fig. 29.1

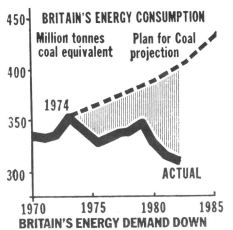

BRITAIN'S ENERGY DEMAND DOWN

INVESTMENT UP

Reprinted from the Sunday Times

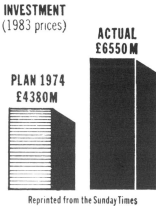

PRODUCTIVITY DOWN

TODAY'S RACING

ASCOT

2.0—HYPERION STAKES
(2 y o), 7f.

1, ITSAMAZING (G. Starkey—G. Harwood); 2, Split Image; 3, Vienna Belle.

S.P.: 6-1 1st, 15-8 fav. 2nd, 8-1 3rd.—8 ran.

Tote: £4.30; £1.10, £1.20, £2.50. Dual forecast: £4.30. Straight forecast: £16.23.—2l.; Head.

2.30—PRINCESS ROYAL STAKES, 1m. 4f.

1, ONE WAY STREET (L. Piggott—H. Cecil); 2, Allegedly Blue; 3, Llinos.

S.P.: 10-1 1st, 8-1 2nd, 20-1 3rd. Mpani 4-1 fav.—11 ran.

Tote: £7; £2.10, £2.20, £6.80. Dual forecast: £32. Straight forecast: £74.01.—5l.; ¾l.

TOP JOCKEYS

	W	M	£1 Stake
S Cauthen	122	728	−97.00
P Eddery	100	573	−55.29
L Piggott	94	448	−71.72
W R Swinburn	89	510	−64.23
T Ives	85	619	−193.45
W Carson	80	582	−162.50
G Duffield	78	650	−169.09
B Rouse	63	633	−172.90
T Quinn	57	330	+75.22
B Raymond	57	511	−164.78
G Starkey	56	352	−142.66
J Reid	55	583	−250.00

DIVISION I

	P	W	D	L	F	A	P
Arsenal	10	7	1	2	22	11	22
Tottenham	10	6	1	3	21	10	19
Sheff. Wed.	10	5	3	2	19	14	18
Man Utd	10	4	5	1	19	9	17
Nottm For.	10	5	2	3	19	14	17
Everton	10	5	2	3	18	18	17
Newcastle	10	4	3	3	20	20	15
West Ham	10	4	3	3	13	16	15
Sunderl'nd	10	3	5	2	13	12	14
Chelsea	10	3	4	3	13	10	13
South'mpt'n.	10	3	4	3	14	14	13
Aston Villa	10	4	1	5	15	20	13
West Brom	10	3	3	4	17	14	12
Ipswich T	10	2	6	2	12	12	12
Q.P.R.	9	2	5	2	17	18	11
Liverpool	10	2	5	3	12	13	11
Norwich	10	2	4	4	12	16	10
Coventry C	10	2	3	5	7	12	9
Luton	10	2	3	5	12	19	9
Leicester	10	2	3	5	13	22	9
Watford	10	1	4	5	18	23	7
STOKE C.	9	1	4	4	9	18	7

TOP SCORERS

DIVISION ONE: Bannister (QPR) 12, Falco (Tottenham) 11, Thompson (WBA) 10.

DIVISION TWO: Aldridge (Oxford) 10, Stevens (Shrewsbury) 10, Hamilton (Oxford) 9, Thompson (Blackburn) 9.

DIVISION THREE: Wilson (Derby) 13, Randall (Bristol Rovers) 9.

DIVISION FOUR: Adcock (Colchester) 9, Clayton (Tranmere) 9, Phillips (Hereford) 9, Steel (Wrexham) 9.

DIVISION I

Chelsea	2	Watford	3
Coventry C	1	Newcastle	1
Everton	2	Aston Villa	1
Ipswich T	1	Q.P.R.	1
Leicester	1	Arsenal	4
Luton	1	Sheff. Wed.	2
Man Utd	5	West Ham	1
STOKE C.	1	South'mpt'n.	3
Sunderl'nd	2	Norwich	1
West Brom	4	Nottm For.	1

■ HIGHEST SCORE: 5, Manchester United. HIGHEST AGGREGATE: 7, Airdrie 4, Clyde 3.

■ Total number of goals scored in yesterday's English and Scottish League games: 183.

Fig. 29.2

Newspaper articles sometimes rely very heavily on statistical data, particularly for sports results and for financial aspects of the business world. Examples of these are seen in Figs. 29.2 and 29.3.

Fig. 29.3

Local stock prices

BUYERS have appeared for EVODE in some strength on favourable view of their recent acquisition of Carter Bros. and the consequent diversification into polyethylene pipes and plastic film.

FOSECO-MINSEP plan to give their Foszoc building, chemicals and equipment division, a firm base in North America by an agreed bid for Gibson-Homans.

WEDGWOOD are continuing to attract investment and Warburg Investment Management have now increased their holding to more than 18 per cent.

A.I. Industrial Products 25p Ord.	33-35+1
Berisfords 25p Ord.	108-112+3
Berisford S. & W. 25p Ord.	192-196+5
Wm. Boulton 10p Ord.	5½-6½
Century Oils 10p Ord.	72-75
E.R.F. (Holdings) 25p Ord.	40-43-1
Evode Holdings 20p Ord.	114-118+8
Foseco Minsep 25p Ord.	177-181+2
R. Goodwin & Sons 10p Ord.	18-20-1
J. Hewitt (Fenton) 25p Ord.	53-57
I.C.L. 25p Ord.	94-97
Johnson Matthey £1 Ord.	106-110-2
Longton Industrial Holdings 25p Ord.	57-60-1
Marling Industries 10p Ord.	55-58+2
Norcros 25p Ord.	167-171-1
Staffs. Potteries (Holdings) 25p Ord.	75-77-1
Wade Potteries 10p Ord.	77-80
Waterford Glass 5p Ord.	31-33+½
Wedgwood 25p Ord.	177-180+8
Arthur Wood & Son (Longport) 5p Ord.	59-61
A.J. Worthington (Holdings) 10p Ord.	28-31

£500 BOND WINNERS

DERBYSHIRE and STAFFS.

3AW	492680	11PZ	585409
5AW	851480	18PK	929098
11AZ	929087	6QP	971420
14AZ	387883	7QZ	750857
17AF	187272	RL	009972
24AL	389353	RP	366530
26AS	884564	11RP	918352
32AT	382461	16RF	133776
32AW	123324	21RL	764417
1CW	438089	22RT	910087
2DL	323962	25RT	454721
3DP	657312	4SZ	250675
4DP	111730	4TF	476699
5DN	611288	12TP	820779
5DT	865978	13TL	438537
7EL	997009	15TT	187593
11EZ	021061	17TB	729593
11EZ	639103	12VT	755043
3FT	661570	14VT	375437
4HS	971132	16VN	137095
5HZ	723672	22VS	291413
4JN	481159	9WZ	621992
2KN	694954	19WP	585534
11KL	206154	20WP	634297
13KS	092764	10YN	656817
18KB	872751	12YW	029941
6LL	399332	14YF	725474
9LB	818537	4ZZ	596573
8PP	921116	5ZW	997706

Originally statistics began as a study of such things as wealth, industrial output, agricultural production, imports and other quantities of interest to a particular country, which might be studied in detail and perhaps compared with similar results of other countries.

Today, statistics has become the study of many types of data. They are used in all walks of life and affect us all sometimes without us realizing it.

Further areas in which statistics are used (apart from the previously described uses) are advertizing, stock control, sales trends, market research, T.V. ratings, the study of weather and many many more.

Facts are often required by a variety of people so that they can decide whether to

(a) change things to improve them

or (b) leave things unchanged.

For instance, the manufacturer of a Washing Powder may want to know:

(a) how many people use their brand

(b) how many people use brand X.

A manufacturer of light-bulbs would need to know how many hours his light-bulbs will last.

A local council highway planners' department may wish to know if building a new road would:

(a) reduce traffic jams,

(b) cause a rise in the number of accidents,

(c) damage nearby houses.

Activities

In Fig. 29.4 you will see quite a large variety of statistical information removed from magazines, newspapers and other sources over a period of one week. Look through your own local and national newspapers and magazines and any other material that you may have and see if you can find thirty different items which could be classed as statistical information. Fix these into a scrap-book, writing next to each from where the article came.

Just do this small exercise for **one** week only and you will be surprised how many items you can find. See if you can pass the thirty mark.

DATE	DESTINATION	NIGHTS	ACCOMMODATION		DEP. AIRPORT	FINAL PRICE
12 Nov	Costa Blanca	14	Economy	F/B	Birmingham	£163
12 Nov	Mallorca	14	Economy	H/B	Birmingham	£164
17 Nov	Costa del Sol	7	Apartment	A/O	Birmingham	£136
17 Nov	Costa del Sol	14	Apartment	A/O	Manchester	£165
19 Nov	Costa Blanca	7	Economy	F/B	Gatwick	£98
25 Nov	Tangier	7	Premium	H/B	Gatwick	£102
25 Nov	Tangier	14	Premium	H/B	Manchester	£162
26 Nov	Mallorca	7	Economy	H/B	Gatwick	£106
26 Nov	Mallorca	7	Economy	H/B	E. Midlands	£122
26 Nov	Costa Blanca	7	Premium	F/B	Manchester	£124
30 Nov	Costa Blanca	7	Premium	F/B	E. Midlands	£121
30 Nov	Costa Blanca	7	Economy	F/B	Luton	£105

Code: H/B = Half Board F/B = Full Board A/O = Accommodation Only. B/B = Bed and Breakfast.

Holidays (National)

Example of the 2% (4.2% A.P.R.) Scheme	MICRA 1·0 'L'
Cash price	£3846.00
On the road charges	£160.00
Total price	£4006.00
Deposit 33⅓%	£1335.00
Finance charges 2%	£106.76
Monthly payment 24 x	£115.74
WEEKLY EQUIVALENT	**£26.71**
Total credit price	£4122.76
CUSTOMER SAVING	**£481.00**

Customer savings compared to typical 11% in

Car Prices (National)

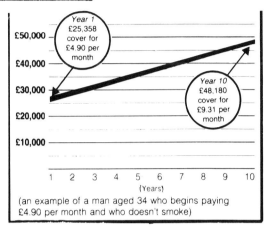

Year 1 £25,358 cover for £4.90 per month

Year 10 £48,180 cover for £9.31 per month

(an example of a man aged 34 who begins paying £4.90 per month and who doesn't smoke)

Insurance (Brochure)

BENEFITS PAYABLE ON DEATH

You pay monthly		£4	£8	£12	£20
YOUR AGE NOW		YOUR BENEFITS			
Male	Female	£	£	£	£
—	50	2000	4665	7331	12662
—	51	1884	4396	6907	11931
—	52	1777	4145	6514	11250
—	53	1674	3906	6138	10602
50	54	1578	3681	5784	9991
51	55	1487	3470	5452	9417
52	56	1400	3267	5133	8866
53	57	1318	3075	4832	8347
54	58	1241	2896	4550	7859
55	59	1176	2744	4311	7446
56	60	1107	2582	4037	7008
57	61	981	2156	3330	5679
58	62	929	2042	3154	5379
59	63	881	1935	2989	5097
60	64	837	1838	2840	4842
61	65	793	1743	2692	4592

Insurance Benefits (Local)

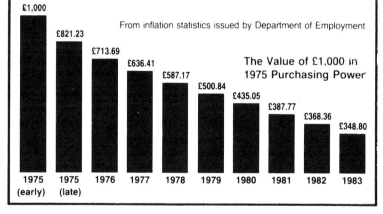

What inflation has done to the value of £1,000 since 1975

As you can see from this chart, £1,000 worth of insurance bought at the beginning of 1975 was worth only £348.80 by the end of 1983 in protecting your family, and is now worth even less.

From inflation statistics issued by Department of Employment

The Value of £1,000 in 1975 Purchasing Power

£1,000 | £821.23 | £713.69 | £636.41 | £587.17 | £500.84 | £435.05 | £387.77 | £368.36 | £348.80

1975 (early) | 1975 (late) | 1976 | 1977 | 1978 | 1979 | 1980 | 1981 | 1982 | 1983

TOP TV   **TOP VIDEO**   **TOP POPS**

For week ending Oct. 7. Figure in millions.

1 Coronation St. (Wed) . ITV 16.85
2 Coronation St. (Mon) . ITV 16.50
3 Fresh Fields .... ITV 16.40
4 Duty Free .... ITV 14.75
5 Benny Hill Show .... ITV 14.65
6 The Glory Boys .... ITV 14.35
7 Just Good Friends .. BBC-1 13.90
8 Tenko BBC-1 13.70
9 Paul Daniels Magic Show
 BBC-1 13.00
10 Play Your Cards Right ITV 12.95

This week's Top Ten video rentals, Last week in brackets.

1 (1) Sudden Impact—Clint Eastwood.
2 (2) Footloose Lori Singer.
3 (5) Tootsie Dustin Hoffman.
4 (3) An Officer And A Gentleman Richard Gere.
5 (-) Children Of The Corn— Peter Horton.
6 (6) Wargames—Matthew Broderick.
7 (4) Jaws 3 Louis Gossett Jr.
8 (9) Fawlty Towers—The Germans John Cleese.
9 (10) Krull Ken Marshall.
10 (-) Porky's 2—Dan Monohon.

Last week in brackets

1 (2) Freedom—Wham!
2 (1) War Song—Culture Club
3 (3) I Just Called To Say I Love You—Stevie Wonder
4 (5) No More Lonely Nights—Paul McCartney
5 (6) Together In Electric Dreams—Phil Oakey Giorgio Morodes
6 (4) Drive—The Cars
7 (9) Shout To The Top—Style Council
8 (14) Missing You John Waite
9 (16) I'm Gonna Tear Your Playhouse Down—Paul Young
10 (17) Skin Deep—Stranglers

Top of the Pops etc. (National)

FONTWELL RESULTS
Good to soft

2.00: DR. PEPPER (P. Corrigan, 9-2), 1; Playfields (7-2)f, 2; Rib Law (5-1), 3. Polar Express 7-2jf, 8 ran. 15, dist. (P. Haynes). Tote: £3.50; £1.10, £1.10, £2.10. Df: £6.70. Csf: £18.46. Tricast: £66.85. NRs: Donaghmoyne, Chosen.

2.30: IT'S TOUGH (Dunwoody, 14-1), 1; French Captain (11-1), 2; Paddy O'Malley (8-1), 3. Corston Lad 7-2f. 20 ran. 6, 12. (S. Woodman). Tote: £27.80; £5.80, £2.60, £2.60. Df: £185.80. Csf: £152.22.

3.00: HELLO KILLINEY (J. Francome, 7-2), 1; Cool Gin (4-1), 2; Sanhedrin (8-1), 3. 12 ran. ¾, 15. (J. Jenkins). Tote: £3.40; £2.10, £1.80, £2.20. Df: £10.90. Csf: £16.96. NR: Batula Prince.

3.30: BROTHER PARTISAN (C Smith, 12-1), 1; Come On Gracie (4-1f), 2; Thunder Rock (10-1), 3. 20 ran, 10, dist. (W Musson). Tote: £25.80; £4.90, £1.40, £8.00. Df: £90.10; Csf: £60.95.

4.0: TOM TAILOR (A Webber, 15-2), 1; Crowning Moment (12-1), 2; Hopeful Answer (20-1), 3. Zellda's Fancy 4f. 13 ran. 1½, 10. (R. Armytage). Tote: £8.10; £3.30, £4.00, £3.40. Df: £28.80; Csf: £84.56; Tricast: £1,566.63. NR: Moon Dreamer.

4.30: TROPICAL MIST (C Brown, 2-1), 1; Quite A Night (20-1), 2; Reeman (12-1), 3. 18 ran. 15, 5. (D Elsworth). Tote: £2.90; £2.00, £1.90, £3.60. Df: £6.20; Csf: £17.36. NRs: Landseer, Wordsworth.

Placepot: Not won.

RACING BRIEF

GOING: Good
COURSE: (Altitude 215ft.) Left-hand oval mile. Run-in 300y.
PLACEPOT: All six races.
TRICASTS: All handicaps of 10 or more declared.
TOP JOCKEYS (riding today): H Davies 17, Philip Hobbs 17, M Williams 16, S Smith Eccles 15, J Frost 13, P Richards 13, R Linley 12.
TOP TRAINERS (with runners today): J Jenkins 30, J Thorne 20, D Barons 17, D Elsworth 12, D Gandolfo 12.

Horse-Racing (National)

SPEEDWAY

BRITISH LEAGUE: Reading 32 (Andersson 11, Shirra 9). Ipswich 46 (Sanders 10, Niemi 10).

BRITISH LEAGUE TABLE
(Includes all matches up to Sunday, August 5)

		Home			Away					
	P	W	D	L	W	D	L	F	A	Pts+/−
Ipswich	12	6	0	0	5	0	1	537	397	22 +10
Wimbledon	15	8	0	1	2	0	4	602	567	20 +2
Belle Vue	12	8	0	0	1	1	2	557	379	19 +3
Newcastle	19	7	0	3	0	0	9	682½	795½	14 −6
Cradley Heath	10	4	0	1	2	1	2	417	362	13 +3
Reading	8	4	0	0	2	0	2	352½	270½	12 +4
Wolver'pton	12	5	0	2	1	0	4	461	472	12 −2
Sheffield	16	4	0	2	2	0	8	606	642	12 =
Swindon	11	4	1	1	1	0	4	434½	423½	11 −1
Oxford	8	4	0	1	1	0	2	320½	303½	10 =
Coventry	15	5	0	3	0	0	7	591	576	10 −6
King's Lynn	10	3	0	2	0	0	5	380	399	10 +4
Eastbourne	15	4	0	3	1	0	7	562	604	10 −4
Poole	11	4	1	1	0	0	5	404	454	9 −3
Halifax	11	3	1	1	0	1	5	395	463	8 −2
Exeter	15	4	0	1	0	0	10	487	681	8 −2

National Speedway

STAFFS. ALLIANCE

	P.	W.	D.	L.	P.
Fenton Poole D.	9	7	1	1	15
Eccleshall	9	6	1	2	13
Kidsgrove Y.A.	7	6	0	1	12
Brownhills Y.A.	10	5	2	3	12
Florence Coll.	9	5	1	3	11
Meir Park	9	5	1	3	11
Ash Inn	8	4	2	2	10
Foley	9	4	1	4	7
Stone O.A.	8	4	1	3	9
Madeley W.S.	9	2	4	3	8
Edwards Eng.	9	3	2	4	8
Burslem Town	9	2	2	5	6
Cheadle Town	9	2	1	6	5
Rists Utd.	8	2	0	6	4
Asager Town	8	1	2	5	4
Michelin A.C.	10	1	1	8	3

Local Soccer

Tunstall dominoes

	P.	W.	D.	L.	P.
Great Britain	7	6	0	1	12
Goldenhill WMC.	7	5	1	1	11
Goldenhill BL.	7	4	2	1	10
Elephant & C	7	4	2	1	10
Windmill	7	4	2	1	10
Butt Lane WMC	7	4	1	2	9
Goose Inn	7	4	0	3	8
Leopard	7	4	0	3	8
Cheshire Cheese	7	3	1	3	7
Coach & Horses	7	2	3	2	7
Smallthorne Vic.	7	3	1	3	7

Local Dominoes

DARTS

Rizla - Daily Mirror County Championship (Women's results in brackets): Beds 9, Cornwall 3 (3-2); Brecon 0, Somerset 12 (1-4); Bucks 7, Devon 5 (4-1); Cheshire 4, Derby 8 (3-2); Cleveland 7, Leics. 5 (3-2);

Local Cribbage

Newcastle L.V.A. Cribbage

	P.	W.	D.	L.	P.
Knutton	9	6	2	1	14
Newcastle WMC.	9	5	3	1	13
Newc. & H. CC.	9	4	2	3	10
Silverdale CC	9	4	2	3	10
Oxford Arms	9	5	0	4	10
Crown (Sil.)	9	4	2	3	10
Bird In Hand	9	4	1	4	9
Black Horse	9	4	1	4	9
Seabridge	9	3	2	4	8
Swan	9	3	3	4	7
London-rd BC	9	2	2	5	6
Duke of York	9	1	0	8	2

SCOTTISH SECOND DIVISION

	P	W	D	L		W	D	L	F	A	Pts
Dunfermline	11	4	1	0	13	.	5	0	1	12	4..19
Alloa	11	3	3	0	10	3..4	1	0	7	3..18
Montrose	11	4	0	1	9	6..4	0	2	8	6..16
Stenhsemuir	11	2	2	2	6	8..2	2	1	5	4..12
Cowdenbth	11	4	0	2	14	7..1	1	3	5	6..11
Qn of Sth	11	2	2	1	10	6..1	3	2	7	10..11
Berwick	11	3	1	2	8	5..1	1	3	3	8..10
Stranraer	11	3	0	2	8	5..2	0	4	5	12..10
Queens Pk	11	2	0	3	10	7..2	1	3	8	14.. 9
Raith	11	2	1	3	6	7..1	2	2	6	10.. 9
Albion R	11	1	0	4	5	9..3	1	2	10	12.. 9
Arbroath	11	1	1	4	5	12..2	1	2	5	6.. 8
Stirling A	11	0	2	3	6	9..2	1	3	6	6.. 7
E Stirling	11	0	3	3	5	8..0	2	3	7	14.. 5

Scottish Soccer

Soccer Club Results

National Pools Checks

SEQUENCES

SINCE A HOME SCORE DRAW		SINCE A DRAW	
Berwick	18	Fulham	19
Dundee	16	Preston	16
Chelsea	15	Grimsby	14
Man City	15	Tranmere	14
Barnsley	13	Cardiff	12
Bury	13	Notts Co.	12
Forfar	13	Airdrie	11
Sheff Utd.	10	Birmingham	11
Shrewsbury	10	Crewe	11
West Ham	10	Arsenal	10

SINCE AN AWAY SCORE DRAW			
		St. Mirren	10
		Wimbledon	10
Bradford C.	28	Albion	9
Northamptn	24	C. Palace	9
Chesterfield	21	Falkirk	9
Derby	16	Tottenham	9
Falkirk	14	Wrexham	9
Notts Co.	13	Bolton	8
Orient	13	Oxford	8
Dumbarton	12	Swansea	8
Torquay	12		
Alloa	11	SINCE A DEFEAT	

SINCE A SCORE DRAW			
		Alloa	12
Notts Co.	24	Barnsley	8
Fulham	22	Sheff. Wed.	8
Bolton	20	Blackburn	7
Airdrie	16	Southampton	7
		Airdrie	6
Preston	16	Chesterfield	6
Forfar	15	Arsenal	6
Chesterfield	14	Hartlepool	5

		SINCE A HOME WIN	
Cowdenbeath	14	Aldershot	6
Grimsby	14	Cambridge	5
Northampt	14	East Fife	5
Tranmere	14	Watford	5
Brighton	13	Arbroath	4
Birmingham	12	Bournemth	3
Cardiff	12	Coventry	3
St. Mirren	12	Exeter	3
Crewe	11	Sheff. Utd.	3
Reading	11		

SINCE A WIN		SINCE A HOME DRAW	
		Dundee	16
Morton	9	Man City	15
Bournemth	8	Chelsea	11
Cambridge	8	Sheff. Utd.	10
East Fife	8	Shrewsbury	10
Sheff. Utd.	7	Hamilton	9
Stoke	7	Barnsley	7
Clyde	6		
Preston	6	SINCE A HOME DEFEAT	
Charlton	4	Hereford	16
C. Palace	4	Norwich	10
Dundee	4	Tottenham	10
Gillingham	4	Blackpool	9
Norwich	4	Bristol R.	9
		Rotherham	9
		Sunderland	9
		Portsmouth	8
		Millwall	7

SINCE AN AWAY WIN	
Derby	19
Wolves	15
Clyde	11
Bolton	10
Newport	9
Q.P.R.	6

SINCE AN AWAY DRAW	
Falkirk	14
Bradford C.	13
Orient	13
Northamptn	12
Charlton	10
Fulham	10

SINCE AN AWAY DEFEAT	
Darlington	8
Alloa	5
Airdrie	3
Sheff. Wed.	3

SNOOKER

Benson & Hedges World Amateur Championship (Dublin).—V. Saenthong (Thailand) bt K. Sirisomo (Sri Lanka) 4-0:

PONTOON CHART

	Sept		Oct				Sept		Oct				Sept		Oct		
	22	29	6	13	20		22	29	6	13	20		22	29	6	13	20
Aberdeen	2	4	1	2	4	Dundee U	2	0	1	0	1	Oxford Utd	2	4	0	2	5
Airdrie	1	5	2	4	2	Dunfermline	0	1	2	4	2	Partick T	2	2	1	2	1
Albion R	3	1	3	0	0	East Fife	2	0	1	0	2	Peterboro	3	0	2	3	1
Aldershot	0	3	0	0	0	E Stirling	2	0	1	0	2	Plymouth	2	6	0	1	1
Alloa	1	3	3	1	0	Everton	2	5	0	2	1	Portsmth	3	2	2	3	2
Arbroath	0	1	0	2	2	Exeter C	0	0	2	1	1	Port Vale	2	0	2	2	2
Arsenal	2	4	2	1	4	Falkirk	3	1	1	0	6	Preston	0	4	0	0	1
A Villa	0	0	3	1	2	Forfar A	3	1	1	0	4	Qn of Sth	1	1	2	3	3
Ayr Utd	1	3	3	2	3	Fulham	0	2	2	2	3	Queen's Pk	2	1	1	3	0
Barnsley	1	5	2	1	0	Gillingham	3	1	1	0	2	Q. P. R.	5	1	2	1	2
Berwick	2	0	0	0	0	Grimsby	1	3	2	2	3	Raith Rov	0	2	1	1	0
Birmingham	2	1	0	0	0	Halifax	1	0	0	1	0	Rangers	0	0	3	2	3
Blackburn	3	2	3	2	1	Hamilton	2	3	0	0	3	Reading	0	1	1	2	3
Blackpool	1	3	1	1	0	Hartlepool	1	3	2	2	1	Rochdale	0	1	1	3	3
Bolton W	7	0	1	2	4	Hearts	3	3	2	2	1	Rotherham	3	3	2	3	2
Bournemth	1	0	1	1	1	Hereford	3	1	0	2	2	St. Johnstne	2	0	0	3	2
Bradford C	2	1	2	3	1	Hibernian	1	0	1	2	0	St Mirren	1	1	2	1	1
Brechin C	0	1	2	0	4	Huddersfld	1	0	1	3	1	Scunthorpe	1	4	2	1	1
Brentford	3	2	0	0	5	Hull City	3	2	0	1	0	Sheff Utd	1	2	1	0	1
Brighton	0	2	2	1	0	Ipswich	2	3	0	1	2	Sheff Wed	2	2	2	2	5
Bristol C	2	1	2	3	1	Kilmarnock	0	4	0	3	1	Shrewsbury	0	4	1	3	1

SNOOKER

National Bingo Results

BINGO SERVICE

Daily Mail Casino (Day 100): 31, 8, 28, 4, 12, 5, 18, 36, 19, 17, 29, 22, 7, 14, 6, 10, 2. Extra numbers: 18th, 16; 19th, 9; 20th, 23; 21st, 32; 22nd, 3.

Daily Mirror (Game 125): 36, 25, 80, 74, 62, 14. Who Dares Wins: 28, 33, 10, 42, 09, 50, 21, 36; 31, 39, 16, 45, 12, 17, 30, 59; 28, 08, 30, 35, 38, 48, 45, 60; 24, 40, 39, 49, 45, 54, 58, 07; 42, 45, 31, 46, 20, 58, 10, 12; 31, 59, 24, 58, 40, 48, 60, 55; 54, 24, 30, 48, 12, 45, 50, 09; 39, 48, 47, 17, 27, 58, 28, 30; 17, 27, 41, 43, 60, 01, 36, 55; 33, 43, 59, 50, 08, 10, 48, 46. £1 Million Accumulator: 40, 10.

Daily Star (Game 17): 79, 31, 2, 89, 15, 75, 64, 46, 70, 81.

Sun (Game 180): 37, 71, 2, 59, 32, 70, 81, 58, 89, 38, 51, 23, 45.

Fig. 29.4 continued

Unit 30

Statistical population

Data is collected about many populations. A **statistical population** consists of all items about which data is being collected. Table 30.1 below shows some examples of populations.

Data collected	Population
Life of a particular light-bulb	All light-bulbs of the same type
The number of words per line in a particular textbook	All the lines of that textbook
Hair colours of pupils in a class	All the pupils in the class
The jobs of people in the country	All people 16 years of age and over in the country

Table 30.1

When we collect data about a population, it is best if we can:

(a) collect data about all members of the population,

(b) collect data as quickly as possible,

(c) collect data with the minimum of expense.

Most populations are very large, and collecting data of all members would be very slow and expensive. In some cases we may even destroy the whole population, i.e. the light-bulbs would be of no use for sale, after finding their life-span.

In order to overcome these problems, we usually collect data about a population by using what is commonly known as a representative **sample** of the population.

Activities

Collection of data

1 **Population: You**

Find and write down your

(a) age to the nearest month,

(b) height to the nearest cm,

(c) waist size to the nearest cm,

(d) chest size to the nearest cm,

(e) hip size to the nearest cm,

(f) weight to the nearest kg,

(g) shoe size,

(h) hair colour,

(i) eye colour.

2 Population: Your Family (include yourself)

Find and write down

    (a) their favourite breakfast food,

    (b) their favourite drink,

    (c) their favourite colour,

    (d) their eye colours,

    (e) their hair colours,

    (f) their ages,

    (g) their favourite T.V. programmes,

    (h) the time that they usually go to bed.

Add more, if you think of some other things.

3 Population: Your Schoolfriends (include yourself)

Ask the same questions as in Question **1**, and record your answers in a table similar to Table 30.2. Use as many of your friends as you can for this exercise.

Name	Age	Height	Waist	Chest	Hips	Weight	Shoe size	Hair	Eyes
Me John Jane Elizabeth Graham ⋮ Etc.									

Table 30.2

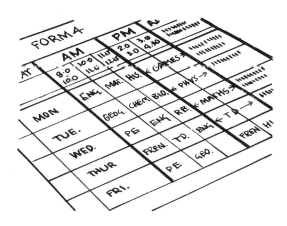

4 Using a suitable population, i.e. class or year group, collect information on

    Hobbies

or **Pets**

or **Favourite School Subjects**

Analyse the information to see if you can discover the most popular of each of the above topics.

N.B. You must use a population of at least thirty, if your results are going to be of any significant value.

5 Using as large a population as possible, conduct your own survey to find the most popular T.V. shows. Use headings such as

Children's Programmes,

Comedy Programmes,

Drama Programmes,

Popular 'Soap Opera' Programmes, i.e. *Dallas, Crossroads, Coronation Street* etc.,

News Programmes,

Sports Programmes,

or any other definite types of programmes that you can think of.

N.B. An interesting and useful exercise would be to limit choices, and see if your results are the same. That is, do you get the same results by asking, 'Do you like best, *Dallas, Crossroads* or *Coronation Street*?' as when you ask, 'Which Soap Opera programme do you like best?'

Unit 31

Sampling

A sample is made up of some of the members of the population.

A good (representative) sample is one in which the results we obtain could be taken as true for the total population.

To obtain a good sample, we must choose the sample members carefully by following these guidelines.

(a) Choosing at random. This means that every member of the population has an equal chance of being chosen.

(b) Choosing a sample large enough to satisfy the size of the population being investigated.

(c) Choosing a sample that is in no way biased (favoured).

A completely unbiased sample from a population should result, if the sample is totally random and large enough.

A fraction or percentage of the sample should then be the same fraction or percentage of the whole population. The sample is hence a representative sample.

Fig. 32.3

Unit 32

Methods of collecting data

32.1 Introduction

Data can be collected by the following.

(a) Questioning people and recording their replies – known as Questionnaires.

(b) Observation – watching and recording.

(c) Experimental work and recording the results.

(d) Finding data, in published books, already collected by other people.

We shall look now at a few specific examples of data collection.

Finding the petrol consumption of your own family car over the past six months, may prove to be difficult to work out without precise records of petrol purchases and mileages.

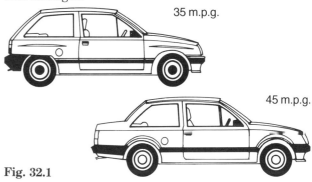

Fig. 32.1

It might be far easier to count the number of pupils in your own class with a birthday in January, because this data is easier to collect.

Fig. 32.2

On the other hand, we might measure the heights or weights of this same group.

Petrol consumption, numbers of pupils, or heights of pupils etc., are the things we wish to study. They are known as **variables**.

32.2 Variables

Variables fall into two distinct types: **discrete** and **continuous**.

A **discrete variable** is one which can only have certain definite values, more often than not, whole numbers, e.g. the number of peas in a pod must be a definite value, in this case a whole number. There might be 5 peas in one pod and 7 in another etc., but there cannot be 4.53 peas in any one pod.

Certain values of **discrete** variables are not in whole numbers. In shoe sizes there are the 'half' sizes. As a child's foot grows the shoe sizes may be 2, $2\frac{1}{2}$, 3, $3\frac{1}{2}$ but, no matter the size of the foot, we cannot buy a size 3.25. Shoes can only be bought in certain definite sizes.

The various values of a **discrete** variable can usually be obtained by counting. The number of peas per pod can be counted. The number of children taking a size 3 shoe can be counted.

A **continuous variable** is one which can take up any value within a certain range. The different values of a **continuous** variable are usually obtained by some kind of measurement.

Suppose we consider the actual length of a child's foot as it grows. Between the ages of 9 and 13 years, the foot may have grown from 19 cm to 24 cm and obviously there is no length between 19 cm and 24 cm that the foot did not measure at some time. At one point in time it would have measured 19.75 cm and at another time it was 22.462 cm etc. The length of the foot, we can say, varied continuously in length between 19 cm and 24 cm.

Other examples might include the child's height or weight which vary continuously and may be measured.

Example 1 The shoe sizes of members of your class is a **discrete** variable.

Example 2 The rainfall (measured in cm) in your town over the past year, is a **continuous** variable.

Activities

1 Make a list of three different discrete variables and three different continuous variables based on any topic you like.

2 Say which of the following variables is discrete and which is continuous.

(a) Train-speed throughout a journey.

(b) Marks of the class in a Maths Examination.

(c) The number of goals scored by a footballer during one season.

(d) The height of a child over the first four years of its life.

(e) The temperature of cooling water at regular time-intervals.

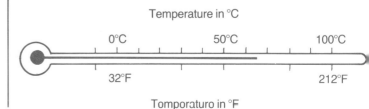

(f) The number of rooms in your house.

(g) The volume of water used by a town throughout the year.

(h) Goals scored by a netball team every week.

(i) Air pressures recorded at a weather station.

(j) The amount of rainfall in Stoke-on-Trent over a ten-year period.

Unit 33

Recording information

By far the best way of recording information is to form a **frequency distribution table**. This is best done by putting the unsorted results into some type of order by using a **tally chart**.

Example In a French test, a group of 40 children scored the marks, shown in Table 33.1, out of a possible 10 marks.

6	7	5	4	4	5	4	6	5	6
7	10	3	6	6	4	7	7	2	4
6	6	8	7	8	7	3	5	7	9
8	7	5	3	2	5	7	1	4	7

Table 33.1

It is very difficult to make much use of this information as it is, but if we draw up a tally chart/frequency table as shown in Table 33.2, the information then becomes quite meaningful.

Marks in French test (10)		
Mark	Tally	Frequency
0		0
1	I	1
2	II	2
3	III	3
4	IIII I	6
5	IIII I	6
6	IIII II	7
7	IIII IIII	10
8	III	3
9	I	1
10	I	1
		40

Table 33.2

From the list of scores, one stroke is marked each time the score occurs. Every fifth stroke is drawn across the previous four, giving blocks of five. It is a good idea to cross out the numbers on the list as they are tallied, in order to avoid confusion.

It is also very important to total the frequency to see that it is the same as the number of scores, i.e. 40 in Table 33.2.

If a number has been missed or recorded twice, then this can be put right by a re-tally.

You must concentrate very hard when you do the tally.

Table 33.3 is a horizontal version of the same frequency table.

Mark	0	1	2	3	4	5	6	7	8	9	10
Frequency	0	1	2	3	6	6	7	10	3	1	1
	(Total 40)										

Table 33.3

The example we have just worked through shows **ungrouped data**. It is ungrouped because we are only talking about a small range of values, i.e. from 1 to 10.

If however, the marks had been given as marks out of 100, we would have had to produce a tally chart of enormous size. In order to avoid this problem, we then have to put the marks into classes or groups (this is known as **grouped data**) such as from 1 to 10, 11 to 20 etc.

Note: Grouped data is fully explained in Volume 2, Unit 24, Statistics.

Activities

Tally charts and frequency distribution

1 Collect the shoe sizes of at least twenty different people and, by using a tally chart, form a frequency distribution of shoe sizes.

2 By using a tally chart, draw up a frequency distribution table for the goals, in Table 33.4, scored by a netball team over a period of matches.

8	6	8	9	7	7	9	5	8	7
2	6	2	5	0	6	3	7	3	1
3	3	5	6	3	6	2	6	1	6

Table 33.4

3 The heights of fifty boys in the same year at school, measured to the nearest cm, were recorded as in Table 33.5.

173	167	166	174	170	168	173	169	167	172
172	169	174	168	170	175	173	168	169	167
167	168	169	173	170	170	172	168	170	165
166	169	172	167	168	165	173	168	172	173
176	172	169	171	169	171	169	171	169	170

Table 33.5

Draw up a tally chart and form a frequency distribution table of the boys' heights.

4 Table 33.6 gives the results of 18 football matches played on one particular Saturday.

2–0	2–1
1–1	0–2
2–4	2–0
3–1	1–3
2–1	1–3
3–1	0–2
1–0	2–1
4–0	5–1
2–0	2–4

Table 33.6

Form a frequency table of the total number of goals scored on this particular Saturday in these matches.

Unit 34

Visual representation of data

34.1 Introduction

Having collected the data, its presentation is very important in order for it to be easily noticed and understood.

The most obvious impacts are made by such things as graphs or charts which are carefully coloured or shaded.

The most common ways of showing information are the **pictogram**, the **bar graph**, the **pie chart** and the **line graph**.

34.2 The pictogram (or pictograph or ideograph)

This is a simple way of showing facts using little drawings or symbols. In order to make a good **pictogram** we should think about the following points.

(a) Use small, sensible symbols to represent the data.

(b) Make the symbols simple and clear.

(c) Produce a scale to show exactly what each symbol represents.

(d) Make sure all full symbols are of the same size.

(e) Space the symbols equally.

(f) Draw all symbols for one section of data in a straight line (either vertical or horizontal).

(g) Show data of less than scale size by a part of the symbol, as shown in Figs. 34.1, 34.2 and 34.3.

We usually draw symbols similar to the data to be represented, either vertically or horizontally depending on the data involved.

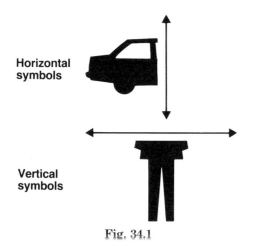

Fig. 34.1

Example (i) Symbols horizontally (see Fig. 34.2)

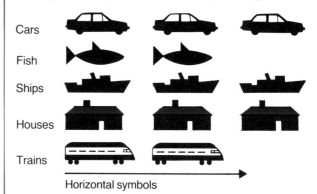

Horizontal symbols

Fig. 34.2

Example (ii) Symbols vertically (see Fig. 34.3)

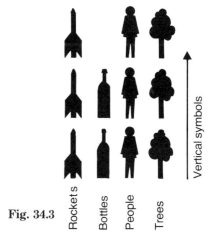

Fig. 34.3

We shall now look closely at two such typical examples.

Example 1 The following seaside resorts recorded hours of sunshine over the month of February 1975, as in Table 34.1.

Brighton	40 hours
Bournemouth	40 hours
Blackpool	35 hours
Scarborough	25 hours

Table 34.1

Construct a pictogram to represent this information. The pictogram could be as in Fig. 34.4.

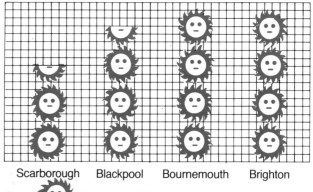

Scarborough   Blackpool   Bournemouth   Brighton

Scale 🌞 Represents 10 hours

Fig. 34.4

Example 2 Study the pictogram, in Fig. 34.5, of bread sales of a bakery over a one week period and write down how many loaves were sold on:

(a) Wednesday

(b) Friday

(c) Sunday (and why?)

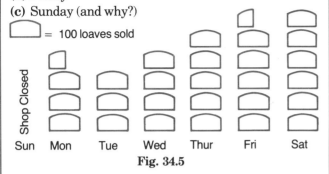

Fig. 34.5

(a) 4 loaves represents four hundred loaves sold.

(b) $5\frac{1}{2}$ loaves represents five hundred and fifty loaves sold.

(c) No loaves sold – shop closed on Sunday.

34.3 The bar graph (or bar chart)

This is usually the most popular method of displaying statistical information and is probably the easiest of all of the four different methods we are studying.

We can display the information on a **bar graph** either vertically (sometimes called a column graph) or horizontally, both ways being equally acceptable.

A bar chart is made up of a series of bars. Each bar is usually separated by a space from other bars. Each bar shows a section of the data to be represented. The length or height of each bar depends on the size of the section of the data it represents.

Bar charts are used to show discrete data.

Note that all the bars are drawn of the same width, and spaces are also of the same width.

N.B. Bars and spaces need not be of the same width.

Example Of 36 teachers in a school, seven teach Maths, nine teach English, six teach Science, four teach Humanities, five teach Art and Crafts, three teach Modern Languages and two teach P.E./Games.

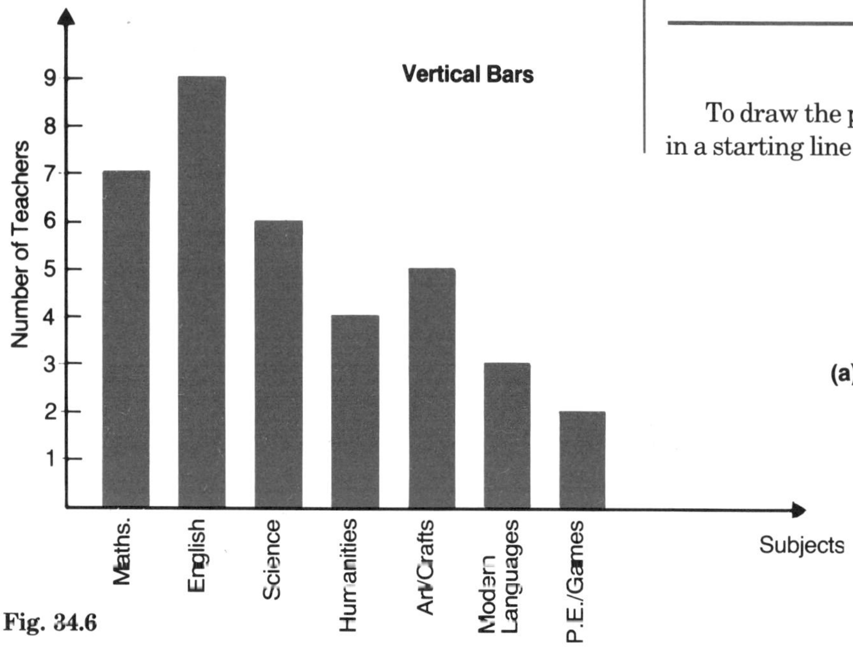

Draw a vertical and a horizontal bar graph (fully labelled) to represent this information.

Fig. 34.6 shows the vertical, and Fig. 34.7 the horizontal, bar graph.

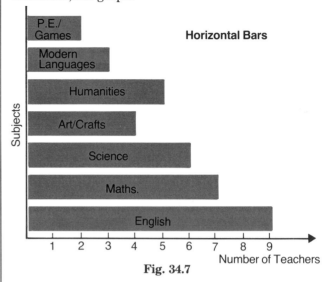

Fig. 34.7

34.4 The pie graph (or pie chart)

This method involves drawing a circle which represents a 'pie' of which each slice represents an item. The size of the slice depends on the size of the item.

The angle at the centre of a circle is 360°.

Example 1 Consider the bar chart example above concerning the 36 teachers in a school.

The pie must be equally divided amongst them. Each teacher must be represented by

$(360° \div 36) = 10°$
Maths will be represented by $7 \times 10° = 70°$
English   „   „   „ $9 \times 10° = 90°$
Science   „   „   „ $6 \times 10° = 60°$
Humanities   „   „   „ $4 \times 10° = 40°$
Art/Crafts   „   „   „ $5 \times 10° = 50°$
Mod. Langs.   „   „ $3 \times 10° = 30°$
PE/Games   „   „   „ $2 \times 10° = \underline{20°}$
$\underline{360°}$

Table 34.2

To draw the pie chart, first draw a circle and mark in a starting line as shown in **(a)**, Fig. 34.8.

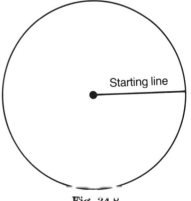

(a)

Fig. 34.8

Fig. 34.6

Using a protractor, from this starting line measure an angle of 70°. This is then the Maths slice of the pie, see **(b)**, Fig. 34.9.

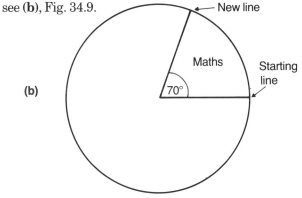

Fig. 34.9

Use the new line drawn in **(b)** to measure the next angle 90° (for English), as shown in **(c)**, Fig. 34.10.

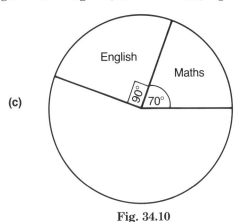

Fig. 34.10

We continue the process until we have completed the full circle. We must obviously be very careful when measuring the angles, otherwise the slices may not fit exactly.

The slices or **sectors** now have to be labelled with the subject names to complete the chart, as in **(d)**, Fig. 34.11.

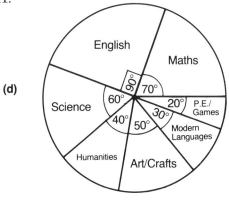

Fig. 34.11

The problem can be operated in reverse, by providing the graph from which the various results can be obtained.

Example 2 The pie chart, in Fig. 34.12, shows how a boy spends his £4 pocket money. How much does he spend on discos? How much on magazines and comics? How much does he save? How much does he spend at the football match?

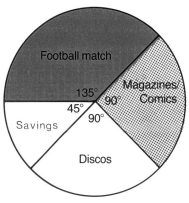

Fig. 34.12

Since 360° represents 400p

$$1° \text{ represents } \frac{400}{360}\text{p}$$

Hence, Discos – 90° represents

$$\frac{400}{360} \times 90 = 100\text{p} = £1$$

Magazines/Comics – 90° represents as above, £1

Savings – 45° represents

$$\frac{400}{360} \times 45 = 50\text{p}$$

Football Match – 135° represents

$$\frac{400}{360} \times 135 = 150\text{p} = £1.50$$

34.5 The line graph (or trend graph)

This is a graph which is usually used to show differences (trends) in sales figures, growth figures etc., whether they be rising or falling as time goes by.

Typical examples of trends include such things as these, below.

(a) Rainfall – up in the winter but down in the summer.

(b) Ice cream sales – up in the summer but down in the winter.

(c) Traffic – up during the rush-hour periods, down during the remainder of the day.

When drawing a trend graph we should use the following guidelines.

(i) On graph paper draw two axes, one vertical and one horizontal.

(ii) Mark the horizontal axis in the time units involved (i.e., seconds, minutes, hours, days etc.).

(iii) Mark the vertical axis in the units of the quantity which is changing with the time.

(iv) Plot each pair of values in the list of data against each other, fixing the position with a vertical (dotted) line.

(v) Join up the tops of the vertical lines with straight lines which then show the trends.

Example The heights of a child are taken at two-yearly intervals between the ages of 9 and 21.

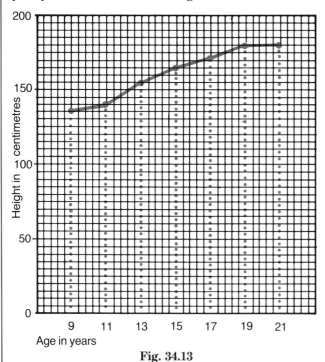

Fig. 34.13

In Fig. 34.13, a line is taken from the age to the corresponding height, and the tops of these lines are connected by straight lines. By studying these straight lines we can see the following information.

(a) The child grows fastest between 11 and 13 years (since the slope of the line is at its steepest there).

(b) The growth rate is quite steady between 13 and 19 years.

(c) Growth after 19 years is nil (since the line is level).

(d) Between 9 and 11 years, the growth is quite slow (a shallow slope).

Activities

Pictograms

1 In a traffic census conducted outside the school gate, the results in Table 34.3 were noted over a one hour period, during a typical weekday.

Cars	13
Buses	8
Lorries	6
Motor Cycles	9
Pedal Cycles	4

Table 34.3

Draw a pictogram to show the above information.

2 Fig. 34.14 is a pictogram showing how many houses were built during 1980, 1981 and 1982.

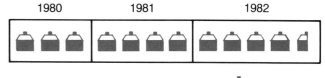

1980   1981   1982

= 50 houses

Fig. 34.14

From the pictogram answer the following.
How many houses were built in
(a) 1980? **(b)** 1981? **(c)** 1982?

3 On a particular day at school, sixty pupils were found to be absent. The reasons for their absence are shown in Table 34.4.

Visiting Doctor	Visiting Clinic	Visiting Dentist	School Trip	Coughs/ Colds
6	5	7	20	22

Table 34.4

Show this information on a vertical pictogram using the following scale:

∧ = 1 pupil   = 2 pupils   = 3 pupils
= 4 pupils

N.B. Horizontal cut-off for vertical pictogram.

4 The pictogram in Fig. 34.15 represents the catches of five anglers during a season of fishing.

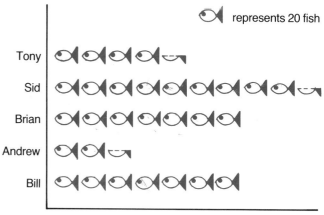

represents 20 fish

Tony
Sid
Brian
Andrew
Bill

Fig. 34.15

Study the pictogram and answer the following questions.
(a) Which two men had caught the same number of fish? How many did each catch?
(b) Which man had a catch of 50 fish?
(c) Which man had a catch of 190 fish?
(d) What size of catch did Tony have?
(e) Which man would have won the fishing prize?
(f) Which man won the 'wooden-spoon'?

Bar graphs

1 Thirty pupils in a class were asked if they had pets and the results are recorded in Table 34.5.

Pet	Cat	Dog	Hamster	Rabbit	Bird	Tortoise	Mouse	No pet
Number of Pupils	6	8	2	3	4	1	1	5

Table 34.5

Draw a bar chart to show the information.

2 The bar chart in Fig. 34.16 shows the way in which a family spends its wages in one month.

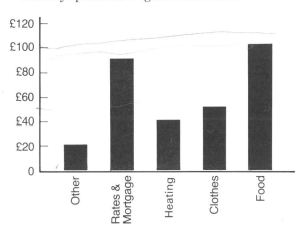

Fig. 34.16

Study the chart and then answer the following.

(a) On what item does the family spend £50 per month? ~~Clothes~~ Clothes

(b) Make a list of all expenses.

(c) Find the total amount of the family wage.

(d) What is the most expensive item that the family has to buy each month? ~~Food~~ Food

3 Draw a bar chart to show the shoe sizes in Table 34.6, from a survey conducted in a school.

Shoe size	3	$3\frac{1}{2}$	4	$4\frac{1}{2}$	5	$5\frac{1}{2}$	6	$6\frac{1}{2}$
Number of Pupils	2	5	6	9	10	7	8	3

Table 34.6

Then answer the following questions.

(a) How many pupils were in the survey sample (i.e. the population size)?

(b) Which shoe size was worn by more people than any other?

(c) Which shoe size was least worn in the sample?

4 Study the horizontal bar chart in Fig. 34.17, which shows the lengths of the longest rivers of the world, and then answer the questions.

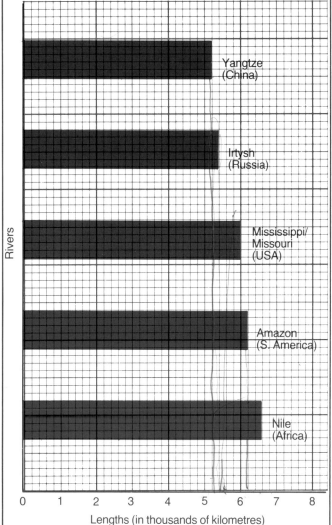

Fig. 34.17

(a) What is the approximate length of the longest river in the world? 6·6

(b) Which river is about 5400 km long? russia

(c) Which river is about 6200 km long? Amazon

(d) What is the approximate length of the Yangtze river? 5200

(e) Why do you think that the graph has been drawn horizontally? don't know

5 Construct a bar chart of your own involving members of your class or your family. Firstly obtain your own frequency distribution table, after performing your own survey using such details as heights (in cm) shoe sizes, ages, pets, or any other detail that may be of interest to you.

Pie charts

1 Construct a pie chart showing the favourite hobbies of a group of twenty children, as shown in Table 34.7.

Fishing	4
Football	6
Skating	5
Cycling	2
Stamp Collecting	3

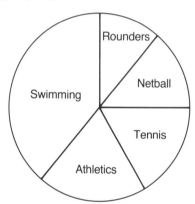

Table 34.7

Explain carefully how you arrived at the angle representing each hobby. Check your calculations to make sure the sectors of your 'pie' total 360°.

2 The pie chart in Fig. 34.18 shows the five favourite sports of a group of girls.

Fig. 34.18

Study the chart carefully and then:

(a) draw a table to show the angle representing each sport;

(b) record on the same table how many pupils the angles represent, using a scale of 5° to one pupil;

(c) find how many girls there are in the group altogether.

3 The cost of a new book at a booksellers is £3.60. This cost is broken down into four parts, as shown in the pie graph in Fig. 34.19.

Fig. 34.19

From the diagram, find the answers to the following questions.

(a) What is the writer's fee?

(b) What is the cost of the materials?

(c) The angle representing the publishing costs?

(d) The actual cost of publishing?

4 Draw a pie chart, using 5 cm radius, to represent the five sections of expenditure of a Local Council shown in Table 34.8 which gives the angle of the sector corresponding to each section.

N.B. Label your diagram clearly and fully.

Section	Angle
Education	225°
Social Services	15°
Environmental Services	45°
Other Services	30°
Inflation	?°

Table 34.8

(a) Find the angle of the Inflation sector.

(b) £720 000 was the total expenditure by the Council. Calculate how much was spent on the Environmental Services.

(c) How much was spent on Other Services?

(d) How much was spent on Social Services?

(e) What was the Education cost?

Line graphs/trend graphs

1 A grocer opened his small shop to the public on January 1st 1976 and his nett (overall after expenses) profit over the following 6 years was as shown in Table 34.9.

Year	1976	1977	1978	1979	1980	1981
Nett Profit	£500	£800	£1000	£2000	£3500	£3000

Table 34.9

Draw a trend graph to show the information above and write,

(a) what happened between 1976 and 1980,

(b) what has happened in 1981, and what may have caused this.

2 A speedway rider rode the number of first places over a seven-year period, as shown in Table 34.10.

Year	1973	1974	1975	1976	1977	1978	1979
No. of victories	58	93	80	46	102	76	65

Table 34.10

Draw a trend graph to show this information, (**N.B.** What type of variable?) and,

(a) comment on his career from 1977 onwards,

(b) say what could have happened to him in 1976.

3 The amount of money shown on a family's bank balance at the end of each month is shown on the trend graph in Fig. 34.20.

(a) Study the graph and suggest a reason why there are very noticeable drops in August and December.

(b) From the graph, complete the distribution table (Table 34.11).

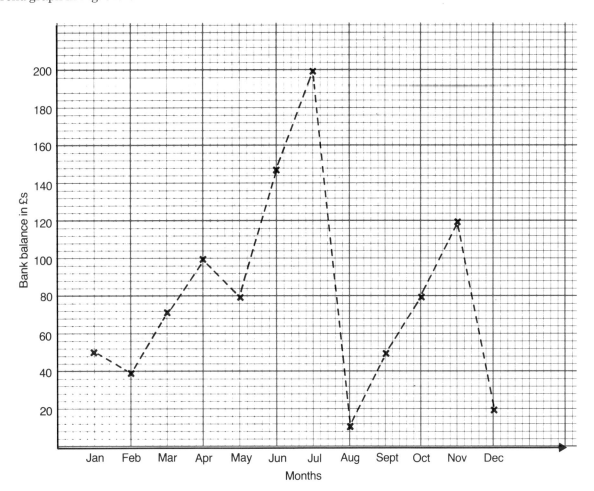

Fig. 34.20

End of month	Jan	Feb	Mar	Apr	May	Jun
Bank Balance (£)		40			80	

End of month	Jul	Aug	Sep	Oct	Nov	Dec
Bank Balance (£)						

Table 34.11

4 Table 34.12 gives information on the population of a village over a number of years. Draw a graph to show the information, showing males and females separately.

N.B. Be very careful with the time scale.

Year	Population	
	Male	Female
1964	530	710
1969	580	730
1974	650	790
1976	690	820
1981	790	900

Table 34.12

Try to comment on the trend.

Miscellaneous problems

1 Thirty pupils gained the marks shown in Table 34.13 in a Maths test. The maximum mark was 10.

5	1	6	5	4	4	5	6	2	8
9	3	2	6	2	3	4	8	7	3
8	9	6	1	7	3	4	7	1	2

Table 34.13

Draw a tally chart and frequency distribution table and then display the information by means of the following.

(a) A bar chart (vertical).

(b) A pie chart (fully labelled).

(c) A pictogram using ⚲ to represent 1 pupil.

2 The frequency distribution table (Table 34.14) illustrates the number of different types of aircraft using an airport during one day.

Type of Aircraft	Concorde	Boeing 747	BAC 1-11	Trident	Light Aircraft
Frequency	5	15	25	20	25

Table 34.14

(a) How many different aircraft used the airport during the day?

(b) Display the information by means of a line graph (**N.B. discrete**, not continuous).

(c) Display the information by means of a pie graph showing clearly the sectors. Label each sector carefully with the type of aircraft and the sector angle.

3 Over a two week period in June 1984, the midday temperatures in °C at a weather station in Staffordshire were recorded as shown in Table 34.15.

Day	M	T	W	T	F	Sa	Su
Temp °C	18	22	21	18	18	20	19

Day	M	T	W	T	F	Sa	Su
Temp °C	27	17	25	16	17	21	20

Table 34.15

(a) Show this information on a trend graph.

(b) Is there any real up or down trend involved?

(c) What is your opinion of the weather during this period?

Unit 35

Misrepresentation of data

Newspapers and magazines often produce graphs to show statistical data but unfortunately the graphs used can easily produce false ideas.

For instance if horizontal, vertical or both scales are altered, startling changes can be made to the shape of the graph.

Example The following graph, in Fig. 35.1 was published in a newspaper article showing the increase in car production over a ten-year period.

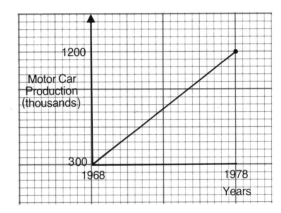

Fig. 35.1

In Fig. 35.2, there are obviously some spectacular results from the same data; production in (**d**) looks far better than in (**b**), for instance.

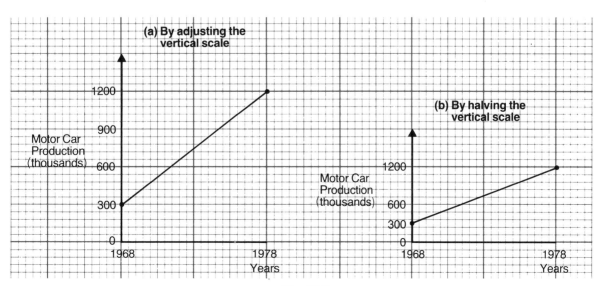

Fig. 35.2

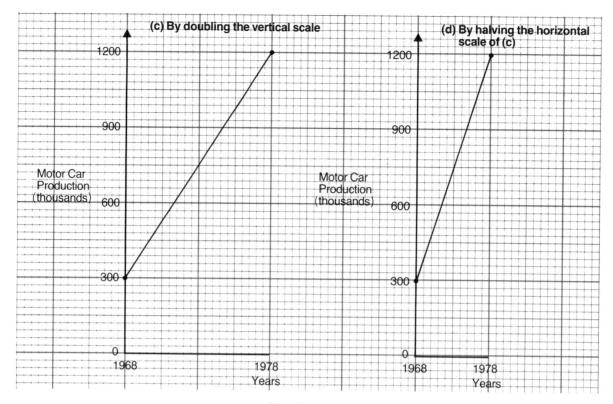

Fig. 35.2 cont.

Another common misuse is to use a type of graph to represent the wrong type of data.

Example A straight-line graph to represent rainfall, as in Fig. 35.3, is a silly idea because although rainfall itself is a continuous variable, the measurement of rainfall – usually performed once daily – is obviously discrete (there is a 24-hour gap between each reading).

The information would best be represented by a bar chart.

In conclusion, there are three main things to look out for when we see a graph.

(a) Is it the correct type of graph to represent the data?

(b) Are the scales realistic?

(c) Could there be any seasonal variations, such as ice-cream sales in winter, rainfall in summer, unemployment in winter etc?

The motto is, do not be fooled by statistics, see if you can make sense of the situation.

Remember the representation may be very poor.

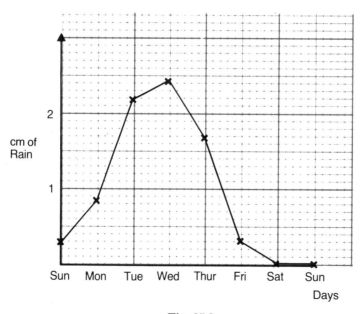

Fig. 35.3

Activities

Good graphs/bad graphs

1 The growth of a company over a 10-year period is shown in the profit figures in Table 35.1.

Draw three or four different trend graphs of the above information; by altering the scales of the axes of the graphs, show how the figures can be made to look completely different.

2 What is wrong with the graph, in Fig. 35.4, showing absentees from a firm due to illness?

Year (ended 1st Jan)	Profit (£ millions)
1981	34
1980	31
1979	30
1978	28
1977	25
1976	23
1975	21
1974	20
1973	18
1972	15

Table 35.1

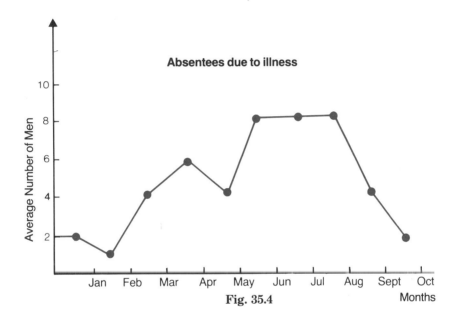

Fig. 35.4

3 What do you think is wrong with the graph shown in Fig. 35.5?

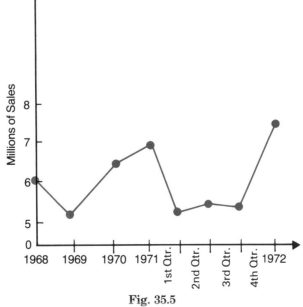

Fig. 35.5

Answers

Unit 1 Whole numbers

Useful sets of numbers (*page 8*)

1 (a) $\{1,2,3,4,5,6,7,8,9\}$ (b) $\{1,3,5,7,9,11\}$
  (c) $\{2,4,6,8,10\}$ (d) $\{2,3,5,7,11,13\}$
  (e) $\{1,4,9,16,25,36,49\}$ (f) $\{21,22,23,24\}$
  (g) $\{31,33,35,37,39\}$ (h) $\{42,44,46,48\}$
  (i) $\{81,100,121,144\}$ (j) $\{23,29,31,37\}$
  (k) $\{8,16,24,32,40,48\}$ (l) $\{12,18,24,30,36\}$
2 even 3 odd 4 even
5 (a) $\{3,31\}$ (b) $\{9,49\}$ (c) $\{3,9,15,39\}$
  (d) $\{3,15\}$ (e) 58 (f) 93

Sequences or series (*page 9*)

1 (a) $9,11$ (b) $10,12$ (c) $17,20$ (d) $32,39$
  (e) $9,4$ (f) $55,44$ (g) $32,64$ (h) $10,5$
  (i) $243,729$ (j) $80,160$ (k) $60\,000,600\,000$
  (l) $5,1$
2 (a) $36,49$ (b) $33,65$ (c) $41,122$ (d) $18,34$
  (e) $23,30$ (f) $17,14$ (g) $45,59$ (h) $67,64$
  (i) $80,110$ (j) $34,55$ (k) $127,255$ (l) $86,342$

Unit 2 Factors and multiples

Factors (*page 10*)

1 (a) $\{1,2,3,4,6,12\}$ (b) $\{1,2,4,5,10,20\}$
  (c) $\{1,5,25\}$ (d) $\{1,2,4,5,8,10,20,40\}$
2 $\{1,2,3,4,5,6,10,12,15,20,30,60\}$

Highest Common Factor (*page 10*)

1 4 2 6 3 5 4 12 5 16
6 7 7 6 8 5 9 9 10 14

Multiples and factors (*page 10*)

1 (a) $\{10,20,30,40\}$ (b) $\{8,16,24\}$
  (c) $\{6,12,18,24,30\}$ (d) $\{12,24,36,48\}$
                any 3 of these
  (e) $\{4,8,12,16,20,24\}$ (f) $\{5,10,15,20\}$
                any 4 of these
  (g) $\{21,24,27,30,33,36,39\}$
  (h) $\{8,16,24,32,40,48,56,64,72,80,88\}$
  (i) $\{25,50,75,100\}$ (j) $\{7,14,21,28,35,42,49\}$

2 (a) 20 (b) 24 (c) 50 (d) 30 (e) 15
  (f) 60 (g) 12 (h) 40 (i) 15 (j) 36

3

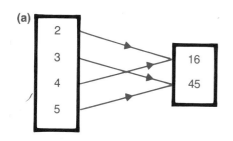

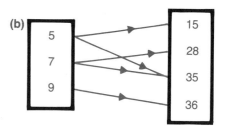

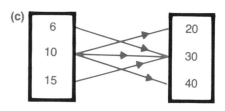

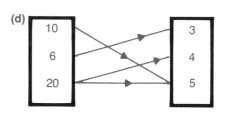

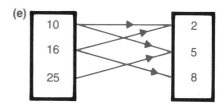

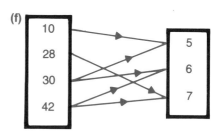

Fig. A2.1

Unit 3 The four rules for whole numbers

Adding and subtracting (*page 13*)

1 (a) 578 (b) 365 (c) 1132 (d) 319 (e) 36 (f) 27
2 (a) 1735 children (b) 1100 boys
3 171 cars
4 Mon – 7500 litres   Tues – 5635 litres   Wed – 4841 litres
  Thur – 6557 litres   Fri – 5717 litres   Sat – 7370 litres
  Total sales for the week – 37 620 litres

Number pictures (*page 14*)

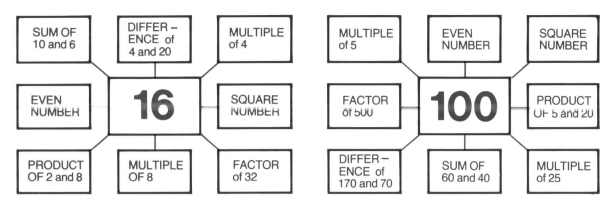

Fig. A3.1

Multiplication and division (*page 16*)

1 (**a**) 1280   (**b**) 540   (**c**) 378   (**d**) 140
    (**e**) 2032   (**f**) 2750   (**g**) 24 706
2 (**a**) 322   (**b**) 2706   (**c**) 12 495   (**d**) 27 370
3 (**a**) 15   (**b**) 23   (**c**) 108   (**d**) 142
    (**e**) 35   (**f**) 14   (**g**) 49   (**h**) 235
4 (**a**) 175 newspapers   (**b**) 1200 copies
    (**c**) 2750 copies   (**d**) 14 000 copies
5 (**a**) 14 km   (**b**) 350 km

Unit 5   Fractional numbers

Equivalent fractions (*page 17*)

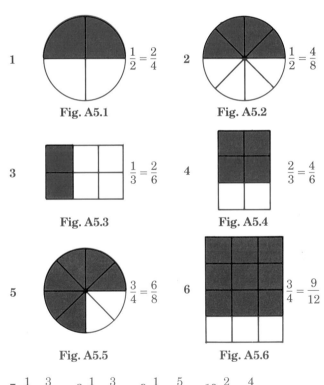

1 $\frac{1}{2} = \frac{2}{4}$ Fig. A5.1

2 $\frac{1}{2} = \frac{4}{8}$ Fig. A5.2

3 $\frac{1}{3} = \frac{2}{6}$ Fig. A5.3

4 $\frac{2}{3} = \frac{4}{6}$ Fig. A5.4

5 $\frac{3}{4} = \frac{6}{8}$ Fig. A5.5

6 $\frac{3}{4} = \frac{9}{12}$ Fig. A5.6

7 $\frac{1}{2} = \frac{3}{6}$ **8** $\frac{1}{3} = \frac{3}{9}$ **9** $\frac{1}{2} = \frac{5}{10}$ **10** $\frac{2}{5} = \frac{4}{10}$

11 $\frac{2}{3} = \frac{8}{12}$ **12** $\frac{1}{6} = \frac{2}{12}$ **13** $\frac{3}{5} = \frac{6}{10}$ **14** $\frac{5}{6} = \frac{10}{12}$

15 (**a**) $\frac{1}{2} = \frac{4}{8}$ (**b**) $\frac{1}{4} = \frac{2}{8}$ (**c**) $\frac{1}{5} = \frac{2}{10}$ (**d**) $\frac{1}{6} = \frac{2}{12}$

      (**e**) $\frac{2}{5} = \frac{8}{20}$ (**f**) $\frac{3}{4} = \frac{15}{20}$ (**g**) $\frac{2}{3} = \frac{8}{12}$ (**h**) $\frac{2}{3} = \frac{6}{9}$

16 (**a**) $\frac{2}{5}$ (**b**) $\frac{1}{5}$ (**c**) $\frac{1}{3}$ (**d**) $\frac{3}{5}$ (**e**) $\frac{2}{3}$

      (**f**) $\frac{1}{4}$ (**g**) $\frac{5}{12}$ (**h**) $\frac{3}{13}$ (**i**) $\frac{2}{3}$ (**j**) $\frac{3}{5}$

17 (**a**) $\frac{1}{2} = \frac{2}{4} = \frac{3}{6} = \frac{4}{8} = \frac{5}{10} = \frac{6}{12} = \frac{10}{20}$

     (**b**) $\frac{1}{3} = \frac{2}{6} = \frac{3}{9} = \frac{4}{12} = \frac{5}{15} = \frac{6}{18} = \frac{10}{30}$

     (**c**) $\frac{1}{4} = \frac{2}{8} = \frac{4}{16} = \frac{5}{20} = \frac{6}{24} = \frac{8}{32} = \frac{10}{40}$

     (**d**) $\frac{3}{4} = \frac{6}{8} = \frac{9}{12} = \frac{12}{16} = \frac{15}{20} = \frac{24}{32} = \frac{30}{40}$

     (**e**) $\frac{2}{3} = \frac{4}{6} = \frac{6}{9} = \frac{8}{12} = \frac{10}{15} = \frac{16}{24} = \frac{20}{30}$

     (**f**) $\frac{3}{5} = \frac{6}{10} = \frac{9}{15} = \frac{12}{20} = \frac{15}{25} = \frac{24}{40} = \frac{30}{50}$

Improper fractions and mixed numbers (*page 19*)

1 $1\frac{3}{4} = \frac{7}{4}$ **2** $2\frac{1}{5} = \frac{11}{5}$ **3** $3\frac{2}{3} = \frac{11}{3}$ **4** $1\frac{4}{5} = \frac{9}{5}$

5 $2\frac{3}{8} = \frac{19}{8}$ **6** $5\frac{1}{3} = \frac{16}{3}$ **7** $1\frac{7}{10} = \frac{17}{10}$ **8** $4\frac{1}{5} = \frac{21}{5}$

9 $2\frac{1}{6} = \frac{13}{6}$ **10** $10\frac{1}{3} = \frac{31}{3}$ **11** $5\frac{1}{2} = \frac{11}{2}$ **12** $1\frac{5}{6} = \frac{11}{6}$

13 $\frac{5}{4} = 1\frac{1}{4}$ **14** $\frac{7}{3} = 2\frac{1}{3}$ **15** $\frac{15}{2} = 7\frac{1}{2}$ **16** $\frac{23}{6} = 3\frac{5}{6}$

17 $\frac{30}{7} = 4\frac{7}{7}$ **18** $\frac{23}{5} = 4\frac{3}{5}$ **19** $\frac{53}{10} = 5\frac{0}{10}$ **20** $\frac{17}{8} = 2\frac{1}{8}$

21 $\frac{21}{2} = 10\frac{1}{2}$ **22** $\frac{19}{3} = 6\frac{1}{3}$ **23** $\frac{25}{12} = 2\frac{1}{12}$ **24** $\frac{20}{9} = 2\frac{2}{9}$

Comparing fractions (*page 20*)

1 <   **2** =   **3** >   **4** =   **5** >   **6** >
7 <   **8** >   **9** >   **10** =   **11** <   **12** <

13 $\frac{1}{4}, \frac{1}{3}, \frac{1}{2}$ **16** $\frac{1}{2}, \frac{7}{12}, \frac{4}{6}, \frac{3}{4}$

14 $\frac{1}{6}, \frac{1}{3}, \frac{3}{8}, \frac{1}{2}$ **17** $\frac{1}{4}, \frac{3}{10}, \frac{3}{8}, \frac{2}{5}$

15 $\frac{7}{12}, \frac{3}{5}, \frac{2}{3}, \frac{3}{4}$

Unit 6   Operations on fractions

Addition and subtraction (*page 22*)

1 (**a**) $\frac{8}{10}$ (**b**) $\frac{3}{4}$ (**c**) $\frac{9}{8} = 1\frac{1}{8}$ (**d**) $\frac{11}{10} = 1\frac{1}{10}$

     (**e**) $\frac{17}{12} = 1\frac{5}{12}$ (**f**) $3\frac{7}{10}$ (**g**) $6\frac{1}{6}$ (**h**) $5\frac{8}{15}$

2 (**a**) $\frac{4}{8} = \frac{1}{2}$ (**b**) $\frac{3}{6} = \frac{1}{2}$ (**c**) $\frac{3}{12} = \frac{1}{4}$ (**d**) $\frac{4}{15}$

     (**e**) $\frac{4}{6} = \frac{2}{3}$ (**f**) $\frac{19}{20}$ (**g**) $1\frac{9}{10}$ (**h**) $1\frac{7}{12}$

3 He saves $\frac{5}{12}$ of his pocket money.

Multiplication and division (*page 22*)

1 (a) $\frac{15}{8} = 1\frac{7}{8}$ (b) $\frac{12}{5} = 2\frac{2}{5}$ (c) $15\frac{3}{4}$ (d) $\frac{1}{4}$

   (e) $\frac{2}{15}$ (f) $11\frac{1}{3}$ (g) 4   (h) 27

2 (a) $\frac{1}{4}$ (b) $\frac{1}{2}$ (c) $2\frac{2}{9}$ (d) $\frac{27}{32}$

   (e) $\frac{4}{7}$ (f) $5\frac{5}{8}$ (g) 4   (h) $4\frac{1}{5}$

3 It will take $3\frac{3}{8}$ hours.

Unit 7 Decimal numbers

Addition and subtraction (*page 23*)

1 (a) 13.3   (b) 9.37   (c) 11.57   (d) 27.805
   (e) 19.25
2 (a) 2.5   (b) 1.6   (c) 1.55   (d) 3.5   (e) £2.05
3 (a) 0.26 seconds   (b) 0.07 seconds

Multiplication and division (*page 23*)

1 (a) 10.2   (b) 3.9   (c) 24.25   (d) 3.2   (e) 0.79
   (f) 11.45   (g) 346.8   (h) 47   (i) 137.5   (j) 6.67
   (k) 2.555   (l) 1.11   (m) 4.8   (n) 7.5   (o) 7
2 (a) £14.85   (b) £4.35

Unit 8 Percentages (*page 24*)

Table 8.1

$10\% = \frac{10}{100} = \frac{1}{10} = 0.10$	$15\% = \frac{15}{100} = \frac{3}{20} = 0.15$
$30\% = \frac{30}{100} = \frac{3}{10} = 0.30$	$25\% = \frac{25}{100} = \frac{1}{4} = 0.25$
$40\% = \frac{40}{100} = \frac{4}{10} = 0.40$	$75\% = \frac{75}{100} = \frac{3}{4} = 0.75$
$50\% = \frac{50}{100} = \frac{1}{2} = 0.50$	$5\% = \frac{5}{100} = \frac{1}{20} = 0.05$
$60\% = \frac{60}{100} = \frac{6}{10} = 0.60$	$2\frac{1}{2}\% = \frac{5}{200} = \frac{1}{40} = 0.025$
$70\% = \frac{70}{100} = \frac{7}{10} = 0.70$	$7\frac{1}{2}\% = \frac{15}{200} = \frac{3}{40} = 0.075$
$80\% = \frac{80}{100} = \frac{8}{10} = 0.80$	$12\frac{1}{2}\% = \frac{25}{200} = \frac{1}{8} = 0.125$
$90\% = \frac{90}{100} = \frac{9}{10} = 0.90$	$150\% = \frac{150}{100} = 1\frac{1}{2} = 1.50$

Table A8.1

Unit 9 Linking fractions, decimals and percentages

To find a percentage of something (*page 25*)

1 £12   **2** £3   **3** £12.50   **4** £0.60
5 £8   **6** £4.50   **7** £7.50   **8** £6
9 £10   **10** £3   **11** 150   **12** 10

To express a fraction as a percentage (*page 25*)

1 (a) 50%   (b) 25%   (c) 40%   (d) 75%
   (e) 15%   (f) 84%   (g) 90%   (h) 85%
2 70%   **3** 60%
4 (a) 15% absent   (b) 85% present

Unit 10 Money

Money operations (*page 27*)

1 (a) 10p   (b) 20p   (c) £1 coin   (d) 50p   (e) 20p
2 10   **3** 10   **4** 5   **5** 86   **6** 10p, 5p, 5p

7 20p, 20p, 10p   **8** 5p, 2p, 2p, 1p   **9** £1, £1, £1, 50p, 20p
10 £1, 50p, 20p, 2p
11 £1.95   **12** £10.39   **13** £18.20   **14** £1.28
15 £7.65   **16** Pete saves £3 more.
17 (a) £20.19   (b) £32.39   (c) £4.55   (d) £1.41
18 (a) £6.75   (b) £11.18   (c) £13.11   (d) £2.33
19 (a) £283.60   (b) £46.20   (c) £199   (d) £14.75
20 (a) £31.15   (b) £59   (c) £975
21 £8.40   **22** £31.25   **23** £231.60
24 (a) 58p   (b) £3.85   (c) £1.15   (d) 45p
25 (a)

3 @ 32p =	96p
6 @ 8p =	48p
4 @ 18p =	72p
2 @ 28p =	56p
	£2.72

   (b) 28p
   (c) 4 coins (20p, 5p, 2p, 1p)
26 £146

Shopping bills (*page 28*)

1

(a)	(b)	(c)	(d)
18p	41p	£2.40	43p
£1.90	42p	£1.20	65p
32p	84p	96p	74p
£2.40	£1.67	£1.32	72p
		£5.88	£2.54

2 (a) 24p   (b) 32p   (c) 7p   (d) 11p   (e) £1.65
      96p
      1.92
      70p
      £5.23

More money operations (*page 29*)

1 (a) (i) 16p   (ii) 96p
   (b) (i) 80p   (ii) £4
   (c) (i) £3.95   (ii) £19.75
   (d) (i) 16p   (ii) £1.92
   (e) (i) 16p   (ii) £1.12
2 (a) £4.10   (b) £5   (c) 24p   (d) £15   (e) £8.40
   (f) £27.50   (g) £165   (h) £1.12   (i) £42   (j) £35
3 (a) £10   (b) £2.25   (c) £8.80   (d) £1.08   (e) 80p
4 80p   **5** (a) £78   (b) £22   **6** (a) 33 cards   (b) 5p
7 £5.80   **8** £641.30

Unit 11 Length

Metric length (*page 30*)

1 (a) (i) 8 cm   (ii) 80 mm
   (b) (i) 11 cm   (ii) 110 mm
   (c) (i) 6.5 cm   (ii) 65 mm
   (d) (i) 8.5 cm   (ii) 85 mm
   (e) (i) 2.3 cm   (ii) 23 mm
   (f) (i) 5.8 cm   (ii) 58 mm
   (g) (i) 0.7 cm   (ii) 7 mm
2 (a) 20 mm   (b) 60 mm   (c) 45 mm   (d) 110 mm
   (e) 17 mm   (f) 72 mm   (g) 8 mm   (h) 231 mm
   (i) 64 mm   (j) 1 mm
3 (a) 5 cm   (b) 9 cm   (c) 7.5 cm   (d) 24 cm
   (e) 2.6 cm   (f) 2.1 cm   (g) 0.5 cm   (h) 19.2 cm
   (i) 8.8 cm   (j) 0.4 cm
4 (a) 2 m   (b) 9 m   (c) 4.5 m   (d) 7.8 m
   (e) 1.45 m   (f) 0.5 m   (g) 0.05 m   (h) 3.09 m
5 (a) 500 cm   (b) 1100 cm   (c) 550 cm   (d) 285 cm
   (e) 70 cm   (f) 25 cm   (g) 3 cm   (h) 510 cm
6 (a) 5 km   (b) 3.5 km   (c) 1.355 km   (d) 0.75 km
   (e) 1.95 km   (f) 0.3 km   (g) 0.03 km
   (h) 0.003 km
7 (a) 7000 m   (b) 2600 m   (c) 1250 m   (d) 485 m
   (e) 3080 m   (f) 70 m   (g) 700 m   (h) 9 m
8 (a) 8.78 m   (b) 366 cm   (c) 9.5 cm   (d) 59 mm
   (e) 8.521 km   (f) 5435 m
9 (a) 3.4 cm   (b) 4.7 cm   (c) 15 mm   (d) 215 cm
   (e) 83 cm   (f) 2.25 m   (g) 1750 m   (h) 2.855 km
   (i) 9.350 km   (j) 12.25 m
10 18 blocks   **11** 40 cm   **12** (a) 14 cm   (b) 140 mm
13 13 km (in 5 days)

Unit 12   Mass

Operations involving units of mass (*page 32*)

1 (a) t   (b) g   (c) kg   (d) mg   (e) g   (f) kg
2 (a) 5000 kg   (b) 9000 g   (c) 4000 mg   (d) 3500 g
   (e) 2300 kg   (f) 800 mg   (g) 3.42 t   (h) 0.475 g
   (i) 2.625 kg   (j) 5340 g
3 12 kg   **4** 18.45 kg   **5** (a) 0.55 kg   (b) 550 g
6 2865 g   **7** 775 g

Unit 13   Capacity

Operations involving capacity (*page 33*)

1 (a) 3000 ml   (b) 2400 ml   (c) 1265 ml   (d) 800 ml
   (e) 1050 ml   (f) 7 l   (g) 0.7 l   (h) 0.07 l
   (i) 0.007 l   (j) 2.555 l
2 200 doses   **3** 5 glasses   **4** 112.5 litres
5 (a) 14 glasses   (b) 100 ml
6 6 glasses   **7** 750 ml   **8** 25 days   **9** 40 bottles
10 3 km

Using metric units generally (*page 34*)

1 (a) g   (b) m or cm   (c) m   (d) mm   (e) l
   (f) kg   (g) km   (h) mg or g   (i) ml   (j) m
   (k) mg   (l) kg
2 24 litres   **3** 20 lengths   **4** 12 m   **5** 15.75 kg
6 20 laps   **7** 20 g   **8** 14 m

Unit 14   Time

Operations involving units of time (*page 37*)

1 Clock B = 9.05 = five minutes past nine.
   Clock C = 12.40 = twenty minutes to one.
   Clock D = 5.55 = five minutes to six.
2 (a) 120 seconds   (b) 300 seconds   (c) 1200 seconds
   (d) 210 seconds   (e) 620 seconds   (f) 3600 seconds
   (g) 375 seconds   (h) 105 seconds
3 (a) 120 minutes   (b) 180 minutes   (c) 330 minutes
   (d) 195 minutes   (e) 140 minutes   (f) 285 minutes
   (g) 1440 minutes   (h) 95 minutes
4 (a) 40 min   (b) 55 min   (c) 20 min   (d) 45 min
   (e) 55 min   (f) 70 min   (g) 40 min   (h) 70 min
   (i) 105 min   (j) 140 min
5 (a) 1 h 15 min   (b) 2 h 30 min   (c) 4 h 10 min
   (d) 2 h 18 min   (e) 2 h 50 min   (f) 4 h 5 min
   (g) 2 h 24 min   (h) 14 h 30 min
6 (a) 44 days   (b) 50 days   (c) 58 days   (d) 35 days
   (e) 68 days   (f) 44 days   (g) 13 days   (h) yes
8 (a) 0115   (b) 0545   (c) 0837   (d) 1150
   (e) 1200   (f) 1235   (g) 1305   (h) 1445   (i) 1830
   (j) 2225   (k) 2355   (l) 0030
9 (a) 12.45 a.m.   (b) 3.20 a.m.   (c) 7.50 a.m.
   (d) 10.15 a.m.   (e) 12.10 p.m.   (f) 1.30 p.m.
   (g) 2.00 p.m.   (h) 3.05 p.m.   (i) 7.10 p.m.
   (j) 9.40 p.m.   (k) 10.17 p.m.   (l) 11.49 p.m.
10 (a) 1 h 45 min   (b) 2 h 32 min   (c) 1 h 30 min
   (d) 2 h 38 min   (e) 0945   (f) 1700   (g) 0705
   (h) 2015   (i) 0510   (j) 2 h 38 min
11 9 h 25 min   **12** 1630   **13** 05.30 a.m.
14 10.15 p.m.   **15** 9.50 a.m.   **16** 12.02 a.m.   **17** 0756
18 (a) Bus A – 40 minutes   Bus B – 30 minutes
      Bus C – 40 minutes
   (b) Bus B, by 10 minutes   (c) 1 h 58 min
   (d) Yes   (e) 10 minutes   (f) 119 minutes
19 (a) 2$\frac{1}{2}$ hours   (b) $\frac{1}{4}$ hour   (c) 2 h 50 min
   (d) 1 h 43 min   (e) 30 minutes   (f) 30 pages

Unit 15   Perimeter

Perimeters of different shapes (*page 41*)

1 (a) 12 cm   (b) 14 cm   (c) 12 cm   (d) 32 cm
   (e) 48 cm   (f) 42 cm   (g) 24 cm   (h) 48 cm
   (i) 26.5 cm   (j) 22.4 cm   (k) 37 cm   (l) 20 cm

Unit 16   Area

Squares and rectangles (*page 44*)

1 (a) 4 cm^2 (b) 9 cm^2 (c) 16 cm^2
2 (a) 49 cm^2 (b) 100 cm^2 (c) 144 cm^2 (d) 1.21 m^2
   (e) 400 mm^2 (f) $\frac{1}{9}$ km^2 (g) 0.25 m^2 (h) $\frac{1}{16}$ cm^2
3 (a) 250 mm^2 (b) 6 cm^2 (c) 15 cm^2
4 (a) 40 cm^2 (b) 44 m^2 (c) 270 cm^2 (d) 9 m^2
   (e) 3 km^2 (f) 180 mm^2 (g) 125 mm^2 (h) 2$\frac{1}{2}$ m^2
5 81 cm^2 **6** 77 mm^2 **7** 2 m   **8** 11 cm
9 9 cm   **10** 8 cm   **11** 300 m^2 **12** 4 m
13 20 pieces   **14** 120 tiles   **15** 108 slabs
16 (a) 85 cm^2 (b) 8500 mm^2 **17** 480 tiles
18 320 slabs   **19** (a) 20 cm   (b) 300 cm^2

Areas of rectangular shapes (*page 45*)

   (a) 26 cm^2 (b) 22 cm^2 (c) 17 cm^2 (d) 28 cm^2
   (e) 71 cm^2 (f) 78 cm^2 (g) 94 cm^2 (h) 96 cm^2
   (i) 45 cm^2 (j) 100 m^2 (k) 100 cm^2 (l) 88 cm^2

Area of borders (*page 46*)

1 (b) 108 cm^2 48 cm^2 60 cm^2
   (c) 150 cm^2 84 cm^2 66 cm^2
   (d) 96 cm^2 60 cm^2 36 cm^2
   (e) 35 cm^2 20 cm^2 15 cm^2
   (f) 60 cm^2 40 cm^2 20 cm^2

Conversion of units (*page 46*)

1 (a) 30 000 cm^2 (b) 120 000 cm^2 (c) 75 000 cm^2
   (d) 42 500 m^2
2 (a) 900 mm^2 (b) 500 mm^2 (c) 250 mm^2
   (d) 175 mm^2
3 (a) 0.75 m^2 (b) 22 m^2 (c) 500 000 m^2
   (d) 1 500 000 m^2
4 (a) 500 cm^2 (b) 50 000 mm^2
5 (i) area = 50 000 cm^2 perimeter = 21 m
   (ii) area = 2 cm^2 perimeter = 90 mm

Areas of triangles and quadrilaterals (*page 49*)

1 (a) 21 cm^2 (b) 18 cm^2 (c) 52$\frac{1}{2}$ mm^2
   (d) 13.5 cm^2 (e) 18.4 cm^2 (f) 50 cm^2
   (g) 132 cm^2 (h) 36 cm^2 (i) 640 mm^2
   (j) 124 cm^2 (k) 294 cm^2 (l) 580 mm^2
2 (a) 96 cm^2 (b) 22 cm^2 (c) 375 mm^2
   (d) 30 cm^2 (e) 143 mm^2 (f) 7.5 m^2
3 (a) 120 cm^2 (b) 35 cm^2 (c) 187 mm^2
   (d) 240 cm^2 (e) 64 cm^2 (f) 67.5 cm^2

Problems on area and perimeter (*page 51*)

1 Lounge, by 0.5 m^2
2 44 m^2
3 31.5 m^2
4 4.6 m^2
5 (a) 32 m^2 (b) 15 m^2 (c) 59 m^2
6 (a) 1425 cm^2 (b) 1600 cm^2 (c) 220 cm
7 (a) area = 24 cm^2 perimeter = 22 cm
   (b) breadth = 15 cm   perimeter = 50 cm
   (c) breadth = 4 mm   area = 24 mm^2
   (d) length = 20 m   perimeter = 62 m
   (e) length = 2$\frac{1}{2}$ cm   area = 12$\frac{1}{2}$ cm^2

Unit 17   Directed numbers

Negative numbers (*page 54*)

1 true   **2** false   **3** true   **4** false   **5** false
6 false   **7** true   **8** false   **9** false   **10** true
11 false   **12** true   **13** false   **14** true   **15** true
16 false   **17** false   **18** false   **19** false   **20** true
21 >   **22** <   **23** <   **24** <   **25** >
26 >   **27** >   **28** <   **29** >   **30** <
31 −2   **32** −1   **33** −3   **34** 0   **35** −3
36 −5   **37** −3   **38** −5   **39** −8   **40** 7
41 4   **42** 5   **43** 4   **44** −1   **45** −5

46 −6	47 −8	48 0	49 5	50 −9
51 −3	52 −2	53 9	54 −2	55 −4
56 −3	57 −7	58 6	59 −1	60 4
61 +3	62 +6	63 +4	64 +8	

Directed number operations (*page 54*)

1 (a) 5°C (b) 2°C (c) 3°C (d) 5°C (e) 9°C
2 (a) 190 m (b) 140 m (c) 290 m (d) 240 m
3 −3°C 4 12°C 5 1250 m 6 12 m

More operations with directed numbers (*page 55*)

1 6	2 3	3 −3	4 −11	5 −13
6 2	7 −2	8 9	9 3	10 13
11 −21	12 −2	13 20	14 0	15 12
16 3	17 −10	18 11	19 11	20 6
21 −30	22 −35	23 15	24 40	25 −4
26 4	27 −11	28 −8	29 7	30 −4

31 My watch is 5 minutes fast.
32 Your watch is 4 minutes slow.
33 I am £50 overdrawn at the bank.
34 The school population decreased by 50 pupils.
35 The party moves 5 km due east.

Unit 18 Collecting like terms (*page 56*)

| 1 8p | 2 17p | 3 12a | 4 10b | 5 9c |
| 6 12d | 7 3e | 8 f | 9 2g | 10 −5h |

11 $7a + 7b$ 12 $4x + 5y$ 13 $13a + 2y$ 14 $3x + y$
15 $5a + 4b$ 16 $x + 5y$ 17 $5m$ 18 $5b$ 19 $2a$
20 $7f + 13$ 21 $8a + 11b$ 22 $3e + g$ 23 $5a − 3b$
24 $3c$ 25 $2m + 4p$ 26 0   27 $a + 2b + 3$
28 $5p − 5q − 3r$ 29 $6e + 4f + g$ 30 $9a − 3b − 4c$
31 $11xy$ 32 $6ab$ 33 $3pq$
34 $2xy + 3x$ 35 $10fg − f − g$ 36 $3abc$
37 $4efg − 2fg$ 38 $5pt + 5rt$ 39 $8a + b + 2ab$
40 $4xy$
41 $4a + 4b = 32$ 　　　　　 42 $9a + 4c = 35$
43 $5b + 4c = 33$ 　　　　　 44 $c + b = 7$
45 $a + 8b = 43$ 　　　　　 46 $a = 3$
47 $2a + 3b = 21$ 　　　　 48 $2a = 6$
49 $10ab = 150$ 　　　　　 50 $4ac = 24$

Unit 20 Simple substitution

Algebraic substitution (*page 58*)

1 15	2 24	3 11	4 13	5 22
6 5	7 7	8 11	9 23	10 $1\frac{1}{2}$
11 12	12 19	13 15	14 32	15 6
16 19	17 0	18 29	19 5	20 1
21 11	22 41	23 16	24 44	25 7
26 30	27 27	28 4	29 4	30 0
31 24	32 12	33 24	34 30	35 2
36 3	37 $3\frac{1}{3}$	38 12	39 12	40 2

Substitution into formulae (*page 58*)

1 (a) 130p (b) 260p
2 (a) 240p (b) 110p
3 (a) 18 cakes (b) 36 cakes
4 (a) 128 lollipops (b) 60 lollipops

Unit 21 Solving simple equations (*page 60*)

A $2x + 3$ B $2y − 5$ C $3b + 7$
D $5q + 11$ E $x + 7 = 13$ F $y − 5 = 4$
1 $x = 8$ 2 $x = 5$ 3 $x = 17$ 4 $x = 11$ 5 $x = 3$
6 $c = 1$ 7 $c = 3$ 8 $a = 7$ 9 $a = 5$ 10 $y = 5$
11 $x = 10$ 12 $x = 14$ 13 $x = 14$ 14 $x = 12$
15 $x = 3$ 16 $a = 11$ 17 $c = 11$ 18 $e = 30$
19 $g = 4$ 20 $g = 15$ 21 $x = 5$ 22 $x = 4$ 23 $x = 20$
24 $x = 5$ 25 $x = 4$ 26 $x = 9$ 27 $x = 9$ 28 $x = 2$
29 $x = 13$ 30 $x = 27$

Unit 22 Simple set theory

Describing sets (*page 63*)

1 $A = \{a, b, c, d, e\}$
  $B = \{$Monday, Tuesday, Wednesday, Thursday,
  　　　　　　　　　　Friday, Saturday, Sunday$\}$
$C = \{$1p, 2p, 5p, 10p, 20p, 50p, £1$\}$
$D = \{$Sept, April, June, November$\}$
$E = \{1, 3, 5, 7, 9\}$ $F = \{10, 12, 14, 16, 18, 20, 22, 24\}$
$G = \{1, 4, 9, 16, 25, 36, 49\}$ $H = \{8, 16, 24, 32, 40, 48\}$
$I = \{$summer, autumn, spring, winter$\}$
$J = \{11, 13, 17, 19, 23, 29\}$
$K = \{v, w, x, y, z\}$
$L = \{1, 2, 4, 5, 10, 20\}$
2 {colours}   3 {fruit}   4 {months beginning with 'J'}
5 {even numbers}   6 {shapes}   7 {multiples of 5}
8 {odd numbers}   9 {metric units}   10 {flowers}
11 {arithmetic signs}

Members of sets (*page 64*)

1 cycle ∈ {vehicles}　　　oak ∈ {trees}
   desk ∈ {furniture}　　　elm ∈ {trees}
   apple ∈ {fruit}　　　　　soccer ∈ {sports}
   car ∈ {vehicles}　　　　tennis ∈ {sports}
   fir ∈ {trees}　　　　　　chair ∈ {furniture}
   table ∈ {furniture}　　　banana ∈ {fruit}
   cricket ∈ {sports}　　　van ∈ {vehicles}
   golf ∈ {sports}
2 (a) f (b) f (c) t (d) f (e) t
  (f) t (g) f (h) t (i) f (j) t
3 Equal sets are (i) A and E (ii) B and C (iii) D and F

Special sets (*page 64*)

1 (a) φ (b) φ (c) not empty (d) φ (e) φ
2 (a) Ø (b) {September} (c) φ (d) φ (e) {2}

Subsets (*page 65*)

1 (a) $\{A, C, H, K\}$ (b) $\{B, I\}$ (c) $\{A, C, F, G, H, L\}$
  (d) $\{G, L\}$ (e) $\{D, E, J, K\}$
2 (a) t (b) t (c) f (d) t (e) f
3 (a) no (b) yes (c) yes (d) no (e) yes

Universal sets (*page 65*)

  (a) $\mathscr{E} = \{$European countries$\}$
  (b) $\mathscr{E} = \{$cars$\}$
  (c) $\mathscr{E} = \{$sports$\}$
  (d) $\mathscr{E} = \{$letters of the alphabet$\}$
  (e) $\mathscr{E} = \{$multiples of 3$\}$
2 (a) {London, Paris, Moscow, Rome}
  (b) $\{2, 4, 6, 8\}$
  (c) {English, Maths, Science, French}
  (d) {triangle, square, rectangle, hexagon}
  (e) {cat, dog, hamster, mouse}

Unit 23 Venn diagrams

Pictures of sets (*page 68*)

1

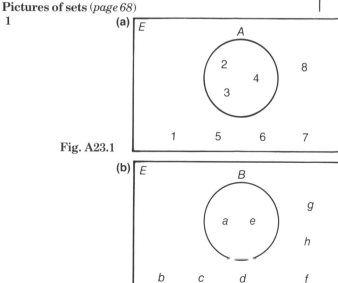

(a)

Fig. A23.1

(b)

Fig. A23.2

(c)

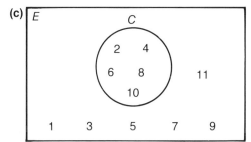

Fig. A23.3

2 (a)

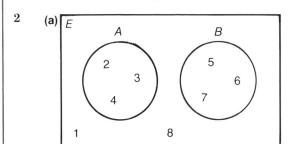

Fig. A23.4

(b)

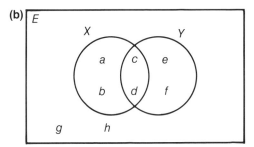

Fig. A23.5

(c)

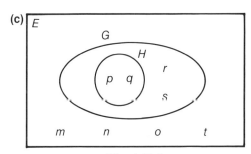

Fig. A23.6

3 (a) 6   **(b)** 7   **(c)** 4   **(d)** 2   **(e)** 3   **(f)** 2

Union of sets (*page 69*)

1 $A \cup B = \{$Roy, Mike, Andy, Matt, Sid, Frank$\}$
2 $F \cup G = \{2, 4, 5, 6, 7, 8\}$
3 $P \cup Q = \{a, b, c, d, e, i, o, u\}$
4 $X \cup Y = \{p, q, r, s, t, u\}$
5 $A \cup B = \{1, 2, 3, 4, 5, 6\}$
6 $L \cup M = \{2, 3, 5, 7, 8\}$
7 $P \cup Q = \{1, 2, 3, 4, 6, 8, 12\}$
8 $X \cup Y = \{m, i, s, l, e, n, g\}$
9 $A \cup B = \{w, r, i, t, e, p, y\}$
10 $X \cup Y = \{p, e, n, c, i, l\}$

11

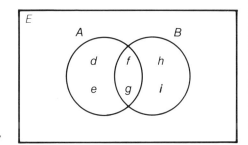

Fig. A23.7

$A \cup B = \{d, e, f, g, h, i\}$

12

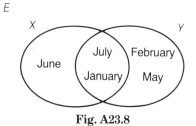

Fig. A23.8

13

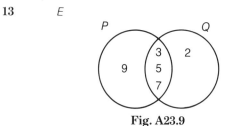

Fig. A23.9

Intersection of sets (*page 69*)

1 $A \cap B = \{$boys in your class who like cricket and football$\}$
2 $X \cap Y = \{$people in your family who like both tea and coffee$\}$
3 $P \cap Q = \{$athletes who are four-minute milers$\}$
4 **(a)** $A \cap B = \{4, 6\}$ **(b)** $A \cap C = \{6\}$
   (c) $B \cap C = \{5, 6, 7\}$
5 $X \cap Y = \{$Bob, Fred$\}$
6 $M \cap N = \{3, 5, 7, 11, 13\}$
7 $X \cap Y = \{$s, o, l$\}$
8

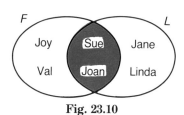

Fig. 23.10

Complement of a set (*page 69*)

1 $\{$even numbers$\}$
2 $\{$boys$\}$
3 $\{$people younger than yourself$\}$
4 $\{$right-handed people$\}$
5 $\{$weekends$\}$
6 **(a)** $A' = \{f, g, h, i, j\}$ **(b)** $B' = \{b, c, d, f, g, h, j\}$
   (c) $A \cup B = \{a, b, c, d, e, i\}$ **(d)** $A \cap B = \{a, e\}$
7 **(a)** $A' = \{5, 7, 8, 10, 11, 13, 14, 16, 17, 19, 20, 22, 23, 25\}$
   (b) $B' = \{5, 6, 7, 8, 9, 11, 12, 13, 14, 15, 16, 17, 18, 19,$ $21, 22, 23, 24, 25\}$
   (c) $C' = \{5, 7, 9, 11, 13, 15, 17, 19, 21, 23, 25\}$
   (d) $A \cap C = \{6, 12, 18, 24\}$
8 **(a)** $A' = \{10, 12, 14, 16, 18, 20\}$
   (b) $B' = \{10, 11, 13, 14, 16, 17, 19, 20\}$
   (c) $C' = \{10, 11, 13, 14, 15, 17, 18, 19\}$
   (d) $D' = \{11, 12, 13, 14, 16, 17, 18, 19\}$
9 **(a)** $A' = \{$r, i, o, n$\}$ **(b)** $B' = \{$e, t, o, n$\}$
   (c) $A \cup B = \{$s, l, a, t, e, r, i$\}$ **(d)** $(A \cup B)' = \{$o, n$\}$
10 **(a)** $A \cup B' = \{1, 2, 3, 5, 6, 7, 9, 10, 11, 13, 14, 15, 17, 18, 19\}$
    (b) $A' \cup B' = \{1, 2, 3, 4, 5, 6 \dots 19\}$
    (c) $A \cap B' = \{5, 10, 15\}$ **(d)** $C' \cap B = \{4, 16, 20\}$
    (e) $C \cap A' = \{8, 9, 11, 12\}$

How many in the set? (*page 70*)

1 **(a)** $n(A) = 12$ **(b)** $n(B) = 7$ **(c)** $n(C) = 10$
   (d) $n(D) = 26$ **(e)** $n(E) = 5$
2 **(a)** $n(A) = 5$ **(b)** $n(B) = 7$ **(c)** $n(A \cap B) = 2$
   (d) $n(A \cup B) = 10$ **(e)** $n(A \cup B)' = 3$

3
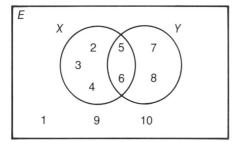

Fig. A23.11

(a) $X \cup Y = \{2, 3, 4, 5, 6, 7, 8\}$
(b) $X \cap Y = \{5, 6\}$ (c) $n(X) = 5$ (d) $n(Y) = 4$
(e) $n(X \cup Y) = 7$ (f) $n(X \cap Y) = 2$
(g) $n(X)' = 5$ (h) $n(Y)' = 6$

4 (a) $A \cap B = \{2, 3, 4\}$ (b) $A \cap C = \{1, 2\}$
   (c) $B \cap C = \{2\}$ (d) $n(A) = 5$ (e) $n(B) = 6$
   (f) $n(C) = 4$
   (g) $A \cup B \cup C = \{1, 2, 3, 4, 5, 6, 7, 8, 11, 12\}$
   (h) $A \cap B \cap C = \{2\}$ (i) $n(A \cup B \cup C = 10$
   (j) $n(A \cap B \cap C) = 1$

Shading sets (*page 70*)

1 (a)
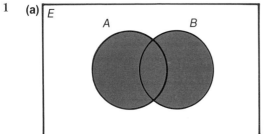

Fig. A23.12

(b)
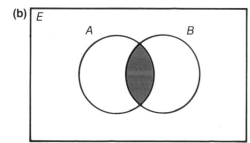

Fig. A23.13

(c)
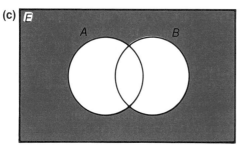

Fig. A23.14

(d)
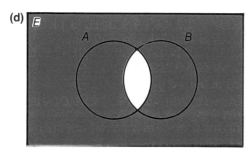

Fig. A23.15

(e)
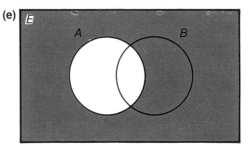

Fig. A23.16

(f)
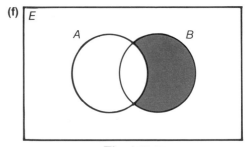

Fig. A23.17

(g)
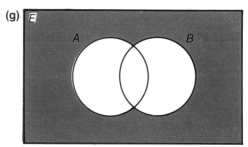

Fig. A23.18

(h)
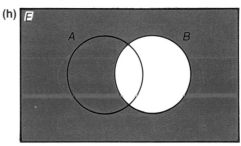

Fig. A23.19

2 (a) $A \cap B$ (b) $(A \cup B)'$ (c) A' (d) $X' \cap Y$

3 (a)
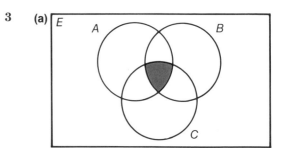

Fig. A23.20

(b)
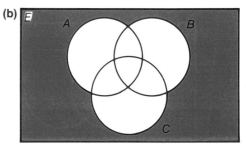

Fig. A23.21

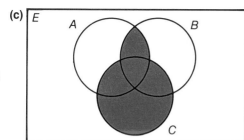

(c)

Fig. A23.22

Unit 24 Straight lines *(page 73)*

2 (a) *CD* and *KL*
  (b) *AB* and *MN*
  (c) *EF* ∥ *GH*, *IJ* ∥ *PQ*, *CD* ∥ *KL*, *AB* ∥ *MN*

Unit 25 Angles

Types of angle *(page 76)*

1 (a) less than 90°   (b) less than 90°
  (c) greater than 90°   (d) greater than 90°
  (e) greater than 90°   (f) greater than 90°
  (g) less than 90°   (h) greater than 90°
2 (a) acute angle   (b) right angle   (c) obtuse angle
  (d) right angle   (e) straight angle   (f) reflex angle
  (g) acute angle   (h) reflex angle

Measuring angles *(page 77)*

2 (a) 31°   (b) 37°   (c) 29°   (d) 50°   (e) 118°
  (f) 130°   (g) 62°   (h) 22°   (i) 164°   (j) 90°
  (k) 77°   (l) 143°
3

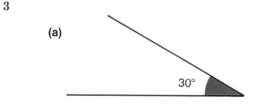

(a)

30°

(b)

60°

(c)

125°

(d)

154°

(e)

97°

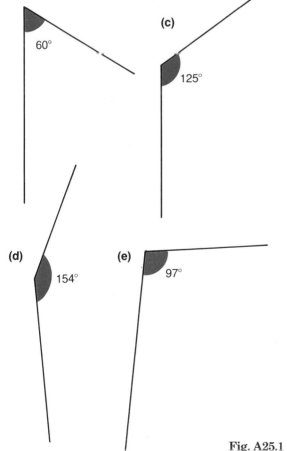

Fig. A25.1

Right angles *(page 78)*

1 (a) 90°   (b) 180°   (c) 270°   (d) 360°
  (e) 540°   (f) 720°
2 (a) 180°   (b) 90°   (c) 270°   (d) 240°
  (e) 120°   (f) 45°   (g) 36°   (h) 30°
3 (a) 3   (b) 6   (c) 9   (d) 7
  (e) 20   (f) 14   (g) 12   (h) 40
4 (a) 35°   (b) 52°   (c) 19°   (d) 63°
  (e) 50°   (f) 107°   (g) 74°   (h) 149°
  (i) 40°   (j) 15°   (k) 150°   (l) 6°

Clock angles *(page 78)*

1 (a) 3 hours   (b) 2 hours   (c) 4 hours
  (d) 7 hours   (e) 10 hours
2 (a) 5 minutes   (b) 30 minutes   (c) 40 minutes
  (d) 25 minutes   (e) 55 minutes
3 (a) 120°   (b) 180°   (c) 270°
  (d) 75°   (e) 75°   (f) 75°
4 (a) 90°   (b) 150°   (c) 210°
  (d) 270°   (e) 420°   (f) 240°
5 (a) 120°   (b) 150°   (c) 60°   (d) 30°
  (e) 105°   (f) 45°   (g) 70°   (h) 20°

Unit 26 Shapes

Triangles *(page 79)*

1 (a) isosceles   (b) scalene   (c) right-angled
  (d) equilateral   (e) obtuse-angled
  (f) right-angled isosceles
2 (a) 52°   (b) 111°   (c) 93°   (d) 41°   (e) 47°
3 95°   4 18°

Special triangles *(page 80)*

1 (a) 48°   (b) 65°   (c) 60°   (d) 44°   (e) 50°
  (f) 22°   (g) 65°   (h) 110°   (i) 45°   (j) 45°
  (k) $71\frac{1}{2}$°   (l) 28°
2 35°, 35°   3 72°

Properties of quadrilaterals *(page 81)*

1 (a) *AB* = *DC*   (b) *BC* = *AD*
  (c) *AX* = *BX* = *CX* = *DX*   (d) *AC* = *BD*
  (e) ∠*AXC* = ∠*BXD*   (f) ∠*AXB* = ∠*CXD*
2 (a) *EF* = *FG* = *GH* = *EH*   (b) *EX* = *FX* = *GX* = *HX*
  (c) *EG* = *FH*   (d) *EG* is perpendicular to *FH*
  (e) ∠*EXF* = 90°
3 (a) *JK* = *ML*   (b) *KL* = *JM*   (c) *JX* = *LX*
  (d) *KX* = *MX*   (e) ∠*KJX* = ∠*XLM*
  (f) ∠*KMJ* = ∠*MKL*
4 (a) *PQ* = *QR*   (b) *PS* = *RS*   (c) *PX* = *RX*
  (d) ∠*QXR* = 90°   (e) ∠*PQX* = ∠*RQX*
  (f) ∠*PSX* = ∠*RSX*

Diagonals *(page 82)*

1 (a) and (b)   2 (a) and (b)   3 (b) and (c)
4 (a) and (b)   5 (b) and (c)

Meet the referee *(page 82)*

1 square   2 rectangle   3 circles   4 kite
5 trapezium   6 rhombus   7 hexagon
8 parallelogram   9 semi-circle   10 triangle
11 trapezium   12 triangle

N.B. No answers given for sections requiring diagrammatic answers

Unit 28 Polygons

Polygon exercises *(page 88)*

2 (a) 108°   (b) 135°   (c) 120°   (d) 144°   (e) 140°
3 (a) 72°   (b) 45°   (c) 60°   (d) 36°   (e) 40°
4 (i) (b), (d), (f)
  (ii) (b), (d)
  (iii) (a), (c), (d), (e), (h)

5

Regular Polygon	Number of sides (n)	Number of triangles	$(2n-4)$ Rt. Angles	Interior Angle	Exterior Angle
Triangle	3	1	2	$60°$	$120°$
Square	4	2	4	$90°$	$90°$
Pentagon	5	3	6	$108°$	$72°$
Hexagon	6	4	8	$120°$	$60°$
Heptagon	7	5	10	$128\frac{4}{7}°$	$51\frac{3}{7}°$
Octagon	8	6	12	$135°$	$45°$
Nonagon	9	7	14	$140°$	$40°$
Decagon	10	8	16	$144°$	$36°$
Dodecagon	12	10	20	$150°$	$30°$

Table A28.1

6 **(c)**   **(d)**

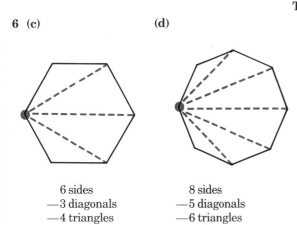

6 sides
—3 diagonals
—4 triangles

8 sides
—5 diagonals
—6 triangles

Fig. A28.1

Thore is a definite relationship between the number of sides of a shape and the number of triangles which can be formed from the diagonals from one vertex, i.e. the number of triangles is always 2 less than the number of sides to the shape.

Unit 29 Collecting information (*page 90*)

You should have collected thirty different statistical items from newspapers, magazines and other sources over a one-week period.

Unit 30 Statistical population

Collection of data (*page 93*)

Activities 1, 2, 3, 4 and **5** are your own personal projects and will provide your own answers which should closely follow the guidelines given to you.

Unit 32 Methods of collecting data

Variables (*page 96*)

Activity 1 will contain your own personal answers. Check them against other examples in the text.

2 **(a)** Train speed throughout a journey is **continuous**.
(b) Marks of a class in a Maths Examination is **discrete**.
(c) Goals scored by a footballer is **discrete**.
(d) The height of a child over the first four years is **continuous**.
(e) The temperature of cooling water is **continuous**.
(f) The number of rooms in your house is **discrete**.

(g) Volume of water used by a town is **continuous**.
(h) Goals scored by a netball team is **discrete**.
(i) Air pressure at a weather station is **continuous**.
(j) Rainfall in Stoke-on-Trent is **continuous**.

Unit 33 Recording information

Tally charts and frequency distribution (*page 98*)

1 You should have a tally chart ranging from the smallest shoe size to the largest shoe size, e.g. see Table A33.1.

Shoe Size	Tally	Frequency
2	I	1
$2\frac{1}{2}$	III	3
3	II	2
$3\frac{1}{2}$	IIII	5
4	IIII I	6
etc		(Total 20)

Table A33.1

2

No. of Goals	Tally	Frequency
0	I	1
1	II	2
2	III	3
3	IIII	5
4		0
5	III	3
6	IIII II	7
7	IIII	4
8	III	3
9	II	2
		30 Matches

No. of Goals per Match	0	1	2	3	4	5	6	7	8	9
Frequency	1	2	3	5	0	3	7	4	3	2

Table A33.2

3

Heights (cm)	Tally	Frequency
165	II	2
166	II	2
167	IIII	5
168	IIII II	7
169	IIII IIII	9
170	IIII I	6
171	III	3
172	IIII I	6
173	IIII I	6
174	II	2
175	I	1
176	I	1
		(Total 50)

Boys' Heights	165	166	167	168	169	170	171	172	173	174	175	176
Frequency	2	2	5	7	9	6	3	6	6	2	1	1

Table A33.3

4 Total number of goals scored in each of the 18 matches is
2, 2, 6, 4, 3, 4, 1, 4, 2, 3, 2, 2, 4, 4, 2, 3, 6, 6

Goals	Tally	Frequency
1	I	1
2	IIII I	6
3	III	3
4	IIII	5
5		0
6	III	3
		18 Matches

Goals in Each Match	1	2	3	4	5	6
Frequency	1	6	3	5	0	3

Table A33.4

Unit 34 Visual representation of data
Pictograms (*page 102*)

1 Cars
   Buses
   Lorries
   M/Cycles
   P/Cycles

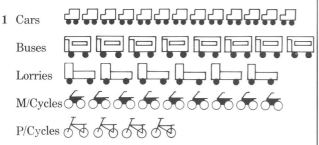

Fig. A34.1

2 **(a)** 1980 – 150 houses built
  (b) 1981 – 200 houses built
  (c) 1982 – 225 houses built

3

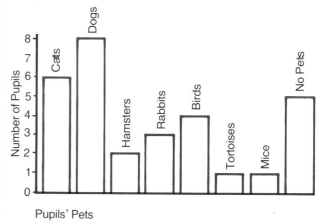

Reasons for Absence

Fig. A34.2

4 **(a)** Bill and Brian had caught the same number of fish,
       i.e. $7 \times 20 = 140$ fish.
  (b) Andrew caught 50 fish.
  (c) Sid caught 190 fish.
  (d) Tony caught 90 fish.
  (e) Sid would have won the fishing prize.
  (f) Andrew would have won the 'wooden spoon' for the
       smallest catch.

Bar graphs (*page 103*)

1

Fig. A34.3

2 **(a)** It spends £50 on clothes.
  (b)
Other	£20
Rates and mortgage	£90
Heating	£40
Clothes	£50
Food	£100

  (c) Family wage is £300
  (d) Most expensive item is food

3

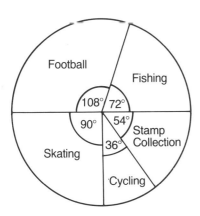

Fig. A34.4

(a) Number of pupils in survey sample = 50.
(b) Size 5 was worn by most.
(c) Size 3 was worn the least.

4 (a) The Nile is approximately 6600 km long.
(b) The Irtysh is approximately 5400 km long.
(c) The Amazon is approximately 6200 km long.
(d) The Yangtze is approximately 5200 km long.
(e) Since we are comparing lengths of rivers, it is more appropriate to draw the graph horizontally rather than vertically.

5 A bar chart of your own design from information concerning heights, shoe sizes etc. of your own class or family.

Pie charts (*page 104*)

1

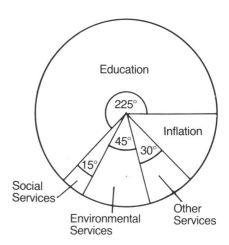

Fig. A34.5

$$20 \text{ children} = 360°$$

$$\therefore \quad 1 \text{ child} \quad = \frac{360}{20} = 18°$$

$$\text{Hence,} \quad \text{Fishing} = 4 \times 18 = \quad 72°$$
$$\text{Football} = 6 \times 18 = 108°$$
$$\text{Skating} = 5 \times 18 = \quad 90°$$
$$\text{Cycling} = 2 \times 18 = \quad 36°$$
$$\text{Stamp collecting} = 3 \times 18 = \quad \underline{54°}$$
$$\text{Total} = \underline{360°}$$

2

Sport	(a) Angle	(b) Number of Pupils 5° = 1 Pupil
Swimming	140°	28
Rounders	40°	8
Netball	50°	10
Tennis	60°	12
Athletics	70°	14

Table A34.1

(c) There are 72 girls altogether in the group.

3 360° represents £3.60
∴ 1° represents 1p.
(a) Writer's fee will be 40p (from 40° sector).
(b) The cost of the materials will be 60p (from 60° sector).
(c) The angle representing the publishing costs will be $360° - (60° + 40° + 90°) = 170°$
(d) The actual cost of publishing will be 170p = £1.70.

4

Fig. A34.6

(a) Angle of Inflation sector is 45°.
(b) 360° represents £720 000
$$1° \text{ represents } £\frac{720\,000}{360} = £2000$$

Environmental Services (45°) will represent £45 × 2000 = £90 000.
(c) Other services (30°) will represent £30 × 2000 = £60 000.
(d) Social Services (15°) will represent £15 × 2000 = £30 000.
(e) Education (225°) will represent £225 × 2000 = £450 000.

Line graphs/trend graphs (*page 104*)

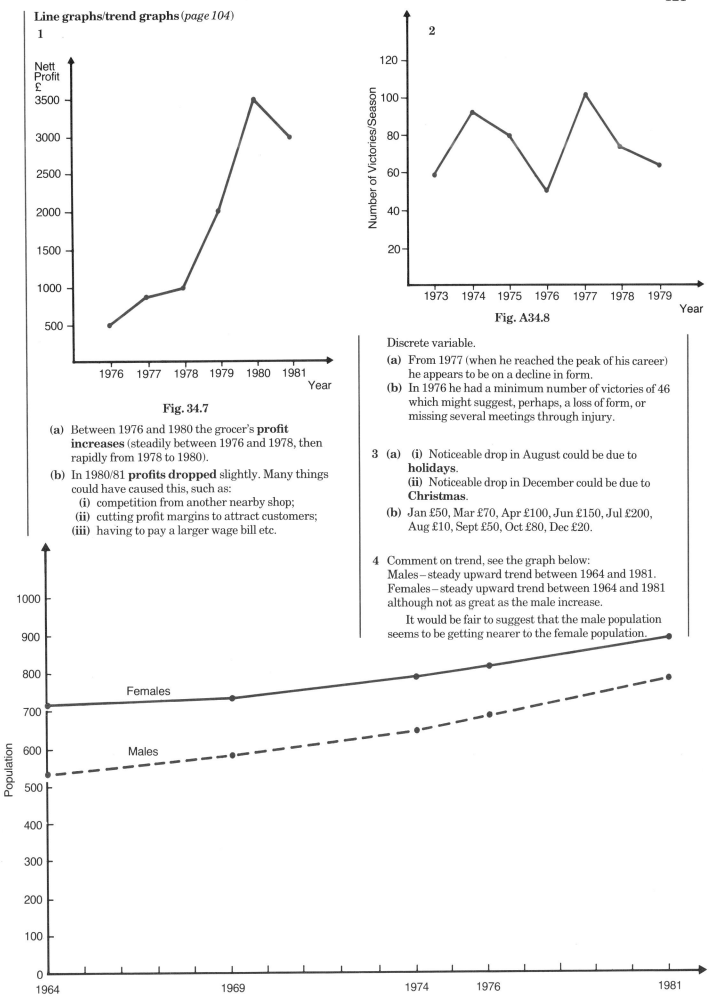

Fig. 34.7

Fig. A34.8

1

(a) Between 1976 and 1980 the grocer's **profit increases** (steadily between 1976 and 1978, then rapidly from 1978 to 1980).

(b) In 1980/81 **profits dropped** slightly. Many things could have caused this, such as:
  (i) competition from another nearby shop;
  (ii) cutting profit margins to attract customers;
  (iii) having to pay a larger wage bill etc.

2

Discrete variable.

(a) From 1977 (when he reached the peak of his career) he appears to be on a decline in form.

(b) In 1976 he had a minimum number of victories of 46 which might suggest, perhaps, a loss of form, or missing several meetings through injury.

3 (a) (i) Noticeable drop in August could be due to **holidays**.
   (ii) Noticeable drop in December could be due to **Christmas**.

(b) Jan £50, Mar £70, Apr £100, Jun £150, Jul £200, Aug £10, Sept £50, Oct £80, Dec £20.

4 Comment on trend, see the graph below:
Males – steady upward trend between 1964 and 1981.
Females – steady upward trend between 1964 and 1981 although not as great as the male increase.

It would be fair to suggest that the male population seems to be getting nearer to the female population.

Fig. A34.9

Miscellaneous problems (*page 106*)

1

Marks	Tally	Frequency
1	III	3
2	IIII	4
3	IIII	4
4	IIII	4
5	III	3
6	IIII	4
7	III	3
8	III	3
9	II	2
	Total	30

Marks (10)	1	2	3	4	5	6	7	8	9	10	
Frequency	3	4	4	4	3	4	3	3	2	0	Total 30

Table A34.2

(a) Bar chart

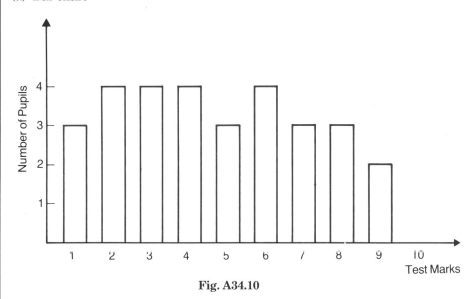

Fig. A34.10

(b) Pie graph

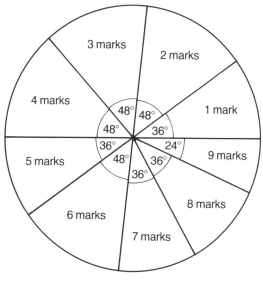

Fig. A34.11

(c) Pictogram

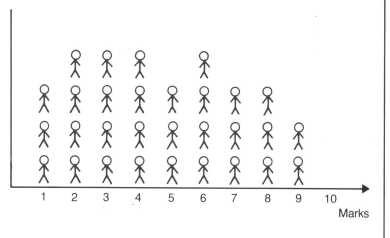

Fig. 34.12

2 (a) Total number of aircraft = 5 + 15 + 25 + 20 + 25
= 90 aircraft

(b) Line graph

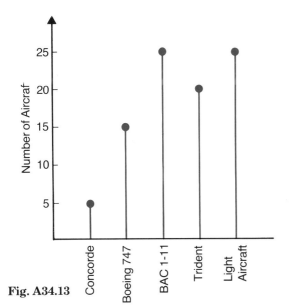

Fig. A34.13

3 *continued from previous column*

(b) No real up and down trend apart from a slight variation on a couple of days.

(c) Since these are only midday temperatures over a certain period, we cannot make any definite conclusions about the weather. There may well be thunderstorms, high winds, cold nights etc. All we can really deduce is that the midday temperatures over this period are reasonably high and remain fairly steady.

(c) Pie graph

BAC 1-11

Boeing 747

100° 60° 20° Concorde

80° 100°

Trident

Light Aircraft

360° = 90 aircraft ∴ aircraft = 40

Fig. A34.14

Unit 35 Misrepresentation of data
Good graphs/bad graphs (*page 109*)

1

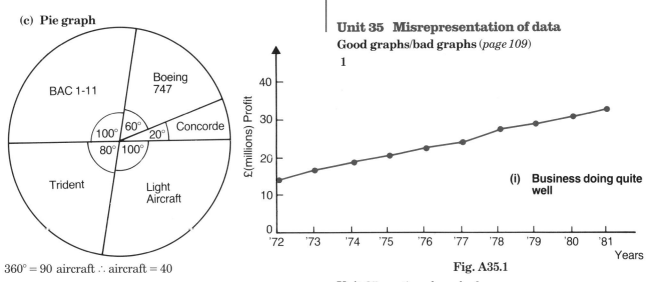

(i) Business doing quite well

Fig. A35.1

Unit 35 *continued overleaf*

3 (a)

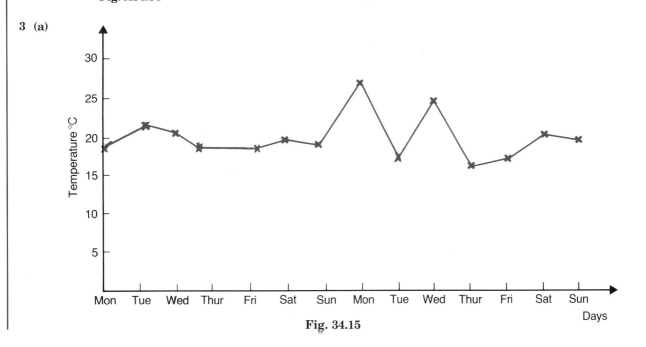

Fig. 34.15

Unit 35 continued

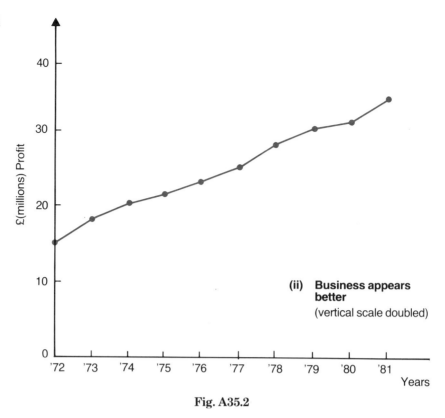

Fig. A35.2

2 It is the wrong type of graph. Rather than a line/trend
graph, since the information is discrete, it would be best
represented by a bar chart.

    Also the graph is unlikely to be true since, generally,
people are more likely to be absent due to illness in
winter months than in summer months.

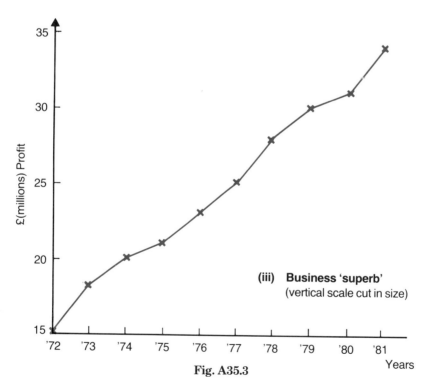

Fig. A35.3

3 This is a terrible graph. Look particularly at the scales.
The vertical scale starts at 5, and 0 to 5 is cut out to
exaggerate the result.

    The horizontal time scale alters in the middle, from
one-year periods to quarters-of-a-year.

    This graph is of very doubtful value.

Useful books for further reading/exercises

Title	Authors	Publisher
Basic Statistics	Devine	Harrap
Headway Maths Books 1–4	Holland & Moses	Hart Davis Educational
Integrated Mathematics Scheme 1MSA1, 1MSA2, B1	Peter Kaner	Bell & Hyman
Mainstream Mathematics Books 1 & 2	Sylvester	Nelson
Mathematics (The Basic Skills)	Llewellyn & Greer	ST(P)
Modern Mathematics for Schools Vols 1 & 2	Scottish Mathematics Group	Blackie Chambers
New General Mathematics Vols 1 & 2	Channon, McLeish Smith, Head	Longman
Ordinary Statistics	Walker, McLean	Edward Arnold
Oxford Comprehensive Mathematics Books 1 & 2	Paling, Wardle	Oxford University Press
Resource Mathematics Levels 1 & 2	Oxford Mathematics Group	John Murray

Glossary

Acute angle An angle less than 90°

Angle The measure of the amount of rotation

Arc Part of the circumference of a circle

Area The size of a surface (measured in square units)

Associative Law $(a*b)*c = a*(b*c)$ where $* = +$ or $\times$ (in this Volume)

Bar graph A representation of a set of frequencies by a set of parallel bars of equal widths, with lengths proportional to the frequencies

Bias Unfair influence, weighted (or lop-sided)

Bisect To cut into two equal parts

Capacity The amount of space enclosed, i.e. internal volume

Commutative law $a*b = b*a$ where $* = +$ or $\times$ (in this Volume)

Complement of a set If A is a subset of a universal set, the subset containing all the elements not in A is the complement of A

Complementary angles A pair of angles which total 90° when added

Continuous data Information gained by measurement

Cubic number The third power of a number; e.g. $8 = 2^3$

Data Given information or detail

Degree A rotation of one three-hundred-and-sixtieth ($\frac{1}{360}$th) part of one revolution

Denominator The term on the bottom line of a common fraction

Diagonal A line joining any two corners of a shape which are not next to each other

Diameter A line passing through the centre of a circle from one point on the circle to another point on the circle

Difference The resulting number after the operation of subtraction

Directed numbers Numbers with either a positive or negative sign in front of them

Discrete data Information gained by counting

Distinct sets (disjoint sets) Sets having no common elements

Distributive law A law linking the operations of addition and multiplication i.e. $a \times (b + c) = (a \times b) + (a \times c)$

Dividend A term used in division; in $a \div b$, a is the dividend

Divisor A term used in division; in $A \div b$, b is the divisor

Empty set A set which has no elements in it

Equation A statement of equality, written to show that two things are equal

Equilateral shape A shape with all sides of equal length

Equivalent sets Sets containing the same elements

Even number An integer which has no remainder when divided by 2

Expression A symbol, or a collection of symbols which are connected by signs of operations (usually $+$ and $-$)

Exterior angle An angle at a vertex of a polygon formed outside the polygon by two adjacent sides, one of which has been extended (produced)

Factors When a number or expression is the product of two or more numbers or expressions, each of the latter is called a factor of the former

Finite set A set which has an end number

Frequency distribution A table of results showing how many times something occurs

Horizontal A line parallel to the earth's surface; a flat line

Improper fraction A common fraction in which the top line (numerator) is bigger than the bottom line (denominator)

Infinite set A set which goes on and on, i.e. it has no end number

Integer A whole number, either positive or negative

Interior angle One of the inside angles of a shape

Intersecting set A set containing element(s) belonging to two or more sets.

Isosceles triangle A triangle with 2 equal sides and 2 equal base angles

Least common multiple L.C.M. is the smallest positive common multiple

Like terms Algebraic terms which can be added or subtracted

Lowest terms A fraction cancelled down to its simplest form

Mass The 'quantity of matter' in a body

Mixed number A number which has a whole number coupled to a fractional number e.g. $2\frac{3}{4}$

Multiple Any integer which has a given integer as a factor, is called a multiple of that factor

Natural numbers Positive integers; whole numbers

Negative numbers Numbers with a minus sign in front of them

Numerator The term on the top line of a common fraction

Obtuse angle An angle between 90° and 180°

Odd number An integer which has a remainder when divided by 2

Parallel lines Lines which never meet, no matter how far they are extended

Parallelogram A 4-sided figure, with opposite sides equal in length, and parallel

Percentage A number expressed in fractional form as a part of 100

Perimeter The distance around the boundary of a figure

Perpendicular A line which is at right angles to another line

Pictogram (pictograph) A graph which uses symbols to represent frequency

Pie chart (pie graph) A circular graph in which the sectors represents the frequency (like slices of a cake)

Polygon The general name for any figure having 3 or more sides, e.g. pentagon is 5-sided, decagon is 10-sided etc

Positive numbers Numbers with a plus sign (or no sign) in front of them

Prime factors Factors which are prime numbers

Prime number Any integer which has only itself and 1 as factors i.e. 2, 3, 5, 7, 11, etc

Product The result of multiplication

Protractor An instrument used for measuring the size of angles

Quadrilateral Any 4-sided figure

Questionnaire Inquiry for data by means of a series of questions

Quotient The result obtained by division

Radius A straight line joining the centre of a circle to any point on the circumference. It is half of the diameter

Rectangle A quadrilateral with two pairs of equal, opposite and parallel sides and 4 right angles

Reflex angle An angle between 180° and 360°

Regular polygon A polygon having sides of the same length and equal interior angles

Rhombus A quadrilateral with opposite sides parallel and sides all of the same length

Right angle An angle of 90°

Sample Part of a total population, used for statistical work

Sampling The process of obtaining a sample of a population for statistical purposes

Scale A system of points placed at known intervals on a line for the purpose of measuring. It may also be used to give a comparison between a real object and a drawing or model of the object

Scalene triangle A triangle with all sides and angles unequal

Sector The part of a circle enclosed by two radii and an arc

Sequence (series) A set of elements written consecutively

Set A collection of things called elements or members

Slant height The sloping height of a triangle (as opposed to its perpendicular height)

Solution The answer, when a problem is solved

Square A quadrilateral with 4 equal sides and 4 right angles, and with opposite sides parallel

Square measure The measurement of area

Square number A number multiplied by itself e.g. $3 \times 3 = 3^2 = 9$

Statistics The study of methods of collecting analyzing and using data

Subset If set A is part of set B, then A is a subset of B

Sum The result of addition

Supplementary angles A pair of angles, the sum of which is 180°

Tally A method of counting frequency in 'bunches' of five

Trapezium A quadrilateral with just one pair of parallel sides

Trend A statistical term for a general tendency in the data

Triangle A polygon with 3 straight sides and 3 interior angles which total 180°

Triangular numbers Numbers which can be represented by a triangular of dots e.g. 3, 6, 10 etc

Union of sets A set containing all the elements of two or more combined sets (but having no repeated elements)

Universal set The set of all those elements under consideration

Variable Any symbol for any member of a set of numbers, points, values etc, which may change in value

Venn diagram A diagram used to represent sets

Vertical line A line in the direction towards or away from the centre of the earth (at right angles to a horizontal line)

Volume The measure of the space occupied by a geometric solid